LIFE IN THE ITINERANCY,

IN ITS RELATIONS TO

THE CIRCUIT AND STATION,

AND TO

THE MINISTER'S HOME AND FAMILY.

BY ONE,

" Who, long devoted to its toils and cares,
Enjoys its triumphs—its reverses shares."

———•———

NEW YORK AND AUBURN:

MILLER, ORTON & CO.,

New York: 25 Park Row.—Auburn: 107 Genesee-st.

1857.

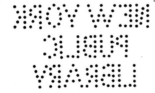

AUBURN:
MILLER, ORTON & MULLIGAN,
STEREOTYPERS AND PRINTERS.

TO

THE WIVES OF METHODIST MINISTERS,

WHO SHARE,

EQUALLY WITH THEIR HUSBANDS,

THE

TRIALS AND TRIUMPHS OF THE ITINERANCY,

These Pages

ARE RESPECTFULLY INSCRIBED,

BY THE AUTHOR.

PREFACE.

It has been the writer's aim in this volume, to furnish the public with a true sketch of life in the Itinerant Ministry. Had it been thought proper to look upon either the sunny or shady side alone, the picture might have been widely different from what is here presented. As will be seen, this course has not been adopted. There is in every part an intermingling of sunshine and shadow, in as exact imitation as may be, of the original from which it is drawn.

While several works illustrating the various features of a settled pastorate have been given to the public, this is, so far as the author's knowledge extends, the first effort to delineate domestic life in the Itinerancy. The numerous biographies of such as have labored in this connection, which have been published within the last few years, are rich in interest, and should be allowed a prominent place in our literature ; but they almost uniformly fail to enter the minister's household, and point out what is being done and suffered in the family circle, as well as on the circuit and station.

Let no one affirm that this is a work of fiction. In no proper sense of the term would such an affirmation be correct. Every incident here narrated has its basis in facts which may be abundantly quoted. It is nothing more nor less than a representation of real life. Extremes on both sides have been studiously avoided. The character drawn, occupies no more than a medium position, and shares only in the every day occurrences of this description of ministerial life.

If it be thought objectionable to thus bring existing evils to light when they might otherwise remain unseen, it may be well to consider that there is no better way of correcting them. Doubtless many such are perpetuated because of their comparative obscurity. Should this humble effort tend in the least to remove them and add strength to the system with which the writer's life is identified, the desire that has prompted it will have been accomplished.

With this end in view, these delineations of scenes in parsonage life are confidingly submitted to a candid christian public.

CONTENTS.

LIFE IN THE ITINERANCY.

CHAPTER I.

CALL TO THE MINISTRY.

"THEN you feel yourself called of God to preach the gospel, do you?" pleasantly asked an elderly minister of a young man seated with him in his study, who had just made his first effort as an " exhorter," under the auspices of the M. E. church.

" Well, yes," said the other with some degree of hesitancy. "That appears to be the path of duty, though myself and friends had marked out another, and quite a different course, which I had formerly hoped to pursue."

" Very likely," responded the clergyman. "The plans that we form must often give way, as they are found to conflict with the will of God. I am happy to learn that you have these convictions, and trust you will fully devote yourself to the work of the ministry."

"I have decided to do so," said the other; "and as soon as the necessary preparation can be made, if the way opens, I shall no longer hesitate to engage in the duties of this holy calling."

George Stanly, who spoke thus, was a young man of more than ordinary talent. Though his parents

A*

were comparatively poor, they had sought to give
him the advantages of a liberal education, and by un-
tiring energy on his own part, he had nearly completed his college course, with the design of immediately entering upon the study of the law.   His
friends, and they were numerous, had encouraged
him in his purpose, and were already looking forward
with high hopes to the time when.he should be in
successful practice ; when, to their astonishment,
they saw him numbered with the fruits of a religious
revival, and subsequently enrolled as a member of
the church.

From the hour of his conversion, young Stanly
turned his attention to the work of saving souls.   The
plans which he had so fondly cherished were at once
abandoned, and it was conceded on all hands that he
was to be a minister.   None doubted his fitness for
the work, nor the sincerity of his motives ; and yet
his immediate companions, including most of his relatives, looked with deep concern on the choice he now
made.   In their estimation, it was a position altogether unworthy his splendid talents, and one which
involved the loss of those fine advantages that had
been heretofore enjoyed.

In accordance with this view, numerous efforts
were made to dissuade him from his purpose.   Visions of wealth and fame were presented before him,
as he was pointed to a successful career in the legal
profession, and these were put in strong contrast with
the life of poverty and toil, so often connected with
the ministry.   He was urged to act, in part at least,
with reference to the wishes of his friends, and listen

to their advice, rather than be carried away with
what they were pleased to call the excitement of the
occasion. But amid all these arguments and entreat-
ies he remained unmoved. The line of duty was
clearly marked out before him, and he felt a "woe"
resting upon his soul, if he attempted to shun it.
Wealth and fame were no longer incentives to his
ambition. These had once occupied the most prominent place among the objects for which he toiled, but
he had now tasted the joys of salvation, and his soul,
filled with higher aspirations, cried out,

> "The love of Christ doth me constrain
> To seek the wandering souls of men,
> With cries, entreaties, tears, to save,—
> To snatch them from the gaping grave,"

In accordance with the custom of the church, an
exhorter's license had already been tendered him, and
in due time he expected to take his place in the conference, and make the pastoral work his business for
life. In reply to the clergyman with whom he was
now conversing, he expressed a wish to pursue his
studies for several years, before entering the Itinerancy; as he felt at present unprepared for the responsible duties of this sacred calling.

"And do you really think it necessary," said his
friend, "to spend so long a time in a theological seminary, in order to become a successful preacher?"

"It seems very important," said George. "I
should not feel at liberty to undertake a work so vast
and far-reaching in its results, without a thorough

preparation. I have always argued that a man should be master of his subject."

"That is right," said the former; "I am glad you entertain such views. Men may say what they will, a minister cannot fully accomplish the work to which he is called, without mental discipline. He must have gifts, natural and cultivated, as well as graces. It is not enough that the spirit of God dwells in him, else, every good man would be a good preacher. But can you not pursue your theological studies, and at the same time be usefully employed in the service of the church? You have now a good begining, and can continue to study *for* the ministry while *in* the ministry."

"Perhaps so," said the young man. "But I should have fears as to my success, without a previous and special work of preparation. If I am correctly informed, the Methodist church at the present day seeks and demands an educated ministry."

"And so she does," was the quick reply. "But she has never required candidates for the sacred office to wait from three to ten years after God calls them, before begining the work. With us, they are expected to be diligent in the acquisition of knowledge, and faithful in the use of it as soon as acquired."

"Can there be any possible objection to taking a theological course under able and distinguished teachers?" asked Mr. Stanly.

"No farther objection than this: He who, like yourself, has a good education to begin with, can go on with the study of theology, and at the same time fill a sphere of extended usefulness. On the circuit

or station, he has time to study as much as his physical constitution will allow, and yet opportunities to
preach to dying men. He who studies thus, will be
likely to become a practical and successful preacher.
Years of usefulness are saved, and Christ is honored
in the service of his chosen ministers."

"I think I see the principle involved," said George.
"But is there not great difficulty in pursuing systematic study while in the regular work? Is not a
preacher's time all occupied in the duties of his
office?"

"Yes, there are difficulties. No places or circumstances are exempt. A minister's business will of
course occupy all his time; but, it is a part of his
business to study. No reasonable congregation will
object to this; and if objections were raised by the
uninformed, they should never be heeded. Again,
in the case supposed, there would be an additional
incentive to this work. An immediate and pressing
demand for the knowledge to be acquired would
scarcely leave it optional with the preacher whether
he would study or not."

"I confess I see the force of your reasoning," replied Mr. Stanly. "Still, I fear I might be tempted
to idleness, and in that case become inefficient."

"You might easily yield to the temptation as others have done," said the clergyman; "but you would
be equally beset in the seminary or college hall. It
is not in the power of circumstance or place to make
students of men. As you well know, many a man
graduates and secures his diploma, without sufficient
preparation to sustain himself on the poorest of our

appointments. Any person who is of such indolent·
habits that he would not become educated in the ministry, would remain uneducated though passing his
whole life in a college. Give a young man a fair
start, and then place him where he will see his deficiencies with every passing day, and if he will not
strive earnestly for the proper cultivation of his mind,
his case is hopeless."

"Am I correctly informed," asked George, after a
moment's pause, "that Adam Clarke obtained his
vast fund of knowledge while engaged in the regular
ministry?"

"Certainly," responded his friend; "that distinguished divine began to preach when very young;
and his ability to write the most profound and learned
biblical commentary of modern ages, was acquired
while traveling the large circuits of his time. Other
instances equally conclusive might also be cited.
Many of our fathers in the ministry, who became
celebrated for their pulpit powers, were educated in
the same way. They were not ignorant men as has
sometimes been represented, though not trained in
the technicalities of the schools. The evidences of
their fitness for their chosen work may be seen on
every hand. As is well known, their success in winning sinners to Christ and building up the church, has
not been surpassed since the days of the apostles."

"I believe you have a course of study, through
which candidates must pass before being admitted to
orders, though I have never examined it," said Mr.
Stanly.

"Yes, and a very good one. But when this is completed, the work of preparation does not end. A Methodist minister is expected to go on with his studies so long as he remains in the work, and this life-long devotion to his books will give him a literary character, independent of the schools."

This strain of conversation was continued until Mr. Stanly began to seriously question the propriety of *waiting* to complete a long course of theological study. His purpose, however, to be, as he had expressed it, "master of his subject," was in no wise shaken. He thought if the way pointed out was practicable, it was to be preferred; especially by one suffering from financial embarrassment, and at the same time ardently desiring to be useful in the vineyard of the Lord. He readily saw that it would require a much greater effort on his part, than to secure the same amount of knowledge in a theological seminary. This he was by no means unwilling to make. After carefully considering the subject in its various bearings, he came to the conclusion, that he would watch the openings of Providence, and be governed accordingly.

It so happened, at this time, that the conference in whose bounds he resided, was in great want of ministers. For some reason, but few young men were turning their attention to this work, and the constituted authorities of the church found it almost impossible to meet the wants of the people. The presiding elder of the district, hearing of Mr. Stanly as a young man of promise, sought an interview with him, and after consultation, proposed that he should connect himself with the Itinerancy, and immediately go forth as a herald of the cross. Though fully conscious that he was not prepared for the work as he should be, Mr. Stanly yielded to the influences around him, and reluctantly consented to the proposition.

A few months only remained before the conference should meet. These were diligently devoted to theological study, and such other preparatory work as the occasion required. A portion of his Sabbaths were spent in the pulpits of his brethren, and those who listened to his preaching felt assured that he was called of God, and duly commissioned for the work to which he was assigned.

CHAPTER II.

THE days and weeks that intervened between the formation of young Stanly's purpose, and the session of conference, sped rapidly away. Almost ere he was aware, he found himself called upon to fulfill his pledge. Though his presence at the conference was not strictly necessary, he determined to be at Andes, the place of meeting, and witness in person the transaction of the business committed to its care. In doing this, he was prompted by a higher motive than the mere gratification of his curiosity. He wished also to study, under more favorable circumstances than he had heretofore enjoyed, the various features of the Itinerant system with which he was about to be connected.

With reference to this subject he was deeply solicitous. Many of his old friends had not yet abandoned the hope of winning him back to his former associations, or at least of securing his attachment to some more fashionable and popular branch of the church. To accomplish this, they had revived the charges of spiritual tyranny on the part of the bishops, and other chief officers who were to be placed over him, and in this manner had trusted to weaken his confidence in the cause he had espoused. The various rumors against the honor of Methodism, which have

2

been kept in circulation from the period of its organization, were, many of them, for the first time brought
to his hearing, and he was warmly urged by these interested pleaders, to make choice of some other mode
of life.

Though not crediting these charges, Mr. Stanly
was far from being able to disprove them. He had
not been reared under religious influences, and consequently knew comparatively little of the government of the church with which he was connected.
Thus far, her doctrines had been the principal subject of his investigations; and these, he felt assured,
were in accordance with the word of God. He now
sought to comprehend her ecclesiastical economy, before farther committing himself to the work of her
ministry.

Actuated by motives of this character, the young
preacher resolved to watch, with a scrutinizing eye,
everything that transpired in the routine of conference business. In his own mind, one thing was certain. He could never submit to a despotism, let it
come in what form it would; and if it were found in
the government of the Methodist Episcopal church,
he must seek his home in some other communion.

With these feelings he reached Andes in time for
the opening of the session. The now sainted McKen-
dree was the presiding bishop, and as most of the
charges referred to, were against the episcopacy, Mr.
Stanly looked on with a jealousy, almost uncharita-
ble from its keenness, as this venerable man performed the duties of his office. It must be confessed
that he had so far listened to the traducers of the

church as to be scarcely able, in this particular, to form an impartial judgment. Still, as day after day passed, he was unable to detect the least exercise of arbitrary power, and the conviction was finally irresistible, that the complaints were unfounded and unjust.

Indeed, he could not discover the possession of authority at all on the part of the bishop, aside from such as grows out of the ordinary duties of a presiding officer, unless it consisted in the power to appoint the preachers to their several fields of labor. Upon this point he remained for some time unsettled. He carefully examined the principle upon which it was based, and attentively considered the evils which grow out of the opposite system, before reaching his conclusion. Thus viewing it, he could not fail to see that this was a scriptural as well as most efficient method of extending the triumphs of Christ's kingdom. For the preachers to relinquish the privileges of bargaining for their places, and the people to yield theirs of electing their pastors, was seen to be a mutual sacrifice for the public good. The whole matter, thus left as by a species of arbitration to a third and disinterested party, was evidently so arranged that while the strifes and heart-burnings of the elective plan were avoided, the work could be carried on in harmony and peace.

Mr. Stanly was also especially benefited by the religious services of the occasion. Able divines expounded the word of God, strong men lifted up their voices in believing prayer, and the whole conference seemed blessed with the gift of sacred song. Notwithstanding the trials and hardships of ministerial life; a degree of contentment and happiness appeared among these brethren that he had never before witnessed. In the "love feast" on Sabbath morning, was heard the testimony of those who had been for half a century in the work, and whose hearts could not fail to be gladdened by the contrast between the past and the present. Some told of glorious revivals through which they had passed during the year, and of the great grace that had rested upon the people. Some referred to afflictions which they had been called to suffer in the loss of friends and kindred, but the grace of God was sufficient for them, and they now rejoiced in the prospect of a happy reünion beyond the grave. A few spoke of hardships, and thanked God that, as soldiers of the cross, they had been enabled to endure, so as not to faint by the way. All were buoyant with hope, and strong in the faith of the gospel. Not a word of complaint fell from the lips of these men of God. They seemed rather to look out upon the whitened harvest with · an earnest and almost impatient desire to go and gather sheaves into the garner of the Lord. "Surely," said Stanly, "these are no ordinary men. Among them shall my lot be cast forever."

In due time the name of George Stanly was enrolled as a member of the conference. He now waited to learn where, in the order of Providence, should be his field of labor. The session was near its close, and these ministers, who had spent a week so pleasantly together, were about to separate. Young Stanly felt that it had been, to him, the most intensely interesting period of his life. Though uncertain of the future, he was moved by an earnest desire to go forth and preach Christ crucified to lost and dying men.

This wish was soon to be gratified. At the close of a protracted evening session, it was announced that the business which had called them together was completed. The conference then joined in singing the parting hymn, so often made use of on such occasions:

"And let our bodies part,
To different climes repair,
Inseparably joined in heart,
The friends of Jesus are."

The devotional exercises ended, the wished for announcements were made, and with glad hearts and joyful steps, these men of God were prepared, with the morning light, to hasten to their designated fields and engage in the duties of their calling. Mr. Stanly was read out as junior preacher on Eaton circuit.

CHAPTER III.

At the close of the conference, our young preacher returned to his home, and prepared for an immediate removal to his newly appointed circuit. As he anticipated, but little encouragement was received from his former friends, most of whom had artfully endeavored to shape his course, and were now extremely mortified at the result of their efforts. A few of his immediate relatives, having exhausted their stock of argument and entreaty, were disposed to ridicule him on account of his final choice, but the greater number wisely concluded henceforth to leave him to himself. Though pained by these manifestations, Mr. Stanly was far from regretting the course he had taken. He had put his hand to the gospel plow, and was not inclined to look back. Nerved by a consciousness of his integrity, he pursued his chosen way with an unfaltering step, and an unwavering faith.

As Eaton was but a few miles distant, he determined to spend the following Sabbath among the people he had been appointed to serve, and then return and complete his outfit. Obtaining the loan of a horse and carriage, he accordingly set out for his circuit. His road led him through a rich and beautiful district, well calculated to inspire the heart of a trav-

eler, and on other occasions Mr. Stanly would have
been highly delighted with the scenery about him.
He was now too much absorbed in thought to give
heed to anything save the duties and responsibilities
of his new position.

Various and conflicting were the emotions that
stirred within him during this brief journey. He
saw, as he had never done before, the importance of
the work assigned him. Before him were a multitude of living yet dying men. In a certain sense their
spiritual interests were being committed to his hands.
He was to preach to them the word of life, to warn
them of their peril, and beseech them to be reconciled
to God. While thus looking out upon the moral
field and surveying the whitened harvest, he was reminded that for the faithful discharge of these duties
an account must be rendered at the judgment seat of
Christ. In the light of this fearful truth, he could
well exclaim, in the impressive language of the poet,

> " 'Tis not a cause of small import,
> The pastor's care demands:
> But what might fill an angel's heart,
> And filled a Savior's hands."

And then as he journeyed, he thought of the cold
and heartless criticisms that would be made on his
efforts, the possibility that he should not succeed as a
preacher, and the disgrace that would be brought on
himself and the church in case of his failure. Viewing the subject thus, his spirits became deeply depressed, and at times he almost wished he had not
accepted the appointment of the conference.

In this state of mind, his heart was involuntarily
lifted to Him who calleth and sendeth forth laborers,
for help.   In answer to prayer the whispers of grace
were heard, " Lo I am with you alway, even unto the
end of the world." His faith at once grasped the
promise, and he felt an assurance that all was well.
From that moment his soul was stayed on God, and
he looked upon the future with a joyous and hopeful
heart.

Mr. Stanly had been so completely absorbed in
these contemplations, that he did not observe the
progress which he made.   Already the village was
before him.   He had never seen it until now, and
from the brow of a hill, was unexpectedly brought in
view of the place.   The horse was brought to a stand,
and the young pastor paused a moment to observe
the scene.   On either side were high hills covered
with rich farming lands, dotted here and there with
the rural homes of their occupants ; while low down
in the valley was the small but beautiful town,
through which ran the murmuring brook, the noise
of whose waterfalls fell like distant music on the lis-
tener's ear.   Three churches, with their spires pointing heavenward, stood side by side, and as he gazed,
he wondered in which he was to preach, and who
were to be his hearers, and where he should find a
home during his stay in their midst.   These, and
numerous like queries passed rapidly through his
mind.

Starting from his reverie, Mr. Stanly hurried on
until he reached the village, and inquired for a
Brother Hallam, on whom he had been directed to

call. As he paused in front of the house to which he was pointed, he could but feel an unusual degree of embarrassment at the thought of the approaching interview. The family within were entire strangers, and he scarcely knew how to introduce himself as a preacher, much less make known the fact that he was one of their appointed pastors. While tying his horse, a strong temptation was presented to turn about and go to a hotel near by, and wait for a more favorable opportunity.

As he thus hesitated, Mr. Hallam chanced to come to the door, and perceiving a stranger, he stepped quickly toward Mr. Stanly, as if suspecting who he was, and at the same time asked, "Is this our new preacher?" On being answered affirmatively, he gave him an earnest shake of the hand, and added, in tones indicating the warmth of his heart, "Walk in, walk in, brother! We shall be happy to make your acquaintance, and hope you will feel at home with us."

Each member of the family extended a similar greeting, and Mr. Stanly felt at once that he was among those who were his friends. He was not anticipating such a welcome. Civility he did expect; but here was a cordiality equal to that extended to the most familiar friend. The young preacher was surprised as well as gratified at these tokens of sympathy with the work in which he was engaged. It is due in justice to say, that this was one of those families with which the church has been so abundantly blessed, where the weary Itinerant finds rest, and receives words of encouragement and counsel.

B

The next day was the Sabbath, and Mr. Stanly was for the first time to appear before his people. It was a beautiful summer's day—such as is wont to inspire the devout heart with gratitude and praise—and as there was a general desire among the people to see and hear the new minister, an unusual number convened in the house of God. Mr. Hallam resided nearly opposite the church, and as the congregation began to assemble, the preacher looked with a kind of exciting interest on the scene before him. The village was small, and most of those who entered the house of worship seemed to come from a distance. Farmers' wagons came ratting along with their rustic but cheerful looking occupants; carriages, bearing those who appeared more fashionable but often less devout; footmen, from the immediate vicinity, and some who gave evidence of having traveled for miles in this primitive fashion; young and old, rich and poor, were wending their way to the place appointed for prayer and praise.

While thus looking out, and musing on the different motives that might actuate these in going to the sanctuary, Mr. Stanly almost forgot that he was the officiating pastor, and that it was time for him to join those who were entering the courts of the Lord's house. With a brief prayer, for he had spent most of the morning in devotional exercises, he left the room, walked across the street, and took his place in the pulpit. He had summoned all the courage at his command, and had hoped and prayed that no special embarrassment might attend this first service. But no sooner did he cast his eye on the congregation, than all his assurance was gone. There was in every countenance such an inquisitive look, that he seemed to be held at a distance, and a tremor ran over his whole frame, until he shook like a leaf in the wind. Never had he seen so trying an hour as this. Could he have looked into one countenance that seemed to appreciate his circumstances, and sympathize with him, he might have found relief. But all were strangers. Not one that could know his embarrassment. Turning from these, he saw truly that his only trust was in God. To him he lifted his heart in silent but believing prayer.

Tremblingly the young pastor arose, and gave the introductory hymn. It was sung with that soul-stirring energy so peculiar to such as worship in spirit and in truth. There was neither organ nor viol, but there was the melody of the heart, as the whole congregation joined in this exercise. The blessing of God seemed to rest upon the people while they sung, and the soul of the preacher caught the hallowed fire. His embarrassment soon passed off, and he was enabled to conduct the remainder of the services with his usual freedom. In after life, Mr. Stanly was frequently heard to say, that if the singing on this occasion had been conducted in the formal and lifeless manner so common at the present time, he should have made so signal a failure in his introduction as possibly to have caused him to abandon the ministry altogether.

At the close of the public service he tarried in the class meeting, and was soon convinced that his lot had fallen among those that loved the Lord. There was something so earnest and so touching in the testimony of these christians, that the idea of being among strangers was at once abandoned. His distrustful timidity had received a rebuke that could not soon be forgotten. The purpose was then formed, never again to look with a suspicious eye on those whom he was appointed to serve. These brethren had received him with open arms and warm hearts, and he was assured that he had already gained a place in their sympathies and their prayers.

Mr. Stanly, thus introduced to the people, became settled among them, and labored during the year with marked success. There were several appointments connected with the circuit, at most of which his congregations were large and respectable, and he had the satisfaction of seeing them increased by frequent conversions and additions to the church. His colleague, the preacher in charge, was a man of age and ripe experience, from whom he derived valuable counsel, and to whom he was greatly indebted for the interest taken in his welfare.

At the termination of the conference year, Mr. Stanly found no occasion to regret his connection with the Itinerancy, nor his appointment to Eaton circuit. A mutual attachment had sprung up between him and his brethren, and his return was anxiously desired. A request was made that such a division of the circuit might be effected as would constitute Eaton village an independent station, and a petition forwarded for the appointment of Mr. S. to its charge.

CHAPTER IV.

Though most of Mr. Stanly's early friends now regarded him with a cold and formal indifference, there
were still unbroken ties that bound him to the home
of his childhood. As the conference year at Eaton
passed away, he availed himself of numerous opportunities to revisit the place of his nativity, and
strengthen the cherished associations of earlier days.
To one of his temperament, there was a kind of in-
describable charm in being allowed to withdraw from
the public gaze; and, disrobed of the artificial restraints thrown around a minister's life, mingle again
in scenes commemorative of the past, until the care-
worn heart should be disburdened of its load, and rejoice in harmony with the genial smiles of nature, as
well as the bounteous provisions of grace.

Thus, while a visitant at the homestead, the young
preacher might be often seen walking leisurely
through the fields, or sitting in solitude beneath the
shade of some spreading tree, intently studying the
volume spread out before him, as his eye traced the
landscape, and his soul from the contemplation of nature, was lifed in grateful adoration to nature's God.
In these studies he greatly delighted; and his soli-
tary walks were frequent and long-continued. On
other occasions, the observer might look upon him as

he chose some familiar path, with a fair one leaning upon his arm, whose bright and cheerful smiles were answered by a manly countenance, lit up with emotions of gladness and delight.

Emily Porter was the only daughter of a respectable and wealthy farmer, residing in the outskirts of the village of Embury. Favored as she had been with the best advantages which a country town could furnish, and possessed of an amiableness of disposition, and loveliness of person rarely combined, she richly merited the universal esteem in which she was held. An unbroken friendship had existed between herself and George Stanly almost from childhood. For some years past, it had been suspected by the friends of the parties, that this principle was ripening into that higher and holier passion by which kindred spirits are united, and in the sight of God made one. Esquire Porter, Emily's father, was not unaware of the attachment existing between "the young folks," and it was generally conceded was far from being displeased on account of it. He had assisted Mr. Stanly in his early efforts to secure an education, and though disappointed at his abandonment of the legal profession, and still more so in his choice of the Itinerant ministry, his interest in the young man's success was scarcely lessened.

When Mr. Stanly became a christian, none rejoiced more heartily than did this pious and devoted family. They were members of the "parish church," as its friends chose to call it, and occupied a prominent place in maintaining its varied interests. The esquire was one of its most efficient officers; and Emi-

ly, who had been several years connected with the
society, was as active in the discharge of religious
duties as the customs of that communion would allow.
When they heard of young Stanly's conversion, they
expected, as a matter of course, that he would connect himself with this branch of the church, and
make his religious interests identical with their own.
Their respect for him was not lessened, however, when
it was seen that he was taking another course; for
they knew him to be honest in his convictions, and
conscientious in the choice which he made.

At first, it was supposed that the intimacy between
George and Emily would be thus broken off; but it
was soon observed that the young man's visits were
as frequent as before, and it was now generally conceded that an agreement of marriage existed between
them. Still it was thought that Miss Porter would
never consent to become the wife of a Methodist
preacher; and those " busy bodies," who are ever active in other people's affairs, predicted a speedy
change in his church relations.

It may appear strange to the general·reader, but it
is nevertheless true, that the good folks at Embury were
so strongly prejudiced against the doctrines and government of the M. E. church, that many of them regarded it as an act of deep disgrace to be engaged in
their support. Reared under such influences, and
possessing but a limited knowledge of the subject,
Emily Porter had shared in these prejudices and been
governed by similar feelings. Vague and indistinct
reports only, had reached her ear, and she knew nothing of the facts of the case, while like thousands of

others, she condemned, unseen and unheard, that which she supposed contrary to reason and the word of God.

Being now led to an investigation of the subject, Miss Porter was greatly surprised at the identity of her own views with the general doctrines of Methodism. She soon learned that the "confession of faith" and the "catechisms" were far from expressing her sentiments, and, though belonging to a Calvinistic communion, she was really no Calvinist. Indeed, she had never before seen the stern and rugged features of this system. The naked deformity of the doctrines of election and reprobation, had not until now been presented to her view. As soon as they were exposed, so that she saw what they were, she was ready to declare herself an Arminian in name, as she had, in fact, ever been at heart.

As her relation to Mr Stanly became more generally understood, Miss Porter was frequently rallied on the prospect before her, especially by those opposed to the religious views which he had adopted. Ordinarily she did not care to defend him in the course he had espoused, and therefore made little or no reply. Most of her friends did not yet know that she had decided to make the same church her spiritual home, and hence they often indulged in a freedom of remark that would not have been otherwise allowable.

"Emily," said Mrs. Deacon Jones on one occasion, "what could have induced George Stanly to join the Methodist church ?"

"I am sure I can't answer for him," said the girl,
with a laugh and a blush.

"It's really a pity, is'nt it!" said the old lady with
a sigh.

"Why, aunt!" inquired a little girl, who was a
great admirer of Mr. Stanly.

"Because he is so talented, and might be so useful,
if he would only take the right course. A man of
any character really degrades himself by doing the
work in which he is now engaged."

"So he does," said another, equally zealous for true
orthodoxy.

"Well, I don't know," responded a third, who was
not a professor of religion. "I presume he is a good
christian, and will do as much good in that church
as in any other. We all believe in having preachers
of the gospel."

"And so we do," said Mrs. Jones: "but Methodism is'nt the gospel. Just think what strange doctrines they hold to, and how they conduct their meetings, and it is enough to convince anybody."

"I don't see anything very bad about the doctrines
they preach," ventured Emily.

"Nor I either," said the non-professor. "I heard
George preach when he was here, and I am sure I
never heard more scriptural doctrine in my life."

"It is because you don't understand doctrine," answered Mrs. Jones. "Most people are so blinded that
they can't. Why, just think; the Methodists hold to
falling from grace, and being saved by their good
works, and all that. They don't admit God's sover-
eignty, but elevate human reason, and become so

puffed up that they say they know they have religion
and live without sin, with a great many other absur-
dities of like character and influence."

"I have devoted some time recently to the study
of their doctrines as put forth by themselves," replied
Miss Porter, "and I have as yet found nothing objectionable. I can honestly say, I do not believe
what our "confession of faith" says about some
men's being predestinated to eternal life, and others
foreordained to everlasting death, with the number
so certain and definite that it can neither be increased
nor diminished. To speak plainly, I am convinced
that their doctrine on this point is right, and ours
wrong."

" O Emily, don't talk so! you have been taught
better than that. I confess," continued the old lady,
"I don't understand the doctrine of the decrees myself, but I believe in it. I learned it in the catechism
when I was a little girl, and have never had reason
to doubt its truth."

"I thought you had given up the old doctrine of
election and reprobation," said the lady who made no
profession. "I am sure your ministers don't preach
it as they used to, years ago."

"Oh, no, " said Mrs. Jones. "It's the bible truth,
but many people won't receive it now as formerly."

"The 'confession of faith' has undergone no
change," said Emily. "It is left out of the little for-
mula which we have heard read so many times when
members join the church, but it is the same in all our
general standards."

The ladies had by this time become deeply inter-

ested in their subject. Mrs. Jones began to fear that
Emily was imbibing a fatal error, and she earnestly
strove to warn her of her danger. Neither of the
parties were very much skilled in theological science,
and after having talked for awhile concerning matters of doctrinal difference without any perceptible
progress, the conversation began to flag, when Mrs.
Jones adopted a new course to effect her object.

"Don't you know," she asked, "that these people
are very ignorant. Just look at their preachers.
They are without education, and go round from place
to place like strolling gypsies. You heard our minister say that many of them could scarcely read."

"Yes, but I don't credit it. I did not then know
but it was true, but I have since learned differently,"
said Emily.

"Well, I believe every word of it," answered the
old lady. "Indeed I know it to be true. My opportunities for observation have been much greater than
yours, Emily. George will rue the day he joined
conference, I can assure you."

"Perhaps he will," said the girl with a degree of
honest indignation, "but not for such reasons as you
name."

Emily knew it was useless to undertake an argument with one whose "opportunities" had been so
great, and did not wish to wound her feelings by contra-
dicting her assertions. She feared she had already
said too much, and resolved to make no further reply. The other ladies continued the conversation for
some time, but without eliciting remark from the one
for whom it was designed.

This Mrs. Deacon Jones belonged to that large class of professed christians, who can see no goodness beyond the pale of their own communion. Though expressing herself freely concerning the doctrines and usages of other churches, she was almost entirely ignorant of both. To a well informed mind, like that of Miss Porter, she appeared as an embodiment of sectarian bigotry, viewing the numerous inroads that were being made on the "standing order," as an infringement of the natural rights of the denomination to which she belonged. And yet Mrs Jones was a woman of an otherwise unexceptional character, and was well deserving the position she occupied as one of the most prominent ladies in the church at Embury.

It was not long before the report was put in circulation that Emily Porter had embraced the doctrinal views held by the Methodist Episcopal church, and was about to become one of its members. She was at once subjected to a trying ordeal. Not only Mrs. Jones, but the whole parish seemed excited. She was expostulated with, times without number, and though avoiding as far as possible all allusion to the subject, was frequently brought in conflict with the opinions of her most respected and beloved friends. Fortunately for her, she was constitutionally cheerful, and these influences had but little weight in depressing her spirits, or controlling her opinions. Her appearance in public was much the same as before, and she joined with her usual vivacity in the familiarities of social life.

With reference to George and Emily, the truth was as had been suspected. Their love had long since been plighted, and an engagement of marriage entered into, though as yet no time had been fixed·for its consummation. Of late, the increased frequency of their interviews indicated its near approach, and it was already whispered that the necessary arrangements were being made.

On one of the bright and beautiful days of early spring, Mr. Stanly might have been seen leaving the cares of his circuit behind, as he set out for his native place. He was wearied with his bachelor life, and oppressed with a sense of his loneliness, and was now resolved to ask that the day might be named when his hopes should be consummated in leading his chosen one to the altar. As might be expected, his heart was full of the subject which interested him ; for he began to think of his wedding day as at hand, when he should no longer be compelled to stem the currents of life and resist their buffetings, alone. Arriving unexpectedly at Esquire Porter's, he was ushered in unannounced, and favored with the pleasure of an informal greeting. The surprise was of a character to increase, rather than diminish his respect for Emily, and as he must return on the morrow, no time was lost in making known the object of his visit.

Emily was not prepared for the request, or at least affected not to be, and presented various reasons for delay. These were met one by one, and refuted ; for our preacher was now eloquent in his pleadings if never before, and ere the evening was spent, it was agreed that the nuptials should be celebrated at the time of the approaching conference, and arrangements made for immediate housekeeping. After va-

rious parleyings, the plan thus formed was agreed to
by Emily's parents, and Mr. Stanly returned the following morning, happy in the results of his brief
visit.

With Miss Porter, the work of preparation was at
once begun. The family mansion at Embury was
soon astir, and by the aid of hired help, the needles
flew, and the business was prosecuted to a successful
issue. Emily was an only daughter, and no pains
were spared on the part of her parents, in giving her
an appropriate setting out. They wished to do all
within their power to render her life happy, as she
should go from under their care and occupy the place
in society which she had now accepted.

Mrs. Porter had told George, in the presence of
Emily, what she had often said to her in private, that
her daughter did not yet understand the duties of a
housekeeper, and this was urged as a reason why
their marriage should be delayed. In reply, Mr.
Stanly had expressed his willingness to take her at his
own risk, and now that the thing was agreed upon,
Emily resolved to disappoint him by becoming ex-
pert in the duties of her new calling. To this end
she busied herself in the kitchen and pantry, sometimes greatly to the amusement, and at others the
mortification of the daughter of the green isle, whose
province she thus invaded. According to Cathe-
rine's judgment, it was no place for a lady, and she often privately declared that her mistress' room was
better than her company.

As the time approached, Emily congratulated herself on her proficiency in what she had undertaken.

Her bread and cakes were as "nice" as those of the kitchen maid herself, and she could draw a smoothing iron over her father's linen to her entire satisfaction. Occasionally, when engaged in this work, a stray thought would come into her mind, as she held a collar to the window, and wondered how it would look in the pulpit. And then she would laugh at herself, and exclaim, in her glee, that she was serving an apprenticeship for a parsonage. At such times, no chidings of her mother could repress the outburstings of her lightsome heart, or prevent exhibitions of the buoyancy of feeling with which she was animated. Though decidedly religious, she was cheerful, almost mirthful, and constitutionally of a merry and happy temperament. While some thought this unfitted her for a minister's wife, Mr. Stanly felt otherwise. To him it seemed that one passing through a life of toil and care, needed just such a companion, and his heart was gladdened by these evidences of her joyous disposition.

The conference year soon reached its termination. Mr. Stanly takes his leave of the people to whom he has ministered, uncertain as to the probabilities of his return, and once more travels the familiar way to Embury. He has reached a great and important point in the history of his life. Excitement hurries him on, and he soon appears among those whose interests are kindled in harmony with his own. One heart, at least, beats with as high hopes, and rejoices with a similar joy.

*　*　*　*　*　*　*

The marriage ceremony is ended, the nuptial song is heard, the echo of farewell voices die away, and the newly married pair are journeying to a distant village, unwearied by the heat of a summer's day, to spend a brief time at the seat of conference, whose session is already commenced. Joyful in each other's affections, they consecrate their united hearts to the work before them, and trusting to the goodness of Him who has thus far crowded their pathway with blessings, they look forward to a bright and happy existence on earth, and an eternally glorious rest in heaven.

CHAPTER V.

THE NEWS.

Mr. Stanly had been at Eaton a year, before it was known that he had any one in view to whom he intended to be married. Perhaps it would have been better for himself, as well as some members of his congregation, had his true position on this point been understood; for Eaton had some intriguing mothers and not a few attractive daughters, who took an especial interest in this subject, and who from time to time had freely discussed his matrimonial prospects. It is not to be presumed, however, that this interest arose from any but the purest of motives—the happiness and usefulness of the minister—after which, as good christians, they were bound to look.

It is often curious, if not instructive, to trace the busy tongue of rumor in her wild and reckless wanderings; but in the case of the young preacher at Eaton, that tongue had been *so* busy, that the task may be considered beyond the reach of the most indefatigable pen. Not aware, on his part, that he was the subject of remark, Mr. Stanly exercised no especial cautiousness in his intercourse with the congregation, but acted in all respects with that freedom, to which, as a pastor, he was justly entitled. His visits among the people were free and familiar; and as he was not detained with household cares, they

occupied no small portion of his time. This fact gave
rise to many of the surmisings of those with whom he
mingled, and led to the well intended, though really
injurious remarks, of such as he recognized among
his warmest personal friends.

Mr. Johnson, the most prominent business man at
Eaton, was a leading member of the society which
Mr. Stanly served. He had three daughters, also connected with the church, and it was supposed by many,
who knew of the pastor's frequent calls at his house,
that one of them would eventually become the occupant of a parsonage. To the mother, and she was
deeply interested in the subject, it was quite evident
that such would be the fact. To aid the young minister in the project, on which she felt assured his heart
was intently fixed, she availed herself of every opportunity to bring the parties together; though she was
not yet sure which of the three was destined to receive
the wished for proposal. Thus, if company was entertained at her house, the preacher was quite sure to
receive an invitation to tea, and, not unfrequently,
matters were so arranged as to detain him at least a
portion of the evening. Before the year had half
expired, the report was in circulation that Mr. Stanly
was paying attention to Miss Johnson, and that a
matrimonial alliance was likely to be the result.

Miss Fenton was also very attentive. She, it seems,
did not credit the report about the Johnsons, and set
herself busily at work in counteracting the influence
which might be there exerted. No one doubted this
lady's piety or good sense; and that she possessed
rare qualities for a minister's wife, was beyond ques-

tion. Active in all the affairs of the church; and
especially so when Mr. Stanly was present, she was
considered by many as the most likely of any in the
circuit to win the prize. It is true, her zeal sometimes made her appear a little officious, but her evident desire to do good, excused her in the minds of
the people, by whom she was highly and almost universally respected.

Several others were named in the same connection.
Miss Manchester, though a number of years older
than Mr. Stanly, was favorably spoken of by her
friends, and at times almost pressed upon his attention. She herself manifested no particular interest
in the matter; while two or three younger ladies that
were "talked of," probably had not the slightest wish
for such a consummation, and did not even dream
that their names were mentioned in this category.

Mr. Stanly remained entirely ignorant of all these
schemes, and of course acted with as much independence, as though they had no existence. It is true,
matters sometimes looked as if there was a design in
what was intended to appear accidental, but having
no idea that there was anything, either in himself or
his position, sufficiently attractive to lead to such results, he dismissed his thoughts at once, and continued
as before.

Thus affairs remained until the session of conference. In accordance with the request of the official
board, Eaton was separated from the circuit, and constituted a station, to which Mr. Stanly was duly appointed. The news of his reäppointment was received with pleasure, and especially so by the John-

sons, who were by this time wonderfully attached to their preacher. Already the mother began to lay fresh plans for a conquest, and the result was considered by no means doubtful.

There were others equally confident. Miss Fenton saw in the return of the young pastor the prospective consummation of her hopes, and could not fail to be pleased. The friends of Miss Manchester, also, took courage, though they were less obnoxious than the others named, to the suspicion of seeking the accomplishment of the wished for event.

- A few days intervened between the termination of the conference and Mr. Stanly's appearance at Eaton. At the close of one of these, Mr. Johnson came in from his store, bringing his usual number of letters and papers, and, with the exception of the latest daily, throwing them on the sitting room table, he sat down to read. Mrs Johnson and the young ladies were also present, when Julia, the eldest of the three, perceiving the Christian Advocate and Journal, languidly took it up, with the remark, that she was going to see if it contained the conference appointments. Casting her eye over the paper, she replied to her own saying, by expressing her disappointment in not finding them.

"Look at the marriages, Julia," said Eliza; "perhaps some one that we are acquainted with is married."

Julia did as she was directed; for like many other ladies, she regarded this as the most important department of a newspaper, and therefore did not need to be asked the second time. The Advocate was scarcely turned and folded, when she exclaimed, almost at the top of her voice,

"O mother, come here! look at this paper; Brother Stanly is married!"

"Pshaw! child, I don't believe a word of it," said Mrs. Johnson.

"He is! he is!" said Eliza; "it is here, in the Advocate."

"It can't be our Brother Stanly I am sure," answered the mother, "it must be some one else. Let me see."

Taking the paper, she stepped to the window and read aloud:

"In Embury, June 22, by Rev. W. L. King, Rev. George Stanly of Eaton, to Miss Emily Porter of the former place."

"Emily Porter! Emily Porter! who is she? I'd like to know," exclaimed Mrs. Johnson.

"Why did'nt he tell folks he was going to be married?" said Julia, petulantly. "I don't believe in a minister's keeping things so private. It is little short of deception."

"I dare say it is some new thing," answered Eliza. "It can't be that he was engaged when he used to call here and visit with us."

"Not unless he is wonderfully deceitful," said the mother. "Who would have thought it. Brother Stanly get married and no one know anything about it."

"Well," said Julia," his usefulness is ended, so far, at least, as this place is concerned."

"So it is," added the mother.

During this brief but excited conversation, Mr.
Johnson had laid aside his newspaper, and pushed
his spectacles on to his forehead, and now sat as if
musing on the scene before him. He finally interrupted the ladies, by saying that he could not see
that a preacher was under any more obligation to tell
his business to everybody than any one else ; and for
his part he was glad Mr. Stanly was married. Mrs.
Johnson still insisted that in so important a matter,
the preacher should have taken advice, especially of
the more judicious members of the church. This
course according to her view, would have saved him
the trouble which he must now endure. She took it
for granted that the choice made was not a good one,
and was already resolved to be highly displeased with
the personal appearance, as well as the conduct of
the bride.

Her husband resumed his reading as though nothing had happened, but the conversation among the
ladies was serious and long continued. They wondered, again and again, how he came to have her—if
she was handsome, or rich, or educated, or what it
could have been that gave direction to his choice.
But the parties having no knowledge on which to base
conclusions, as a matter of course, none were reached.
Upon one point, alone, all were agreed—Mr. Stanly's
usefulness at Eaton was at an end, and, in the em-
phatic language of Mrs. Johnson, it was "a real pity"
the conference had sent him back.

The Johnsons were not alone in being excited. Miss
Fenton and her sympathizers were greatly grieved for
the good of the society, for they were quite certain

no stranger could be as useful among them as one of
their own number, in whom they had confidence, and
who, from personal acquaintance, knew their wants.
Surely, said they, Brother Stanly should have consulted our interests better than thus to bring in one who
cannot possibly appreciate the peculiarities of the
Eaton church.

The friends of Miss Manchester also gave free expressions of regret at this ill-advised step. They
feared, after all, that their minister did not care for
his people as he ought, for if he had done so, he
would have certainly taken advice and been governed
by their opinions. Thus comments were freely made
by one and another, on a subject, concerning which,
every one was without the slightest knowledge.

All, however, were not disposed to find fault. The
larger and better portion of community had sense
enough to know, that a minister should marry the
person of his own choice. They saw that he was under no more obligation to consult the whole neighborhood, and settle the question by the weight of
public opinion, than was any and every other man.
To such, the news was far from being unpleasant.
They were disposed to hope for the best, and at all
events were willing to suspend judgment, until there
was a fair opportunity for its exercise. As to the
idea that a minister should marry to please his parishioners, they saw at once that it was simply ridiculous. No more foolish claim could possibly be set
up, and many of them were pleased to know that Mr.
Stanly had put it at defiance. This class had been
sorely afflicted by the gossip and intriguing which

had been apparent during the past year, and felt sensibly relieved now that it must end.

In the meantime, there was a general anxiety for the coming of the pastor among them. Disguise it as they might, the whole congregation felt an interest in the appearance and habits of the bride, as though she were to become a member of their own households. She was already regarded as belonging to them, and as they had no choice in her selection, they waited with the greater impatience for an opportunity to pass upon her merits.

CHAPTER VI.

THE BRIDE.

THE good people of Eaton were not long destined to remain in suspense with regard to the subject that thus excited them. Mr. Stanly and his lady had returned to Embury, and were busily preparing for their settlement in the station with which they were connected. A few days only were required, as but little remained to be done, and it was soon announced that all things were in readiness for the young couple to go forth and " set up for themselves."

The morning of their departure awakened emotions in Emily's heart to which she had hitherto been a stranger. For months gone by she had been looking forward to this hour with unusual interest, and had supposed herself prepared to meet it, without yielding the mastery to those struggling sensibilities, which the bare thought of separation from the loved ones of her youth, did not fail to call into being. In this the young bride was greatly mistaken. When she came to the point that the home of her childhood was to be abandoned, and the friends on whom she had ever relied for counsel and support left behind, she could but feel that an important crisis in her history had been reached.

Burdened with these reflections, she rose long before the opening of the day, and sought her accus-

C   4

tomed place of private prayer. She wished once
more in her secret chamber to kneel as she had been
taught from infancy, and call upon God for wisdom
to guide and grace to support in the trials and conflicts of life. It was here that she had often been
comforted and blessed; but such was now her agitation that she could scarcely compose herself for the
much loved task. Memories of the past came rush-
ing upon her mind, while vague and indistinct visions
of the future flitted before her, as she attempted for
the last time in this hallowed place to pay her morning devotions. She knelt, but could not pray. Unnumbered little things that had seemed buried and
forgotten rose up before her, and reminded her of
early joys; while every object about the old homestead wore a new and most interesting aspect. Until now she had not known that she loved these associations so tenderly. Never before had they been so
dear to her heart. She was ready to exclaim,

> "A thousand thoughts of all things dear,
> Like shadows o'er me sweep;
> I leave my sunny childhood here,
> O, therefore let me weep."

True, there was one source of relief. The place of
her destination was not distant, and she might often
come and mingle in the scenes now being left behind. But then she must come as a visitor. The
charm would be broken, when she felt that it was no
longer her home. Just now, what volumes existed
in that blessed word.

At length the storm of contending emotions was

hushed, and with calm assurance, she lifted her voice in prayer. Past mercies were gratefully acknowledged, and future blessings earnestly sought. That burdened soul was stayed on God, and all was peace, and hope, and joy.

By this time, the whole house was astir, and Emily met the different members of the family with that cheerful air which was characteristic of her life. Not a word escaped her concerning the struggle that had passed within, and no one suspected the depth of feeling which she had indulged.

There were others in that house whose hearts were melted and whose eyes wept on this occasion. It is not necessary to dwell on a father's anxiety or a mother's love. Mr. and Mrs. Porter knew but little of Itinerant life, and that little was far from inspiring them with hope. They had seen something of ministerial cares and trials in connection with their own settled pastorate, and knew them to be of no ordinary character. It was natural to suppose that the Itinerancy must contend with still greater difficulties. It had been their earnest wish that George and Emily might have selected some other mode of life, but when the choice was made, convictions of duty forbade their interference, and they were now doing all they could to render them happy and successful in their chosen work.

The sun had just passed the meridian of one of the finest days of summer, when George and Emily set out for Eaton. Mr. Stanly could not fail to contrast the present journey with the similar one which he had made a year before. How widely different the feelings that influenced him. He was no more a stranger to those with whom he was to sojourn, and that oppressive sense of loneliness, with which he was then burdened, was now gone. Friends were ready to greet him and bid him welcome. He saw their pleasant faces and anticipated their congratulations. And then there was one beside him to share his joys, and be his companion in all his sorrows. His soul exulted in the prospect; and he inwardly rejoiced as he neared his field of labor, and contemplated the work in which he was to be engaged.

Not so with Emily. Exceedingly timid, and unaccustomed to mingle in the society of strangers, she instinctively shrunk from the approaching interviews. She had been weeping over the recollections of the past, and had found relief; but a much severer trial was now before her. More than once she expressed her fears, and alluded to her embarrassment; but George, fully conscious of her worth, had no misgivings. He assured her that she would be met with cordiality and treated with kindness; and named some of his warm friends with whom he was certain she would be pleased. Though crediting all that he said of the people of Eaton, Emily was still fearful, as a sense of her inability to meet their wants and expectations pressed upon her.

Arriving at the village, Mr. Stanly met several of his brethren before reaching the place where he had chosen to call. These recognized him with a smile and a bow as he passed them in the street; but Emily could not fail to see that she was the one on whom their attention was fixed. No sooner did the recogni-

tion take place, than her husband seemed left out of
the question, as an inquisitive look was cast at her.
She had thrown aside her veil, that a better view of
the town might be obtained, but was soon glad to
restore it, and hide herself from the penetrating gaze
of the strangers.

The door of Mr. Hallam, where they were to call,
was soon reached, and the same cordial welcome was
extended by the members of this christian family, that
had been given to the young pastor when he came
among them friendless and alone. Emily was entirely
unacquainted with Methodist usages, and was agreeably surprised at the cordiality with which they were received. It was not a formal and affected politeness,
after the manner of the times, but an expression of
real and affectionate kindness, which, with a word,
dispelled all her fears, and relieved her from her anticipated embarrassment. At the pressing invitation
of Mr. and Mrs. Hallam, it was soon arranged that
this was to be their home until a residence could be
procured, and the preliminaries for housekeeping
settled.

During the week following, numerous calls were
made on the preacher and his wife, by such as
wished to form Mrs. Stanly's acquaintance, and extend
to her the usual tokens of regard. With most of those
whom she thus met, Emily was highly pleased, though
in a few instances she could not fail to detect the existence of a feeling other than such as arises from a
desire to promote a cordial and friendly intercourse.
Such was the case with Mrs. Johnson and Mrs. Lewis,
who were among the first that called. These ladies

were exceedingly polite and attentive, but there was a heartlessness in their manner, that clearly revealed the paramount wish to gratify their curiosity, in thus meeting and conversing with the bride.

Mr. Stanly was quick to discover the difference between the past and present in Mrs. Johnson's deportment toward him, and for the first time suspected the real object of her former attentions. He could but be amused at the earnestness with which she looked upon Emily, and though her visit was short, it called into being a train of reflections, valuable in themselves, which might not have been otherwise awakened.

Mrs. Lewis remained sufficiently long to make her complaints of the state of the church, which she declared to be very low and discouraging. She detailed many inconsistencies in its members, and though Mrs. Stanly was an entire stranger, doubtless supposed her deeply interested in the personal affairs of other years. Her tale was concluded by entering bitter complaints against former preachers' wives, all of whom had been sadly deficient, according to her showing, in some or other of the departments of life. They had been extravagant, or proud, or fault-finding, or neglectful to visit the poor, or something else that had greatly impared their usefulness. She now hoped for better things, and anticipated more favorable results.

"Really," said Emily, as soon as she was alone, " I have received quite a lecture on my new duties."

"That woman," said Mr. Stanly, "is never in her element unless she can find fault with somebody."

"I presume it will be my turn now."

"No doubt of it," said George. "You may always depend upon it, that a person who dislikes everybody else will dislike you. When I hear a member complaining of the preachers that have been here before me, I feel quite sure it will be my turn when I am gone."

The pastor and his wife were not mistaken in the estimate put upon their visitor. Her "impressions" were quite unfavorable, and as if of pressing importance, they were speedily put in possession of the public.

CHAPTER VII.

THE SEWING SOCIETY.

"Are you going to the sewing society to-day?" asked Mrs. Smith, as she stepped in at the door of her neighbor, Mrs. Lewis.

"Certainly," was the reply, "and I have been thinking some of us should go over and invite Sister Stanly."

"I think we should, too. She is to be our president, you know."

"A pretty president she'll make," said Mrs. Lewis. "A mere girl brought in among us."

"She appears very well."

"Yes, but just think how young she is," continued Mrs. Lewis.

"I should judge her to be about the age of her husband," said Mrs. Smith; "you would not have had him marry an old woman, would you?"

"He's made a very unwise choice. He ought to have taken into consideration the wants of the society in such a matter. It's a real pity he did'nt consult his people on the subject, as a minister *should* do."

"Shall we go," asked Mrs. Smith, "and give her notice, and invite her to be present this afternoon?"

"Yes, I can go. Suppose we call for Sister Johnson on the way, and have her go with us."

"Very well," was the reply. "She is the secretary, and it belongs to her more properly than to us."

The three ladies were soon at Mr. Hallam's. After a few moments' desultory conversation, they reminded Mr. Stanly of the society meeting, and expressed a wish to have him present. To this he readily consented, as he had been accustomed to attend their gatherings for the purpose of conducting their religious services, and otherwise encouraging their effort. During the preceding year, the greater portion of the sum raised for foreign missions had been secured through this organization, and he had consequently become interested in its success.

This point gained, the provision of the constitution which makes the minister's wife "president," was referred to, and the hope expressed that Mrs. Stanly would find it convenient to take the principal oversight of the society's business. To this, Emily made no immediate reply. Her limited knowledge of what was expected of her in the new position which she occupied, and her natural timidity, prevented the answer to which she was inclined.

She very naturally shrunk from the proffered distinction, and turning to her husband, gave him an appealing look, as if inviting him to interpose in her behalf. He saw her embarrassment, and without difficulty, comprehended her meaning.

"I think," said Mr. Stanly, "some one acquainted with your affairs would be better adapted to such a position than a stranger. I presume you will be obliged to excuse her, though we will do all we can to promote the interests of the society."

C*

"Yes," said Emily venturing to speak, "you will
be kind enough to excuse me from holding any office.
I will work as well as I can, but do not feel capable
of being your president."

"We always expect our minister's wife to take the
lead in everything," said Mrs. Johnson. "If she is
not interested enough to go ahead, we cannot expect
much to be accomplished."

Emily colored deeply at this tart response, but
made no reply. Her husband spoke, however, and
assured the ladies that she did not decline from any
want of interest, but from the circumstance of her
being a stranger, and unacquainted with their manner of doing business. "For," added he, "she has
never yet attended a meeting of the kind, and for this,
if for no other reason, is unfitted for such a position."

"Then she must learn," said Mrs. Smith. "That
is the way with the rest of us."

"Yes," put in Mrs. Lewis, "we all consider it her
place, and she must not shrink from it."

"I am not so sure," said Mr. Stanly, "that it is her
place. I can see no reason for coming to such a conclusion, but very many to the contrary. You have
members of age and experience, who have long been
connected with the society, and who understand its
wants. They should occupy these positions instead
of a stranger. I think Mrs. Stanly is justified in declining your proffer, and trust she will make no change
in her decision."

"I think it ungenerous," interposed Mrs. Hallam,
"to press this matter upon Sister Stanly. We should

be pleased to have her occupy these places if she felt
free to do so, but we certainly have no *claim* on her."

"I think we have," answered Mrs. Lewis. "She
is the preacher's wife and ought to go ahead in all
kinds of benevolent efforts."

"She is under no more obligation of that character," said Mr. Stanly, "than is any and every other
man's wife. She did not marry the circuit."

The pastor's tone was such that the ladies saw their
cause was hopeless. Though young in the ministry,
he could not fail to discover the injustice of the demand, and come to the decision that it should not be
met. The conversation was soon turned upon another
theme, and in a little time the party withdrew, evidently mortified, if not chagrined at the result of their
call.

This affair opened to Emily a new view of ministerial life. Hitherto she had supposed her husband and
not herself in the employ of the church. The idea
had never entered her mind that she was to occupy a
public position, and she now became anxious to know
if these ladies represented the general sentiment of
the society with which she was connected. If so,
she was unexpectedly brought into a new relation to
the world, for which she felt herself entirely unqualified. She had been looking forward with pleasure to
the time when she should be mistress of her own
house, but had never contemplated a settlement over
a congregation. But here was a claim put forward
and tenaciously supported, that drew her from the
retirement of private life and made her a servant of
the public. If this demand was to be allowed, she

must abandon at once all hope of enjoying the endearments of the family circle upon which her heart was so fondly fixed.

"How ridiculous," said George when they were alone ;" people ought to know better than to insist on such an arrangement."

"I think," answered Emily, "I should make a pretty appearance, calling the ladies of Eaton to order, and supervising their business the first time I come among them."

"I imagine you will when you undertake it," said her husband. "I suppose spectators will be admitted while you exercise your dignity and sway your scepter over these willing subjects."

The tears that stood in the eyes of the young wife gave place to a burst of laughter at this sally. Viewed thus, the bare thought of being the presiding genius of "every benevolent effort," awakened her native mirthfulness, and caused her to feel herself again.

"They will not be offended at my refusal, will they?" asked Emily.

"I don't know how that is; but you are right, and ought not to yield your point."

"If you will only help me, I shall contend valiantly," said she. "I scarcely knew what to say until you came to the rescue."

"I presume the subject will come up again this afternoon."

"If you had not promised, we would stay away. I am sure I don't feel like going among a crowd of strangers to-day."

"Don't get disheartened so easily. It will all come

out right in the end," said Mr. Stanly in an encouraging tone.

Mrs. Hallam now came into the room and called attention to some other subject. She saw the troubled expression of Emily's countenance, and did what she could to remove its cause. Still it was evident that a cloud rested upon that fair brow, as the young pastor's wife had begun her course of tuition in the duties and trials of the Itinerancy.

It so happened on that afternoon, that Mr. Hallam's business arrangements were such that his carriage could not go out until a late hour; and as the distance was too great to be walked, Mr. and Mrs. Stanly were accordingly delayed. In the mean time, a much larger number than usual assembled at the place of meeting. It was their first public gathering after the reception of the news that their preacher was married, and many besides those usually interested, came to see, and form the acquaintance of the bride. The important event which had just taken place, became at once the theme of conversation.

" Have you seen the bride ?" inquired one of the young ladies, as Mrs. Clark came into the room,

" I have not. I expected she would be here. Is'nt she coming ? "

" She will be here soon," said Mrs. Johnson. " I called on her and notified her of the meeting and—"

" How does she appear ?" said half a dozen voices at once.

" About like any other young girl. But as I was going to say, I—"

" Is she handsome ? " persisted one of the girls.

"Not exactly ; though we we can't find any fault with her looks. But there is one thing I was going to speak of. We must change our constitution or go without a president."

"Won't she accept the office ?" asked Mrs. Butler.

"She positively declined having anything to do with it."

"What reason does she give ?" inquired another.

"I dare say," interrupted a maiden lady of forty-five, without giving an opportunity for the question to be answered, "it is because she don't like the trouble."

"No that is not the *ostensible* reason," said Mrs. Lewis.

"She maintains it is not her place, and Brother Stanly justified her in her refusal," answered Mrs. Johnson.

"Of course he would," burst forth several of the girls in a giggle.

"Not her place !" exclaimed Mrs. Butler, laying down her work and looking perplexed, as though a new idea had struck her. "I'd like to know what a preacher's wife is for, if it is not to take the lead in such things. I am sure Brother Stanly need not bring her here to play lady."

"Indeed he need not," chimed in Mrs. Smith and Mrs. Lewis together.

"There is nothing clearer to my mind," resumed Mrs. Johnson with an air of authority, "than that she ought to go ahead in all the affairs of the society. She can't have much to do at home, and her time belongs to the church as much as her husband's."

"I expected it would be just so, when I learned he had married her," said Mrs. Lewis.

" Did you know her, then ?"

" No, but I knew how it would be. He ought to have taken advice."

" I presume," said a lady who had thus far kept silent, " Brother Stanly thinks she is his wife and not ours."

" That is about what he said when we called on him," answered Mrs. Smith. ·

"And I think he is correct, too," continued the former. " You say she is young, and of course she must be inexperienced. It is asking altogether too much to require her to take charge of our affairs. In my opinion it is not her place at all.".

" Why Sister Allen !" exclaimed Mrs. Lewis. " You know how much depends on having the minister's wife go ahead in everything. For my part, I had rather he would not be married at all."

" And so had I," responded Mrs. Johnson.

" That may all be, but I presume he married to suit himself and not us. At least we don't appear to be as well pleased with the match as he is."

This last remark caused the ladies a little merriment. It was observed, however, that the fault-finders, especially Mrs. Johnson, writhed under the cutting rebuke. Miss Fenton also blushed deeply, though she had taken no part in the conversation.

For a moment there was a pause. The needles flew with unusual celerity, and each one seemed intent to complete the garment on which she was engaged.

At length Mrs. Allen turned and asked, "What do you think of this subject, Sister Olney?"

The lady addressed was the widow of a traveling preacher, and had passed about fifteen years on the various circuits and stations to which her husband had been appointed. A sigh escaped her as she lifted her eyes from her work, and it was evident that though silent, she had been interested in the colloquy that had been going on.

"I can answer best," said she, "by relating a little of my own experience. When I married Mr. Olney, I was about the same age as is Sister Stanley, and like her, knew but little of what would be expected of me in my new position. As we went on to our first charge, I was exceedingly desirous of pleasing the people, not simply for my own gratification, but as a means of aiding my husband in his efforts to do them good. I had scarcely become settled, when demands like those now made on our preacher's wife, were pressed on me. I knew myself inadequate, and saw before me a score of ladies abundantly competent; but in view of the circumstances I dared not refuse. And so I was put in charge of various benevolent interests, and called upon to attend duties that required far more time than I had to spare. Of course Mr. Olney was obliged to assist me, and this broke up his plans, and we were very soon involved in needless though serious trouble.

"For example: I was called to the charge of the young ladies' bible class, was made the principal officer in the female missionary society, and at the same time chosen chief directress of the sewing circle. In addition, I soon learned that I was expected to visit the sick, and make frequent calls on all the members of the society. Well, I attempted to do it. Mr. Olney's salary was small and we could not afford to keep a girl, and thus the housework was also on my hands. I can assure you there was enough to do; my hands, and head, and heart were full. And, notwithstanding all this, I was frequently invited out, with the additional remark, 'You can't have anything to detain you at home.'

"In this way I continued for two or three years, constantly harassed and distressed. At length my health gave out. I could not endure the burden, and then the people wondered why ministers had such sickly wives, and why it was necessary to keep a hired girl at the parsonage, not once suspecting that they themselves were at fault. New troubles now arose. Our increased expenses involved us in debt, and we were more than once accused of being extravagant.

"At one of our removals, my husband advised me to decline all these positions, and I did so, much to the discomfiture of some of the sisters, who thought me unwilling to do my duty. I now found some relief, but it was too late to regain the health and vigor that had been needlessly stricken down. In looking back upon those years, I can candidly say that a great proportion of the severest trials of my parsonage life, resulted from similar claims to those now imposed on Sister Stanly. I am glad she is disposed to reject them from the beginning, and as soon as I have an opportunity, I shall advise her to be firm in her refusal."

"But don't you think, Sister Olney, that it belongs to the minister's wife to go ahead in these things?" said Mrs. Lewis.

"Not at all. She is but a private member of the church, is frequently a stranger, and no more obligated to 'go ahead' as you term it, than any other person."

"So I think" said Mrs. Allen, "though it would be pleasant to have her do so if it was only consistent."

Just then it was announced that Mr. Stanly and his wife were at the door, and the conversation ceased. They were soon in the room. We will allow Emily to give her own account of the introduction, by taking the following extract from a letter written to Miss Boyer, one of her most intimate friends at Embury.

"DEAR CAROLINE:—According to promise, I now sit down to write you a few lines respecting my new position. I cannot describe, neither can you imagine my varied feelings since I have been here. We are staying for the present with a Mr. Hallam, where we expect to remain until we can get settled. It is an exceedingly pleasant family, and they have all taken great pains to make me welcome. Mrs. Hallam and the daughters are so kind and agreeable, I feel already to love them as though they were old and familiar friends.

"A number of ladies called on me during the first few days, and I have met a great many since. Yesterday, in the morning, several of the sisters came in to remind George of the meeting of their sewing society, which was to be held in the afternoon, and at

the same time, invite me to meet with them. They
also informed me that by virtue of their constitution,
I was to become, as the minister's wife, its 'president.' I know you will laugh, dear Carrie, at the
mention of this, but with me it was no laughing matter. Of course I declined the honor, but they insisted
on my acceptance, and seemed hurt at my refusal.

*   *   *   *   *   *

"In the afternoon we rode over to the appointed
place in company with Brother and Sister Hallam,
(you see I begin to say brother and sister since I became a Methodist,) and arriving at a rather late hour,
found a large number already assembled. You can
guess how I felt when going among so many strangers. The door was no sooner reached than I found
myself trembling from head to foot. I was obliged
to make all the effort within my power to appear calm,
but I fear without success.

" I had scarcely laid aside my outer garments when
the ceremony began. I was introduced to Sister
Jones, and Sister Palmer, and Sister Freeman, and
sister this and sister that, for about half an hour.
Sometimes I remembered where I was, and who I
was, and sometimes not; and when the form was gone
through with, I did not know a single person whose
name had been called. Among so many names I re-
collected none.

" As soon as possible, I obtained a seat in one corner, with the hope of finding relief from my embarrassment. But I was greatly mistaken in my expectations. Let me turn my eyes which way I would, I
observed that almost every one was looking at *me*.

My corner seemed to possess unusual attractions. This added to my confusion, as I had not expected to be an object of astonishment, not then even dreaming that a minister's bride must necessarily produce a sensation.

"But there I was. The old folks looked at me, and the young ladies winked at each other, as they peered over their work and exchanged glances, until my perplexity became so great that I was tempted to get up and go out of the room. I think I should have done so, had I been sure I could have reached the door without making some awkward blunder.

"And then the whole house was so still. Not a word was said and I wondered if it was always so. At length a thought struck me; I was the minister's wife, and they were perhaps waiting for me. This thought was so comical that I was half inclined to laugh, and don't know but I should, had I not seen several pairs of roguish eyes fully fixed upon me.

"In this state of things, Sister Hallam seeing my embarrassment—George provokingly enough having gone out with the men folks—came and sat down by my side, and commenced conversation. Others then whispered, and soon there was a general buzz. In the course of an hour, I came to the conclusion that the Eaton ladies could chat and visit equal to ours— *yours* I should have said—at Embury; and who ever knew them at a sewing circle to be silent?

"I supposed the request would be renewed for me to accept the 'presidency,' but it was not. I think they will now settle on some other plan, which they can easily do. I judged from some little circumstan-

ces that two or three of the ladies were offended at
my refusal. The reflection that I had possibly given
offense, pained me much, but I feel I cannot accept
this position."

Such was the introduction of the young and timid
wife to the ladies of Eaton. She preferred and expected to be mostly by herself for a little time, but
this the circumstances did not allow, and she was subjected to the trying ordeal which she has described
above.

To many persons of a different temperament, all
this may seem as an affair of no moment. Not so
with a bashful female of the highest order of sensibilities, just entering upon a new and strange arena. To
her, the side glances, the sly whispers, and the occasional remarks not intended for her, but which she
could not fail to overhear, were occasions of perplexity
and doubt.

It is no wonder that she wrote in her diary for that
day, that the hour of her departure from the sewing
society was the happiest she had seen since her arrival
at Eaton.

CHAPTER VIII.

HOUSEKEEPING.

MR. AND MRS. STANLY were desirous of commencing housekeeping without unnecessary delay. The idea of having a home of their own became more and more fascinating, as they contemplated it in the light of circumstances with which they were now surrounded. Though pleasantly situated at Mr. Hallam's, they did not feel at liberty to tarry long in the reception of hospitalities so kindly and cheerfully tendered. For various reasons, their visit had been already extended to a longer period than they purposed, and it was agreed that an effort should be made, at once, to procure a house.

The society at Eaton, though constituted of the most substantial class of farmers, and village mechanics in good circumstances, had no parsonage. Instead of complying with the recommendation of the conference, and providing a home for the preacher which they were always sure to need, they had uniformly left him to look out for himself. It so happened that the conference held its sessions at a season of the year when but few houses were vacant; and thus the preachers coming on from time to time were subjected to serious inconvenience. Those buildings that were kept to rent were generally taken, unless it was something so out of the way, or out of repair, or held at so unreasonable a price that no one could be found to engage it. In such a case, the only relief for which the owner could hope, was in the coming of the Methodist preacher. With that personage, there was generally no room for choice, and thus disposition was not unfrequently made of the most unmarketable tenement. This state of things had continued at Eaton for many years; and yet no effort was made to remedy the evil.

At first Mr. Stanly could hear of no house at all. He finally learned there was one in the outskirts of the village, but was told that, probably, it was not such as he wanted. Accompanied by Emily he set out to see it. After a walk through a pleasant street, they turned a corner and came to an old dilapidated building, to which they were pointed as the object of their search. It possessed an extremely forbidding exterior, with neither shrub, nor tree, nor flower, to evidence the taste or care of its former occupant or present owner. For a moment the young minister and his wife viewed it in silence, as if afraid to speak. At other times they would not have hesitated an instant. As it was, Mr. Stanly declared he would rather board than settle here, and proposed to pass on without further examination.

"No," said Emily, "let us take a look inside. Appearances you know are often deceitful."

" Come this way, then," said he, passing through a yard to a half closed door in the rear.

" This is the kitchen," said Emily, as she saw her husband pointing to the smoky ceiling. " To be sure, it needs a little whitewashing, and that we can give it," she added with a laugh. "Let us see the parlor and sitting room. O, they are both in one. Here you go up stairs, and there you go down. Is'nt it nice?" and thus she playfully ran on as she looked into each of the apartments.

On almost any other occasion it would have taken but a moment to settle the question now before them. George advocated boarding, though he knew of no suitable place where board could be obtained; but Emily insisted that the old house could be arranged and made comfortable. After much talking and planning the conclusion was reached. They would engage the premises and do the best within their power. They could get along; it was only for one year.

When this decision was reported to Mr. Hallam, he endeavored to change their purpose, but was not able to propose any plan more in accordance with their wishes. Emily could not bear the thought of going out to board. She had labored to get ready for housekeeping, had talked and dreamed of its pleasures, and now that her furniture was purchased, carpets made, and general "setting out" secured, nothing short of it would satisfy her ambition. She insisted upon it, that Mr. Stanly could repair the fence and do various kinds of out-door work which was demanded, while she could scrub the walls, and thus in a little time, by the aid of whitewash and paint, they could make for themselves a comfortable home. In this manner all objections were silenced, the more easily, as the objectors saw no better way than the one pointed out.

The preliminaries thus arranged, the work of repairs was begun in good earnest. With the help of
several sisters who kindly proffered their aid, a complete renovation was soon effected, and the old tenement was pronounced ready for use ; though much
remained to be done as the inmates should afterward
find leisure. Mr. Stanly accordingly ordered their
goods, and when these were unpacked and arranged
according to the fine taste of Emily, it really presented a pleasant and inviting appearance. It must
be confessed, that the new beginners did not otherwise than feel a degree of satisfaction in contemplating the change which had been so speedily effected
by their industry and skill.

It was with no ordinary feelings that George and
Emily entered upon the duties of their new position.
The reflection that they were at their own home, more
than compensated them for the disadvantages suffered.
They no longer felt dependent on the friends that entertained them, and though deprived of many luxuries which they had enjoyed at Mr. Hallam's, but
were not able to supply for themselves, they rejoiced
in the privilege of sitting by a more homely table,
while they could feel that it was their own.

For several weeks after their settlement, Mr. Stanly and his wife were busily engaged in making such
improvements as were necessary to their personal
comfort and convenience. The pastor found his time
so completely taken up in this way, that his studies
were in a great measure suspended and his parochial
duties neglected. He also found himself, as well as
his people, suffering from this want of attention to

D

his appropriate duties. So meager were his prepara-- tions for the pulpit, that he felt a leanness upon his own soul, and saw at a glance that he failed to instruct and profit his hearers.

This change in his manner of preaching was quickly observed by the congregation. Several of his brethren began to express their regrets that he was not able to sustain the interest which he had awakened, without in the least suspecting the reason. He was also complained of, for not visiting as faithfully as before, and strange as it may appear, no one seemed to divine the cause.

Mr. Stanly, who was a close observer of what was transpiring around him, was not slow in coming to the conclusion that more of his energies must be devoted to the appropriate duties of his office. To accomplish this, he struggled hard, seeking to divide his time between the different interests demanding his attention; giving to his conference studies, the duties of the pulpit and altar, and the other claims of the congregation, each its due proportion. His opportunities for miscellaneous reading, and such mental and bodily recreation as his health required, became, in consequence of these unusual labors, extremely limited.

Still he was full of hope. Encouraged by the bright smiles which he ever met at home, he nerved himself for the stern and laborious duties which pressed upon him. His eye of faith caught bright visions of a joyous future, as he trusted in God, and sought the Divine approbation and blessing.

Mr. Stanly had not long enjoyed the bliss of living

in "his own hired house," when he discovered that
his expenses were far exceeding his income. Unnumbered little items presented themselves from day
to day, and it was not many months before all his available means were gone and he was obliged to go in debt.
This was to him a painful necessity; the more so as
he saw it might have been easily avoided, had the
proper provision been made in securing a parsonage.
The strictest economy could not now relieve him, unless a more generous support should be granted by
his brethren, who were abundantly able to keep their
preacher from want.

It may not be uninteresting to take a look into that
department of the Eaton parsonage, as the old house
is now called, over which Mrs. Stanly presides. It is
furnished in good style, though some of the furniture
has been left at Embury for want of room in her present residence. Still she has enough. Everything
seems in order, and the general arrangement cannot
fail to exhibit the good taste of the housekeeper. She
has chosen, for the present at least, to get along without help, and though quite inexperienced, has thus far
succeeded finely. At least Mr. Stanly is sure no one
could do better.

As the winter evenings came on, a great share of
the volumes of the library have found their place, one
by one, in the sitting room below, and Emily, after
the household cares are disposed of, often spends her
leisure hours in reading and writing by her husband's
side. The little trials passed through have not been
sufficient to subdue the buoyancy of spirits with
which she is blessed, or cause her to regret her hus-

band's connection with the ministry. With him she has planned for the prosperity of the station, and from the beginning felt deeply for the interests of the church. With many of her acquaintances she has great reason to be pleased, and friends are already gathered around her, to whom she is ardently attached. Thus the happy months pass on, and though dark shadows sometimes fall across their pathway, the young preacher and his companion recognize the hand of a kind and bountiful Providence, and rejoice in the measure of success which has thus far attended their labors.

CHAPTER IX.

HE who has watched for souls as a faithful servant of the Lord Jesus Christ, can alone tell the struggling emotions of a pastor's heart. To go in and out before the people as their spiritual guide, feeling that deathless interests are depending upon the faithful discharge of the commission received from a risen Redeemer, and that to him a strict account is to be rendered for every opportunity, is to bear a burden of no trifling import. It is true the world has its responsibilities; and these are sometimes sufficient to tax the energies of the human mind to its utmost limit, but the world has no cares equal to those of the christian minister. He is

> "To watch for souls for which the Lord,
> Did heavenly bliss forego;
> For souls, which must forever live
> In rapture or in woe."

From the commencement of Mr. Stanly's labors, he had not been unmindful of the importance of the work committed to his hands. He had looked out on the moral field prepared for the harvest, and had earnestly toiled to gather sheaves into the garner of the Lord. Hitherto he had not labored in vain. His heart was strengthened by the result of his first year's effort, and though since his return from conference,

unexpected difficulties had arisen in his way, he was
in no wise disheartened. Girding himself anew for
the conflict, he pressed toward the prize, trusting in
the God of heaven for success.

During the winter months it was with unfeigned
pleasure that he observed signs of awakening in the
church and congregation. The social meetings became largely attended, and it was evident that the
blessing of God rested upon the preaching of the
word; so that in several instances sinners began to
inquire the way of life, and bow with penitent
hearts at the altar of mercy. Encouraged by these
tokens of the Divine presence, the ever watchful pastor redoubled his diligence, and toiled with increasing earnestness in the vineyard of the Lord.

Hopeful conversions began to occur in connection
with this faithful use of the ordinances of religion.
The youth, for whom he felt an especial interest, were
the principal subjects of the work which followed.
With great rejoicing he led many of these to the
mercy seat, and occasionally had the happiness of
seeing those in middle life, and even in old age, become the willing subjects of the cross. There was
no protracted meeting, and no unusual excitement in
the congregation, yet such was the interest in religious concerns, that the church received numerous and
valuable additions.

To meet the wants of the community at such a time,
required much more than ordinary anxiety and labor.
Mr. Stanly found his pastoral duties rapidly increasing, as he was constrained to visit such as were
seeking religion, and aid them in forming correct

conceptions of duty, and at the same time encourage them to a cheerful compliance with the terms of the gospel. In this manner his time was fully occupied without leaving opportunities for study and calm reflection, which one in his position so much needs.

In addition to the usual and appropriate duties of a minister, many other things were left to divide his time and consume his strength. Thus, if subscription papers were to be circulated or charities collected, as is frequently the case in every appointment, it fell to the lot of the pastor, as no one else was willing to devote his time to the interests of the church, or make the necessary sacrifices for the accomplishment of these ends. In this manner he was frequently obliged to turn aside and serve tables, taking even the oversight of ventilating and warming the house of worship, preparatory to the public services.

The winter passed away and Mr. Stanly was happy in his chosen work. The assiduity with which he toiled diminished not the pleasure experienced in witnessing the triumphs of religion. He rejoiced in the assurance that God was with him in the abundance of his grace, and would sustain him until his work was done.

Emily also shared largely the interest of this revival scene. Entering heartily into the spirit of the occasion, she contributed much to the zeal and spiritual energy of her husband; and though comparatively unseen, was no mean agent employed of God in carrying forward his work. But few understand

the extent to which a minister's influence is graduated by the scenes through which he passes in his
own family circle. Fewer still have thought that
the society he serves has much to do toward making
that circle what it is found to be.

CHAPTER X.

EVERY true minister of the gospel is animated with a deep and fervent love for the souls he seeks to save. This principle, which, next to the love of God, becomes the ruling element of his nature, often leads him to forsake friends and kindred, that he may go forth and preach Christ crucified to lost and dying men. The world has never witnessed a sublimer heroism than has often resulted from the powerful operations of grace, thus brought to bear on the sanctified heart. In a measure this is still seen in every faithful laborer, who cultivates the heritage of the church.

That this love is reciprocal there can be no doubt. The converted sinner in turn finds his heart drawn out in affection for his pastor, and hence, almost ere the parties are aware, a mutual attachment has grown into being. In this respect the relation between a pastor and his people is of a peculiar character. In it may be found congeniality added to intercourse— a concord of mind and temper as well as a confederacy of interests and a union of hopes.

Thus a strong attachment was found existing between the inmates of the Eaton parsonage and the society they served. Mr. Stanly's care for the spiritual welfare of the church, awoke within him a deep

D*   6

interest in behalf of all its members. The ardency of his labors, and the evident sincerity of his motives had established a claim to a place in their affections, which they now gratefully permitted him to occupy. All this is equally true with regard to his companion. Though diffident and retiring in her manners, Mrs. Stanly had looked with a watchful eye upon the cause committed to her husband's hands, and had felt as intensely as he in its behalf. She had not become a convert to the theory that constitutes the minister's wife a sort of public functionary, and though acknowledging herself bound to do all within her power to promote the prosperity of Christ's kingdom among men, she admitted no obligation upon herself, but such as rested with equal weight upon the members of the church in common. Viewing herself in this light, it is not strange that she steadily declined "taking the lead" in those benevolent enterprises which fall by common consent to female hands. She saw around her many, older and wiser than herself, to whom this duty properly belonged, and who had far greater leisure than she could, from her household cares, command.

In this opinion of her relative position, Mrs Stanly was sustained by the sentiments of the most pious and intelligent part of community. Perhaps there were none who might not have been pleased to have honored her with these marks of distinction, but when she declined, there were many who scorned the idea of demanding it as a right, on account of her being the wife of their minister. Among these was Mrs. Olney, who freely advised her on the subject, Mrs.

Allen and Mrs. Hallam, together with others of similar spirit. It will be remembered that these ladies had
kindly defended her decision in the matter of the sewing society, when her motives were rudely assailed,
and her character misrepresented, by persons equally
ignorant of both. Her stay at Mr. Hallam's while
becoming settled, had given rise to an intimacy with
that family of no ordinary nature.

On all occasions of trial or embarrassment, Emily
had gone with entire freedom and unburdened herself to Sister Hallam, who by her kindness of spirit
and appositeness of counsel, had almost supplied a
mother's place from the day she left the parental
roof. So intimate had the parties become, that all
conventional formalities were thrown aside, and the
two households ran freely together as one. This privilege was a source of pleasure, which Emily could not
fail to appreciate. It made up, in part at least, for
the loss of those friends with whom she had been
accustomed to mingle in other days. New ties
were thus formed in the place of old ones broken,
and the young wife no longer felt herself among
strangers.

But it was soon discovered that this kindness and
consequent intimacy, provoked a feeling of an opposite character. There are always some who look with
a kind of jealous eye upon the preacher's family; and
the church at Eaton formed no exception to the general rule. Such was Mrs. Johnson, who had ever
treated Emily with a due degree of courtesy when in
her presence, but had at the same time maintained an
air of stateliness and dignity, that forbade all ap-

proaches to familiarity. Mrs. Smith was also fashionable and polite, and had no higher ambition than to ape the Johnsons and Lewises; and these, with a few others, felt inclined to complain that Mrs. Stanly showed partiality in her intercourse with her neighbors.

It will be remembered that the unpleasant affair of the sewing society, grew out of the claims set up by these ladies, and it was evident that they were still profoundly impressed with the theory which was then put forth. According to their view, a preacher's wife must not choose her friends, and associate with them according to the well known laws of the human mind, but must do all her visiting and calling on the stoical principle of taking the community in course, without private friendships, or the cultivation of pleasing associations. They were, therefore, much afflicted by the partiality shown in these frequent calls at Mr. Hallam's. Acting in accordance with their favorite idea, it was made a theme of public conversation, until quite a number entered into similar views, and shared the dissatisfied feeling which now began to be exhibited.

Mrs. Stanly, all unconscious of what was thought and said, continued her intercourse with Mrs. Hallam. It was to her a source of comfort not to be estimated, to have one with whom she might commune and advise, with reference to all her little trials and difficulties. It had not entered her heart that there was a single person disposed to murmur or complain for such a cause. She was not yet schooled in the selfishness of the world in which she lived; for let it be disguised as it may by a professed desire for the good of society, the real cause of this feeling had its existence in the baser propensities of human nature.

Mrs. Johnson now resolved to " have a talk" with the unsuspecting object of her dislike. She was not sure but duty called her to warn Mrs. Stanly of the error into which she was falling ; at least to inform her of what was said on the subject of her visits. Burdened with the importance of her mission, she appeared at the parsonage with her usual formalities and more than usual compliments. It so happened that Mr. Stanly was also in, though it would have been much more pleasant for the visitor to have seen Emily and conversed with her alone. After various preliminaries by way of preparation for the subject which was to follow, Mrs. Johnson began by inquiring,

" Have you called on Brother Miles lately ? I was there not long since, and he complained that you and Sister Stanly slighted him. I dropped in to tell you, so that you might remove the hardness by going often to see him."

Mr. Stanly colored slightly, and hesitated a moment before making reply. This Brother Miles was a most inveterate fault-finder, and the pastor was well aware had no just cause of complaint. Though a member of the church, he lived in constant neglect of its services, and only kept up a sufficient observation on its affairs to enable him to indulge his favorite propensity.

" I was there not long since," he at length answered.

"He is quite a particular man, you know, and needs a little attention," she added.

"So I perceive," said the pastor, with an evident wish to dismiss the subject, without saying all that was in his mind.

"I trust *you* will call, also, Sister Stanly."

"I have been there once," was the reply, "though Mrs. Miles has never called on me. So you perceive I have already overstepped the rules of etiquette in my desire to see her."

"But you should not wait for people to call on you," said Mrs. Johnson.

"Isn't that the rule," asked Emily, "when a stranger comes into a place?"

"Yes, to be sure; but with a preacher's wife it is different."

"I was not aware of it, though I have in several instances made the first call."

"O, yes," continued Mrs. Johnson, "*you* must not be particular in these matters."

"I think I have not been, or I should not have gone to Brother Miles'. And then," continued Emily, "when I was there I heard nothing but complaints against former preachers and their wives, and I expected it would be the same about me when I was away. I think I shall not go again until she visits me."

"She never visits the preachers," said Mrs. Johnson.

"Really," interrupted Mr. Stanly, "I don't think Brother and Sister Miles have any cause of complaint."

"Perhaps not, but he is very particular, and so is

she, as to that matter; and we ought to try and gratify them. We are to ' become all things to all men,' you know."

The pastor smiled at this ludicrous application of the apostle's language, but seemingly taking no notice of it, remarked that they had paid the Mileses all the attention that was their due.

" But they are not the only ones that think you show partiality," persisted Mrs. Johnson. "Sister Stanly calls at Mr. Hallam's quite frequently. It is this that creates a jealousy among the members. Remember, we all have equal claims on you."

" I did not know that any body had a claim on *me*," said Emily, looking a little puzzled.

" And I cannot consent to any such claim," replied her husband, with some earnestness. " I acknowledge it to be my duty to visit among the people, and that this grows out of my relation to them as their pastor. But my wife sustains no different relation to the community than does any other christian woman. In my opinion it is just as much the duty of Sister Miles to visit by course as of Mrs. Stanly."

" We look upon the preacher's wife as an example for all to follow, and expect her to devote her time to the interests of the church," answered Mrs. Johnson.

" I see no reason for such a claim," said Mr. Stanly, "and as you have heard me say before, can never consent to it. I suppose she may have her friends as well as others, and is at liberty to conform to the rules of society around her, providing they do not conflict with religious duty. I am in the employ of the church—she is not. If she is to do a minister's work, suppose we have her ordained, and set regularly at it."

This playful remark caused a little laughter, and Mrs. Stanly replied that she had not yet received any evidence of a Divine call to the sacred office, and should therefore give up its honors and responsibilities to her husband.

The subject was here dropped. Neither of the parties seemed inclined to discuss it further, though both had much more in their hearts than they had expressed. Mrs. Johnson had not the slightest sympathy with the Mileses, and had taken up their complaint simply to get at the real cause of her dissatisfaction. She was extremely mortified at the position taken by her pastor, and being unable to refute it, made a few commonplace remarks, and withdrew.

She was no sooner gone, than the young wife burst into tears. The imperative and unreasonable demand made upon her, and the manifest disposition to find fault, awakened feelings which she could not control. She felt herself entirely unqualified for a minister's wife, if such were the duties of her position; and the "we" which Mrs. Johnson was careful to employ seemed to imply that she did not speak for herself, but for the society at large. Several incidents had occurred since her coming to Eaton that were calculated to deepen this impression.

And yet what could be more unreasonable. This theory allowed her no reciprocation of kind offices on the part of those around her, and no genial flow of soul toward those she loved. Indeed, she must not love at all. She was the property of the church, and must be a stoic at heart and in life.

Had it really come to this? Could she have no endearments, no delightful associations, no private walks, no *home?* Alas, for the peace and happiness of a minister's family. There are too many who would, in this thoughtless manner, destroy them both.

Mr. Stanly was also troubled at this intermeddling with the affairs of his wife. Since their settlement at Eaton, her hands and heart had been full. His income did not allow the luxury of hired help, and he was satisfied she had done all she could. He was aware that his own visits among his members had been less frequent during this than the preceding year, but he had been compelled to repair houses, build fences, and fit up for himself a place in which to live, as well as attend to the domestic cares of his new relation. To his own mind there was a sufficient excuse for any apparent delinquency. He knew not how general might be the dissatisfaction shadowed forth in this visit of Mrs. Johnson, and this very uncertainty increased his perplexity. It is not to be wondered at that the heart of the young minister sunk within him, as he contemplated his position, without the aid of experience and counsel.

Long and earnestly was the conversation kept up between George and Emily. Occasionally an unbidden thought of retiring from the work would force itself upon their attention, but refusing, for the present, at least, to entertain it, they decided, after a careful examination of the past, to go forward in the name of the Lord, leaving the results in His hand.

Notwithstanding the expostulations of Mrs. Johnson, Emily had recourse to her tried and familiar friend, Sister Hallam. She soon became satisfied, from the representation of this excellent woman, that the fears which agitated her were groundless, and that comparatively few shared the prejudices which had been so ungenerously pressed upon her attention.

CHAPTER XI.

CLOSING SCENES.

How swift the flight of time. Days, and months, and years are like a tale that is told. The past becomes as a dream of the night,—the present is as a shadow that fleeëth quickly away.

Mr. Stanly had scarcely become settled in his new abode, and begun to gather around him the endearments of home, when the time came for his removal. Though the change before him had been anticipated, and in a measure provided for, it was still with most unpleasant feelings that he contemplated its near approach. Eaton was the place where he had commenced his ministry, and his attachment to the people had steadily increased from the beginning of his labors. It was in many respects a pleasant and agreeable station, and the two past years had been the happiest of his life.

Mrs. Stanly would have also gladly remained. Notwithstanding the little trials that had fallen especially to her lot, she was, on the whole, quite contented and happy. Numerous friends had gathered around, whom she could not fail to love. When she came a stranger among them, unacquainted with their usages, and ignorant of what was expected of one in her position, they had kindly given her a place in their sympathies and prayers, and bestowed upon her many tokens of respect. She was glad to love them in return, and, doubtful as to the future, could but regret the necessity of the approaching separation.

Both the pastor and his wife were willing, however, to yield to the constitution of the church. They believed the Itinerancy to be a most efficient means for spreading the gospel, and could see many reasons for its perpetuity. Their regrets, therefore, were in no wise to be confounded with a disposition to complain.

Though Mr. Stanly had found many difficulties in his way, his second term had been more than ordinarily successful. The congregation had steadily increased, numerous additions had been made to the society, a small debt which had embarrassed the church for years was paid off, and the benevolent contributions of the members generally were greatly increased. It was conceded, on all hands, that much of this success was due to the energy and perseverance of the pastor, who had labored in these various departments with unabated zeal. It is no wonder, then, that the people indulged still more earnest regrets than did the preacher, at the change before them.

In the matter of "quarterage," or, in other words, the preacher's salary, there was yet a large deficiency. Mr. Stanly was so immediately interested in this subject, that he had considered it beyond his province; and while looking to all the other interests of the station, had left this where the discipline directs, in the hands of the official members of the church. These were good men, and generally skilled in business matters of their own, but, for some reason, they allowed this whole subject to sleep on their hands. Whenever the deficiencies were alluded to, they contented themselves with the remark that it would all come out right in the end, and thus gave it no serious attention. They now began to bestir themselves, as if to make up for their delinquencies during the year by a fitful effort at its close.

And then came farewell visits and other scenes indicative of the friendship of a grateful people toward a faithful pastor. Various little mementoes were placed in his hands, by those desiring to be had in remembrance, while a multitude of kind wishes and earnest prayers were freely offered for his future success.

In these offerings Emily was almost uniformly remembered. Though but one year at Eaton, she had won upon the hearts of the people, and, so far as her acquaintance extended, secured their esteem. Even Mrs. Johnson, Mrs. Lewis, and their co-workers, were her friends, and had intended her no real evil. A mistaken judgment and a thoughtlessness as to results, had led them to the course they pursued. They now manifested their friendship with as much cordiality as any in the congregation.

Under such circumstances, the pastor and his companion felt embarrassed to be obliged to go away. Even the old house in which they lived began to possess its attractions, as they saw in every apartment evidences of their care and skill. Had it been possible, they would have gladly remained, and shared for years to come in the trials and triumphs of this people. But there was no alternative; and arrangements were being already made to go, they knew not where. It was this uncertainty that gave rise to much of their aversion to the contemplated change.

The last Sabbath came, and the congregation turned out in unusual numbers to hear the preacher's parting words. He did not choose to present a formal farewell discourse, and yet his remarks were adapted to the peculiar circumstances connected with the occasion. A voice of warning was raised against the dangers that crowd the christian's pathway, and words of encouragement given, as his hearers were referred to the strong arm of the Almighty, and urged to flee to the rock that was cleft to take them in. And then the speaker called attention to that great and glorious day, when the friends that now part shall meet again, and enter upon the unbroken rest prepared on high for the people of God. He spoke of the hope he entertained of gaining that heavenly abode, and meeting those with whom he here worshipped, as they should assemble in the house not made with hands, eternal and in the heavens.

As he thus pointed to the final resting place of the faithful, he was himself deeply moved, as were those who heard him. On every hand, there were evidences of a grateful people's love in the falling tears and hearty responses with which the retiring pastor's admonitions and parting counsels were received. It was hard thus to go away, but blessed to be followed by the sympathies of a praying people.

The following day was the appointed time to leave

for the seat of conference. Emily was to spend the
week among her friends at Embury, which was on
Mr. Stanly's way. An early hour on the morning of
their departure had been fixed for the final settlement with the stewards, who were not able until that
time to make the necessary reports. They accordingly called at the parsonage just as everything was in
readiness for the journey, and paid over the sum
which had been collected. It wanted about forty
dollars of making up the amount allowed by these
same men at the beginning of the year, whose duty it
was to estimate the pastor's current expenses, and
who had limited the amount to the sum of three hundred dollars.

And yet they seemed to look upon the deficiency
as a matter of no special moment. It was not an unusual affair for their ministers to go away unpaid, and
they had thus lost all sense of the injustice and wrong
which they were committing. They well knew that
Mr. Stanly had contracted debts for his support during the year, in reliance upon his salary, and that he
had no other means of cancelling them; but with a
statement of their difficulty in raising funds, the subject was coolly dismissed.

To this procedure, Mr. Stanly made no remonstrance. He could not fail to see the iniquity of the
transaction, but for fear of giving offense, or laying
himself liable to the suspicion of preaching the gospel from mercenary motives, he concluded to keep
silent. He knew that neither of these men would
presume to treat the common day laborer in this manner, after he had toiled through weary months in the

cultivation of their farms, and yet he could see no moral difference in the two cases. He was also well aware that if either member of the official board would devote a single day to the duties of his office, the whole difficulty might be remedied. This had not been done, and he must now suffer from their negligence.

With a heavy heart, the preacher called at a store on the corner, and paid out the pittance remaining after withholding sufficient to defray his expenses to conference, and then drove out of the village. Thoughts of debts and impatient creditors crowded upon him, and the young wife also let fall an occasional tear, as she approached the home of her childhood. Still, nothing was said by either of our travelers that revealed their emotions. It seemed as if each was afraid to speak, upon a subject so dark and cheerless.

The reader may ask why a faithful and successful laborer was thus left unprovided for, and whether it was from a want of ability, or a lack of disposition, that those whom he had served allowed him to suffer. It was neither. There was wealth enough in the church to support a pastor with the utmost ease. There was also a general wish that he should have his full pay. But amid so many friends, no one took sufficient interest in the subject to follow it up to a successful issue. As it was everybody's business, nobody attended to it. The preacher uttered no complaints, and the people presumed he was satisfied. Thus, through negligence more than anything else, he was left to suffering and want.

To one uninitiated in this manner of doing business, this will doubtless seem like open dishonesty. At

Eaton no one viewed it in so serious a light. The congregation had done by Mr. Stanly as well as by their ministers in general. Their former pastors had consented to report them paid in full, and they expected the same at his hands. Thus they had been educated to this course, and not being likely to suffer by comparison in the conference minutes with surrounding charges, they thought nothing of it.

Eaton was not alone in turning off its minister but partially supported. The same evil prevailed in many other places, and Mr. Stanly learned by intercourse with his brethren at conference, that no small number were similarly embarrassed.

E 7

CHAPTER XII.

AT the session of Conference now held, Mr. Stanly was received in full connection, and admitted to deacon's orders. He had passed the customory term of probation, and had not only proved an acceptable preacher, but was looked upon as promising extensive usefulness in his future labors. Though young in the ministry, his services were desired by several appointments in the vicinity of his former charge, where his reputation as a minister was already established.

For some reason he was sent to none of these, but found himself put down for Lyndon, a station of respectable rank, about forty miles from Eaton. Though personally a stranger in the place of his destination, he was rather pleased than otherwise with the appointment, and prepared for an immediate removal. A day or two only was taken up in visiting friends at Embury, when the process of packing, boxing, and loading goods was entered upon, and pushed to a speedy conclusion. This required no small amount of labor, and as the change occurred in the hottest days of summer, it was of an exceedingly exhausting character. The expense of moving was also found to reach no inconsiderable sum, and

Mr. Stanly was obliged to increase the debts already contracted. Had it not been for this financial embarrassment, he could have gone to his new field of labor with a light and joyous heart. As it was, he carried with him a burden that deeply depressed his spirits, and in a degree unfitted him for his high and holy work.

Lyndon had now become the object upon which the young minister's thoughts were placed, and for which his plans were formed. He had not as many misgivings with reference to his reception, as had been indulged on a former occasion of like character, but felt, if possible, a still greater responsibility resting upon him, as a minister of the gospel. The experience of two years had more clearly taught him the magnitude of the work, and the necessity of divine aid in its performance.

All things in readiness, Mr. and Mrs. Stanly set out for their new home. The morning—for they were away at an early hour—was pleasant and agreeable, and as the way led them through the picturesque scenery of hills and valleys clothed in the richest verdure of summer, they could but enjoy the ride. For some time a lively conversation was kept up, but as the sun neared the meridian, and clouds of dust began to arise and beat in upon them, the heat was too oppressive to allow their vivacity its usual play. Under these influences, they gradually sunk into silent musings, and longed for that rest and quiet which had been for some time past denied them. Occasionally Mr. Stanly, in his effort to be cheerful, would sing a verse of some familiar hymn, or seek to

relieve the tediousness of the hour by a playful remark as objects of criticism met his eye, and furnished occasion for his wit.

"Come, cheer up, Em.," said he, with a sort of
sportiveness in which he sometimes indulged, "we
shall soon be at Lyndon, and then you can rest at
your leisure."

"Fine opportunities for rest, I should judge," said
she, with a laugh, "in cleaning house, unpacking
goods, and getting settled. I remember too well
what a time we had at Eaton, to think of rest."

"Well, but we are not going to Eaton now."

"It may be worse, for aught you and I know,"
was the reply.

"I think not," said George; "from all I can learn,
I am hoping better things. We shall not be obliged
to hunt up a house. The parsonage will be ready
for us."

"I wish our goods were in it, so that we could go
directly there. I don't enjoy staying *on the town*, as
I suppose we shall have to, for a while."

"We shall find friends who will gladly entertain
us."

"I wish I could get the dust out of my eyes before seeing them," said she. "A pretty appearance
we shall make among strangers to-night."

"Yes," answered Mr. Stanly, in a more serious
tone, "and the opinions they form at the first interview will last all the year. It is hard getting rid of
first impressions, you know."

"I would not care so much, if our usefulness was
not affected by these impressions. We are both too

nearly worn out to be ourselves, at present, and yet
I suppose the people will make no allowance."

"Our brethren generally mean well, and from
what I can hear of those at Lyndon, I judge them to
be of the right stamp."

"If I only had Sister Hallam there," said Emily,
"how glad I'd be."

Here the conversation flagged, though both were
busily engaged in thought. The last range of hills
was being crossed, and the rich valley in which they
sought a home was spread out before them. Nothing could be more inviting, and yet the fine view
was lost in its effect upon the troubled mind of the
young wife, who grew more and more pensive as the
hours flew wearily away. At length she introduced
the subject concerning which she was troubled.

"George," she asked, "how do you expect to pay
the debts we have contracted at Eaton?"

"Aha! you are turning financier, are you? I
imagine there will be no trouble now."

"But tell me. I confess I don't see the way quite
so clear as you affect to."

"Don't let us be troubled about that; sufficient to
the day is the evil thereof."

"Yes, but," persisted Emily, "both the evil and
the day are upon us."

"Well, really, *I* can't tell," answered Mr. Stanley.
"The most that I can do is to trust in the Lord and
hope for the best. There was no necessity for my
being thus embarrassed. Eaton charge was abundantly able to support me."

"They are better able to pay a minister there than at Lyndon, are they not?" inquired Mrs. Stanly.

" I suppose they are, but they have never been educated to do their duty. All their finances are left in a hap-hazard condition. Many of the brethren seem to have no conscience on this subject at all."

" And the preacher must suffer the consequences!"

" So it seems. If they had made a donation visit, as was at one time contemplated, the debts might have been avoided. But two or three brethren opposed that, on the principle that it was not proper to constitute their minister an object of charity in the eyes of the people, and this plea prevailed."

"I like the principle well enough, if it had only been carried out. As it is, they have made us proper objects of charity by their penuriousness, and then interfered to prevent our receiving it. Did those who so conscientiously opposed the donation, pay liberally?"

" Far from it. They were the last men to be liberal. At the time, I supposed their objections well intended, but I have since adopted a contrary opinion."

The conversation on this subject was long continued, and yet the young Itinerants were able to reach no favorable conclusion. They were in debt, with no immediate prospect of relief. All that could be done was to adopt a resolution to economize for the future, with the hope of becoming at least no more deeply involved. Still, they were unable to tell where their new method should begin. In clothing they had been far from extravagant in their outlays, the wardrobe which Emily brought from her

home being yet ample. Their table had been uniformly supplied with very plain though comfortable
fare, while Mr. Stanly's library and periodical list
was absolutely meager. But there was no other remedy, "they must study economy."

Under these circumstances the pastor and his wife
had to guard diligently against a disposition to murmur. They loved the Eaton society, and had done
their utmost to promote its interests. They could
but feel deeply wronged by the want of liberality
which had been manifested in return, and the neglect of the church to do them simple justice. For
more than this they did not ask at the hands of any
people.

It was nearly evening when Mr. Stanly pointed
to the spires that marked the village of Lyndon.
He had never been there, and as it was now to be
his home, was very naturally interested in the objects which met his eye. The sun, that had been
pouring his fiercest rays on the parched up earth
during the day, was just sinking from the view of
the observer, and the cool breezes were springing
up and imparting new vigor to the weary travelers
as they entered the outskirts of the town. It was a
scene of beauty and unsurpassed loveliness, as the
village, surrounded by distant mountain ranges, was
spread out before them. A large manufacturing establishment was seen at the left, the hum of whose
wheels and spindles was already heard; while nearly
opposite was the village burying-ground, with its silent dead and solemn lessons; in close proximity to
which, came the residences of the living with their

gardens and walks, their trees and flowers;—all be-
speaking the existence of wealth and enterprise, and
a cultivated taste, and at the same time inspiring the
devout heart with thanksgiving and praise to Him
from whose liberal hand is derived every perfect gift.

The parsonage, which was beside the church, was
soon reached. As Mr. Stanly drove up, several men
were standing in and around the door, while a number of ladies were seen passing to and fro by the open
windows. The introduction was soon over. Cordial
welcomes were extended to the new pastor and his
companion—who did not alight from their carriage—
and arrangements made by which they were directed
to the house of a Brother Burton to spend the night.
They soon found themselves in a pleasant family, surrounded with the luxuries as well as the comforts of
life, and evidently accustomed to entertain ministers
of the Gospel. These first impressions of Lyndon
were decidedly encouraging, and led both the preacher
and his wife to hope for the best.

During the evening Mr. Stanly made such inquiries concerning the state of the church as the circumstances would allow, and from all that he could learn
was highly pleased with his location. Mr. Burton
had a son in the ministry, and had long since resolved
to treat every Itinerant as he would wish that son to
be treated. In this determination he was heartily
sustained by all the members of his family. Hence,
their house was ever open to such as in the order of
Providence were thrown within reach of their hospitalities. Possessed of wealth and influence, secured
by industry and sterling integrity, they occupied a

prominent position in the church at Lyndon, where they had for many years devoted themselves with ardent zeal to the work of the Lord.

How pleasant for the weary laborer when cast down and partially discouraged, to find friends of this character, and share in hospitalities thus freely tendered. The personal disadvantages growing out of the Itinerant system have been in a great measure overcome by the existence of these traits, which it has so strong a tendency to develop.

Early on the following morning, Mrs. Burton proposed a visit to the parsonage. The invitation was cheerfully accepted, as Emily was anxious to make her plans, and get the house in readiness for their goods which were expected during the day. A few moments' walk brought them to the desired place. The yard in front was filled with shrubs and flowers, betokening the care of its former occupants, and inviting the new comers to a like exercise of the finer sensibilities; while every object around bore a cheerful aspect, in strong contrast with the circumstances of the previous year, of which she could not fail to be reminded.

The house was no sooner entered, than the reasons for the presence of so many persons on the preceding day were fully comprehended. Since the other preacher had moved out, it had been papered and painted within, and at the same time so thoroughly cleaned as to be prepared for immediate occupation. To the preacher and his wife, everything around seemed to say, "here the people care for their minister."

E*

The teamsters having charge of their goods soon made their appearance. This was the signal for several brethren and sisters to come and proffer their assistance. They scarcely waited for Mr. Stanly's consent, before engaging at the work to be done. Boxes were opened, carpets put down, bedsteads set up, and before night came the whole house was in order. "Surely," said Mrs. Burton, "this is an illustration of the old adage, 'many hands make light work.'"

After some consultation, in which they were urged to return to Mr. Burton's, Mr. Stanly and Emily decided to remain in the parsonage. They could, as they said, procure some articles from the bakery to commence with, and should prefer, for the present, to be at their own house. A smile passed between the ladies at the mention of the bakery, but Emily did not suspect what it meant, until some time after a boy came to the door, and setting down a basket, said, "Mrs. Peck wishes you to accept this, as you may need it to begin with."

Emily opened the basket and found a bountiful supply of pies and choice cake, which the good woman had prepared for the new minister's wife. She had scarcely put them away, when a pale little girl tapped at the door, and with a blush on her cheek, and a mild, sweet voice, betokening some embarrassment, said, "Mother has sent this to Mrs. Stanly to begin housekeeping with. Please accept it, ma'am."

It was a similar gift. With scarcely a word except a "thank you," Mrs. Stanly took out the contents of the pail, and turned away to hide a tear that, strangely

enough, just at that moment came coursing its way
down her cheek. No sooner was she alone, than
other tears followed the intruder, and she no longer
sought to restrain them.

Why should she weep? Ah! there was something ·
so touching in the unaffected friendship of this people, that she could not avoid it. She was here a
stranger, yet treated as a sister or a daughter by those
whom she for the first time now met. The people
seemed already to love her and care for her, instead
of looking on with the cold and criticising spirit which
she had anticipated.

But this was not all. Mrs. Burton came with a
larger supply than either of the others, and notwithstanding what had been previously brought in, insisted on its acceptance. Another lady also called
and inquired if anything had been received. If not,
she would send over her husband; but if she had
been anticipated by others, would wait until some
other time. Emily learned that this was Mrs. Cary,
the wife of one of the class-leaders, living almost at
the next door, though she had neither seen nor heard
anything of the family till now.

Our young housekeeper was no sooner alone than
a pleasant thought struck her, and though she was a
minister's wife, she resolved to indulge her wonted
girlishness by playing a surprise upon Mr. Stanly,
who was busily engaged in an upper room, and knew
nothing of what had taken place below. Her table
was quickly spread and arranged in her happiest
style, and all that had been brought—enough for a
large household—placed upon it, when she called,

"George! George! our tea is in readiness."

"You wish me to go to the bakery, do you?"

"Not at all, I thank you; the arrangements are all made."

Mr. Stanly looked a little surprised on coming into the kitchen, and after a moment's pause, remarked, "Aye: Sister Burton has been here, I conclude."

"Yes, but not she alone."

Emily then related the incidents that had occurred, and referred to the feelings by which she had been moved. Mr. Stanly was also affected. The value of the gifts was comparatively nothing, but the spirit that prompted them was most highly prized. From that hour the pastor and his companion felt themselves among tried and reliable friends. In other words, they were at home.

CHAPTER XIII.

THE NEW STATION.

HAVING seen the preacher thus settled in his new and comfortable home, let us now cast an eye over the station he was appointed to serve. In point of wealth and numbers, it was one of the weakest in the conference; but being located in a large village, and surrounded with an enterprising and intelligent community, it took rank among the most important charges, and demanded the first class of ministerial talent.

By great effort on their own part, and considerable help from abroad, the little society had some time since succeeded in building a church and parsonage, though left with a heavy debt, which had been a source of serious embarrassment. To sustain the interests of Methodism in such a manner as to encourage the hope of final success, a small missionary appropriation had been made from year to year, upon which the preachers had in a great measure relied for support. By a favorable turn of affairs, the demands against their church property had been recently cancelled, and the missionary appropriation was accordingly withdrawn; so that for the future, the membership were thrown upon their own resources.

The society at Lyndon, though possessing but little of this world's goods, were accounted rich in faith,

and had ever been ambitious to do their Master's bidding. They had nobly contended with the difficulties
of other days, and now that these were in a measure
removed, were prepared to engage with earnest hearts
in the work of the Lord. Mr. Burton might be regarded as in all respects the leading man in the
church. Of its members, he alone could be called
wealthy, though Mr. Spaulding and several other farmers residing at a little distance, were in easy circumstances, and at the same time liberal supporters
of its financial interests. Aside from these, the congregation was mostly made up of mechanics and day
laborers, not able to contribute largely, but presenting with gladness such offerings as were within their
power. It will be seen, therefore, that Mr. Stanly's
prospect of a support that would enable him to pay
off his debts, was not very flattering. The membership, not more than eighty in all, were scarcely able
to meet the expenses of their own pastor, without paying arrearages for other charges, a hundred fold more
competent than themselves. Yet with all their poverty, the Lyndon preacher was never allowed to go
away in debt for expenses incurred in *their* service.
To do more than this, under present circumstances,
they could not hope.

The reader has already had a view, in the greeting
extended to the new pastor, of the spirit manifested
by the members of this church. It may be well to
remark that this was no fitful display, or mere out-
gushing of transient emotions, but a real index to the
feelings of all the parties concerned. Let it not be
supposed, however, that there were no discordant ele-

ments. A portion only of the membership has yet
been seen. There are others standing aloof, who will
by-and-by come forward with their peculiarities, in
strong contrast with what has been witnessed.

Leaving these for the present, it is sufficient to say
that Brothers Cary, Burton and Smith were the class-
leaders; while prominent among the stewards may
be named Mr. Spaulding, and his opposite in temperament and character, Mr. Steele. These latter
had the principal oversight of the society's temporal
affairs, and were expected to keep an especial eye on
the wants of the preacher's family.

The little Lyndon church did not simply show their
zeal by the offerings they brought into the store-
house of the Lord. A deep religious feeling pervaded the members, that was allowed to give tone to
all their transactions. This could be seen alike in
their prayer and class meetings, their household devotions, and the more public services of the sanctuary.
With this state of things, the pastor could not fail to
be pleased: and from the first he entered heartily into
their plans, and as a standard bearer of the cross, led
the people forward in the way of life.

CHAPTER XIV.

OLD MRS. BLAKIE.

THE auspicious beginning at Lyndon augured a prosperous year. The friendship manifested toward the new preacher at his introduction, did not lesson with the lapse of time, but rather increased as a more extensive acquaintance developed those social and religious excellences by which it was merited.

After all, Lyndon was not a paradise. Difficulties existed as in other places, and there were sufficient to try the patience and prove the faith of the pastor, who encountered and sought to overcome them. These exhibited themselves from time to time, as will be seen in the course of our narrative.

Not long after Mr. Stanly's settlement, a lady called, and introduced herself to Emily as Mrs. Blakie. She apologized for not having come in sooner, for, as she said, it had always been a point with her to visit the new preacher, and give him an insight into the affairs of the society, as soon as he came among them. She was sorry Brother Stanly was not at home, for she wanted to have a plain talk with him, with reference to the low state of the church, and the way in which it was to be remedied. Without waiting for any response from Emily, she began her story and ran on with a railroad speed. She had been, as she informed her auditor, a member of that society from

its organization, and her "experience" taught her
many things that no stranger could possibly understand. A detailed history of the scandal of the last
ten years was then drawn out, in which the charac-
ters of both ministers and people were freely handled.
In her estimation, everything was passing at a false
estimate. The best members of the church were
overlooked and forgotten, while worthless persons were
elevated and put forward. Old fashioned Methodism
was rapidly dying out, as everybody was after the
popularity and fashion of the world, and unless something was done quickly, she was sure the whole
church would be ruined. Indeed, her zeal knew no
bounds as she talked about a "holy church," without
which sinners could never be converted and saved.

While the old lady thus talked, Emily was at first
quite at a loss what to say in reply. She soon felt
relieved on this point, by observing that the time was
fully occupied without the exercise of her gifts, and
wisely concluded to keep silent. She saw that the
spirit indulged was not that of the gospel, but did not
feel at liberty to reprove a stranger so much older
and more "experienced" than herself, and so allowed
her visitor to go on with her backbiting to her heart's
content. Mrs. Blakie observed the respectful silence,
and no doubt thought the preacher's wife deeply interested in the subject of her discourse.

At length there came a pause, and Mrs. Stanly
could do no less than ask, if there were not among
them, at least a few spiritual and devoted members.

"Only a *very* few," was the answer, and they are

8

never made anything of by the preachers, and so are almost discouraged."

"Who are they?" inquired Emily.

Mrs. Blakie named two or three kindred spirits, but they were persons not before heard of at the parsonage.

"I have never seen them in our social meetings," said Mrs. Stanly. "I am sure they cannot be at all active in the church."

"O, no, we don't enjoy the meetings at the chapel, and so meet o' Tuesday nights at my house."

"I think we have most excellent prayer meetings," answered Emily.

"We used to have, but they are nothing now. The members are getting so proud, and wear so much finery, the Lord won't bless us."

"He will bless those who do right, and worship according to his commandment, will he not?"

"Yes, but the church is all backslid. We used to have prayer meetings so powerful that they could be he'ern all over the village. There was no waiting for one another then. I am afraid we shall never see the like again."

"Perhaps not. But still we may enjoy the Divine blessing ourselves, let others do as they will," answered the preacher's wife.

Just then Mr. Stanly came in, and Emily was glad of the opportunity to escape further conversation, as her visitor turned to him and began her complaints. He listened for a few moments, and then interrupted her by asking,

"What is the object of this narrative, sister?"

Mrs. Blakie was somewhat frustrated by this question, and after a moment's hesitation replied,

"To let the minister know the true state of the church. You are a stranger, and must be ignorant of the character of your members. I am sure it will be for your interest to know the whole truth."

"Haven't you something good to tell me about my brethren and sisters?" asked the pastor. "If you have, I shall be glad to hear it; if you have not, I beg to be excused."

"I am only telling you what is true," said she; "I hope you don't want to cover up iniquity in the church."

"I do not desire a history of past dissensions and strifes," answered Mr. Stanly, "unless you have some commendable purpose to be accomplished by the detail. Before hearing you further, I wan't to know your object."

"I mean all I say for your good," replied the old lady.

"If that be your motive, I will appreciate it; but as I am satisfied your course will do me more harm than good, the same motive will now lead you to desist."

"But I want you to know how things are."

"The apostle says, 'speak evil of no man,' and I suppose it just as bad to listen to scandal as to be the author of it. I cannot hear you further."

The old lady appeared quite offended at this rebuff, and threw out something about ministers being as bad as the people, and arose to go.

"Wait a little," said Mr. Stanly; "there are other

subjects on which I shall feel it a privilege to con-
verse with you. How are you prospering, Sister
Blakie, in religion ? "   •

She could not answer even this question, without
falling upon her favorite theme, the backslidings of
the church, which had made her discontented and
unhappy. She finally confessed she had no religious
enjoyment, but could not be convinced that she was
herself at fault. It all resulted from the times in
which it was her misfortune to live. Their degen-
eracy, especially in their relation to the Methodist
church, destroyed her peace and made her miserable.

As Mrs. Blakie was not allowed to make use of
her peculiar talent, and had no taste for anything
else, she soon withdrew, greatly chagrined at the result of her call. She went immediately to her " spiritual friends," and declared that their new minister
was not willing to have iniquity exposed, and could
not endure plain-dealing; but rather reproved and silenced her on account of her faithfulness. As might
be expected, these were greatly agitated by the result of her mission, and were henceforth furnished
with a new cause of complaint.

"How glad I was," said Emily as soon as Mrs.
Blakie was gone, "that you put a stop to her tattling.
I had become weary of hearing her."

"I cannot consent to listen to these old troubles,"
said her husband, "when no object is sought but the
gratification of personal piques."

"Do you know her then ? "

"No, but I know the spirit she is of."

"There can be no great difficulty in ascertaining that," said Emily.

"It is indeed strange that some persons think a preacher should take an interest in the scandal of the whole town. This woman doubtless supposed she was doing me a favor, in recounting the inconsisten: cies of christians in years gone by, and thus awakening in my mind suspicions, perhaps of my very best brethren. And then, ten chances to one, she would have given a false coloring to every subject which she touched. A mind so greedy as hers for something about which to find fault, is never reliable."

"I presume she has taken offense at what you said, and will hereafter bring you into the list."

"Very likely. I cannot hope to escape such a person's censure, and should consider it a real calamity to have her approbation. As you know, 'the world will love its own.'"

CHAPTER XV.

A few hours after the events of the last chapter, the parsonage was favored with a visit of quite an opposite character. Mr. and Mrs. Burton came in at an early hour of the evening, as they had frequently done before, and engaged in pleasant conversation with their pastor, concerning the state of the church and subjects of like character, in which they felt a mutual interest. This excellent man exerted a blessed influence on the society in Lyndon. Much of his time and attention was devoted to the cause of Christ, and he never allowed an opportunity to pass, when he might add to the happiness of the minister's family, or aid his preacher in the performance of his duties. Quiet and unobtrusive in his manners, possessed of sound judgment and deep piety, he was well qualified to advise, in cases of doubt, and at the same time assist in carrying out the plans already formed.

Nothing could be more pleasing and profitable to a young minister of right spirit, than such intercourse with his brethren. Mr. Stanly did not fail to appreciate it. He had been favored with nothing of the kind on his former charge, and was all the more grateful for its enjoyment in this.

To Emily, such seasons were still more precious. Thrown, like her husband, into the midst of strangers,

she had far less opportunities to form acquaintances;
and such approaches on the part of the people were
accordingly the more highly prized. Besides, Mrs.
Burton's visits were not stiff and formal as is often
the case, but free and social, calling out the best feelings of the human heart, and partaking of the familiarity that marks the intercourse of long and tried
friends.

The conversation on this occasion had not been long
continued, when attention was called to the affair of
the afternoon. "Do you know Sister Blakie?" inquired Emily.

"Yes," said Mr. Burton, "we know her well. Has
she been here yet?"

"She was in to-day, and spent an hour or two."

"I thought it was about time," said Mrs. Burton.
"She calls once or twice on every new preacher, and
relates her story of wrongs. I suppose she gave the
church a fine setting out, did she not, Brother
Stanly."

"Not in my presence. She doubtless would have
done so, but I refused to listen, and she soon left."

"I am glad you reproved her," said Mr. Burton.
"The old lady was once an excellent member of society, but has for a number of years been a source of
vexation to the whole church. She began by being
a great stickler for plain dress, and what she called
old fashioned Methodism. Not content with giving
these their due share of attention, she has finally sunk
everything into a crusade against the church on this
subject. All the weightier matters of the law are set
at defiance, and the means of grace neglected, that

she may indulge her passion for fault-finding with
modern Methodism, and show her contempt for the
fancied evils which she cannot remedy."

"Yes," said Mr. Stanly, "she claimed to be a representative of old fashioned Methodism."

"No great honor to the cause she advocates, I
should judge," said Emily.

"No, replied Mrs. Burton, "she is an injury to the
church. I think we have borne with her as long as
it is our duty."

"Who are those whom she calls 'spiritual' members?" asked Emily.

"They are some half dozen persons like herself—
clannish, fault-finding, and tattling. If I were to venture advice unasked, it would be to disregard them
altogether," answered Mr. Burton.

Mrs. Blakie and her confederates were soon dismissed, and more agreeable topics introduced. In
looking over the affairs of the station, Mr. Burton alluded to several subjects that encouraged the pastor's
heart, and strengthened him for new labors in his appointed field. A case was mentioned that had come
under observation, where an unconverted person had
been awakened by the preaching, and was now earnestly inquiring the way of life. Others were pointed
out, who had been quickened by the pastor's appeals,
and it was thought that a greater seriousness pervaded
the congregation than had been manifest for many
previous years.

Such was the character of the conversation which
occupied the evening. It was designed to benefit the
preacher, and well adapted to that end. Mr. Stanly

felt like laboring with a new impulse, in a field thus promising. How could he fail of success with such men to hold up his hands.

As the visitors arose to go, Mrs. Burton placed a small package in the hands of Emily, with the remark that she wished her to accept it as a present from herself. So saying, she passed out, leaving the preacher and his wife alone, as they opened the bundle and examined its contents. It was a rich pattern for a dress, which the good woman had bought for this purpose.

Emily's eyes moistened at this token of Sister Burton's friendship. She could but feel grateful, and yet it was with peculiar emotions that she looked upon it. Heretofore she had not been dependent on others for either food or raiment, and it seemed almost like beggary to be receiving such gifts. And then she thought of Eaton and her husband's debts. It was just what she needed, and would be so much in their favor, as they economized to meet those claims.

George looked on in silence until it was folded and laid aside. He had listened to his wife's remarks without appearing to give them much attention. His mind was busily awakened to reflections which had been called up by the occasion. The past flitted rapidly before him, and the future rose up in prospect. At length he started from his reverie and remarked,

"One thing is certain: Brother and Sister Burton have a care for their minister."

"Yes," said Emily, turning away to hide a falling tear, "and for his wife also."

F

CHAPTER XVI.

MR. STANLY had not been many months at Lyndon, before the congregation gave evidence of a decided increase of religious interest. The Sabbath services were largely attended, and several persons had already sought the pearl of precious price, and were now rejoicing in the hope of the gospel. Added to this, may be mentioned the fact that a general seriousness prevailed among his hearers, so that both preacher and people felt greatly encouraged, and trusted that the future should be still more highly prosperous.

Just as matters were assuming this most favorable appearance, the pastor was troubled by the rise of new and unexpected difficulties. On the part of some of his members, he could not fail to detect an uneasy and restless spirit, accompanied by an inclination to be dissatisfied with what was taking place. The complaints of Mrs. Blakie and her friends, already alluded to, had been wisely disregarded as unjust and comparatively unimportant. These persons were well known as inveterate fault-finders, and for that reason could do no material injury. But there was another class ill at ease, whose good intentions entitled them to respect, and whose influence in the society was far from being limited. They were those who, actuated by honest purposes, and a sincere desire to promote the interests of the church, were often led into excesses by their mistaken zeal, which a more extensive knowledge would have enabled them to avoid.

A leading spirit among these was Mr. Cary, the class-leader. This brother was generally considered a good man, but was of an ambitious turn of mind, that led him on all occasions to put himself forward, and seek a prominent place in what was going on. If by any means his opinions happened to be disregarded, he made no secret of his dissatisfaction, and not unfrequently arrayed himself against such interests as he was not able to control. Mr. Stanly's predecessor at Lyndon had unfortunately appointed him leader of the Sabbath noon class, and Mr. Cary had already succeeded in imparting his spirit to a considerable number of those associated with him. Apt to reprove, severe in his censures, and confident in his professions, he had won the reputation of being deeply pious among those who mistake these qualities for evidences of a high state of grace. Though meaning well, and doubtless a christian, he was, in fact, far from occupying the position thus assigned him.

At this particular time, Mr. Cary and his associates were deeply afflicted with the want of " life and power" in the services of the church. According to their view, the preaching was too doctrinal, and the meetings altogether too formal to result in a revival. Though evidently not disposed to indulge in fault-finding for its own sake, they were quite free to publicly express their dissatisfaction with the circumstances around them.

This spirit of uneasiness manifested itself in various ways, and sometimes in a manner calculated to awaken feelings of a most unpleasant character. In the social meetings, their prayers, which were earnest and excited, would not unfrequently be a mere rehearsal of the backslidings of christians, or a lamentation over the indifference and lukewarmness of Zion. Even when they prayed for their minister, there would seem an implied censure of his course, not really designed, but very naturally resulting from the feelings which they indulged. The effect of all this, was not simply to dampen their own religious enjoyment, but also to awaken suspicions among others, and weaken the faith of their fellow laborers.

This class of the membership were now anxious that a protracted meeting should be got up, and some distinguished revivalist sent for and placed at its head. Mr. Cary consulted his friends, and found their views so to agree with his own, that he was encouraged in pressing matters to an immediate issue. It was determined that the subject should be broached to the minister; and as Mr. Stanly was known to feel a deep interest in the conversion of sinners, but little doubt was entertained of winning his consent. Mr. Cary, Mr. Havens and Mr. Steele accordingly agreed to call at the parsonage, and consult their pastor on the proposed plan.

It so happened when these brethren visited Mr. Stanly, that Mr. Spaulding, another class-leader as well as steward, was also present. This gentleman was in all respects one of the most judicious members of the church. Controlled by an enlarged and enlightened piety, he was far from sympathizing with the views and feelings of those with whom he now met.

After the customary salutations, and a brief conversation on the ordinary topics of the day, the visitors called attention to the state of the church, and Mr. Stanly was asked what he thought of the prospect of a revival. He answered quite encouragingly, and at the same time alluded to several recent circumstances that had inspired him with hope.

"But," said Mr. Cary, " don't you think something more ought to be done than we are now doing?"

"I suppose," answered Mr. Stanly, "we ought to exercise more diligence, and trust we shall have grace to do so."

"But that's not all," said Mr. Havens in his usually rough and abrupt manner; "we ought to do something to get men converted. This stereotyped method of preaching and praying will never answer."

"Yes," put in Mr. Cary, " we ought to hold extra meetings just now. I believe we may get up a revival just as well as not, if we only use the means."

"And so do I," added Brother Steele.

Mr. Stanly was at a loss what reply to make to these opinions so confidently expressed. After a moment's pause, he assured the brethren that he was willing to do all within his power to promote the welfare of the church, and secure the conversion of souls.

"We don't doubt that," said Mr. Cary, "and we

called to see if you did'nt think it best to start a protracted meeting."

"I had not thought so," was the reply.

"I suppose you believe in protracted meetings,
Brother Stanly," said Mr. Havens.

"Yes, under proper circumstances and on proper
occasions."

"I did not know as it was ever improper to try and
get men converted," said Mr. Cary.

"Nor I either," ejaculated Mr. Steele.

"I suppose," interposed Mr. Spaulding, "Brother
Stanly seeks that end in all his preaching, and in the
use of all the means of grace."

"Certainly," added the pastor; "that is the great
object for which we should always labor. I trust we
shall not lose sight of it for a single moment."

"It ought to be so, I admit," replied the disaffected class-leader, "but in these days of gospel light,
sinners have become so hardened that nothing but
extra means will do. We must aim directly at that
result, or remain without success."

"That is very true," said Mr. Stanly, "and that is
the object of every sermon I preach, and every prayer
meeting I hold.

"But we see no such results, and for one I never
expect to," was the reply.

"It will be according to our faith, I suppose," said
Mr. Spaulding. "If we employ the means of grace
without expecting them to result in the blessings God
has otherwise promised, the responsibility of a failure
will be on ourselves. I think we should look for fruit

from the constant services of the church, as well as from extra meetings."

"Experience has taught us differently, and that is better than theory," said Mr. Cary.

"So it is," continued Mr. Steele, who was a mere echo of the views and feelings of his class-leader.

"I am sorry our preacher don't like protracted meetings, and—"

"I do like them, Brother Havens, and did not intend to intimate the contrary. I think our meetings should be multiplied whenever there is a demand for it. I simply said I saw no such demand at present. A protracted meeting and a revival are not necessarily connected. Either one may, and often does, exist without the other. It is quite possible that there will be a call for such a meeting this winter, but I think there is none now."

"And therein you differ from the members," said Mr. Havens.

"I think not," said Mr. Spaulding. "I have heard no expression of the kind until this evening, and for one I fully agree with the opinions of Brother Stanly."

"Well, it is clear that something must be done, or religion will die out in Lyndon," tartly responded Mr. Havens. "As matters now are, we are going backward pretty fast. I see no hope for better things unless we have a revival. At Jonesville they have started a meeting, and already there is a general break down. Brother Bacon will soon be through there, and then we can get him if we choose."

"I do not think it judicious," said the pastor, "at this time to call in help from abroad. If we will but

look to God for strength, we shall not be dependent
on these ' traveling evangelists,' as our Presbyterian
brethren call them. I am sorry that any of us should
so limit the power of God, as to suppose him capable
of carrying on his work only by these special agencies. Let us rather rejoice that our Heavenly Father
will at the same time bless them and us. It is not
necessary for Brother Bacon to get through at Jonesville, in order to secure the Divine blessing here."

"As we all know, there is an increased seriousness
in our congregation," added Brother Spaulding, " and
we are favored with many indications of the Divine
presence. There have been two or three conversions in my class of late, and I am expecting still
greater things, if we are only faithful to the grace
given."

"Large and attentive congregations are no signs
of religious prosperity," replied Mr. Havens. " Folks
will always go to meeting when they hear nothing to
disturb them. Only let the preaching be practical,
and they are not quite so willing to hear. Brother
Stanly, I don't want to dictate, but I wish you would
be a little more practical in your sermons."

"I will do the best I can in that line, I assure
you. What kind of subjects would you have me
discuss ? "

"Discuss! I would'nt have you discuss anything.
It aint discussion we want. It's something to stir us
up. We have got light enough, give us a little more
heat."

"I preached last Sabbath morning on the necessity
of the new, birth, and on the nature of justifying faith

in the afternoon. Do you call those practical subjects?"

"Well, yes,—not exactly, though. We need exhortation, with startling incidents and anecdotes for illustrations. Why, one of Brother Bacon's anecdotes will accomplish more in a revival than all the rest of his sermon. That's what makes him so successful."

"I prefer to take Christ and his apostles as models of preaching. I believe they never told funny stories," said Mr. Stanly.

"But times have changed since then."

"The depravity of the human heart and the grace of God remain the same. I shall be obliged to differ with you, Brother Havens. Am I not right, Brother Spaulding, in supposing that the great principles of the gospel are to be set forth and urged upon the attention as the best means of effecting the work?"

"Undoubtedly, Brother Stanly. I hope you will never resort to other expedients. God will bless his own word, presented according to the standards which he himself has established."

Messrs. Cary and Havens saw it was of no avail to continue the discussion. They were disappointed, as well as grieved, at Mr. Stanly's position, and especially so by the firmness with which he maintained it. Sincerely desiring the success of the gospel in winning souls to Christ, they had no idea of witnessing such results except in connection with extraordinary efforts. Hence, in protracted meetings, camp meetings, and the like, they were strong in the faith, but on ordinary oc-

F*   9

casions were comparatively indifferent. With others of similar feelings, they were now thoroughly aroused, and were willing to devote all their time and influence to the work of saving souls. The plan adopted by their preacher was altogether too slow and uncertain to suit them. According to their views, there was a regular, systematic plan of producing a revival. The church must be humbled by a bold and fearless denunciation of all its errors and sins, and then the stranger, who alone was expected to do this, could open his mission to the unconverted. This is what they called "judgment beginning at the house of God;" or, in other words, "starting right;" and without it, no matter how many sinners were converted, or wanderers restored, there could be no "revival."

Though Mr. Stanly clearly saw their errror, and was decided in his convictions of duty, he was troubled on account of their remarks. For some time past there had been much to encourage him. The people had come in unusual numbers to hear the word preached, and numerous indications appeared of a hopeful seriousness in the congregation. The class and prayer meetings were well attended, and even now there were several persons inquiring what they must do to be saved. His own soul was engaged in the work, and he had supposed the whole church shared with him this feeling of satisfaction and hope, and was therefore entirely unprepared for what he had heard. What was said about practical preaching and spiritual exercises, was plainly intended as a censure on himself, and fears were awakened that after all, he was mistaken in supposing his people cordially united with him in his favorite work. It is true, Mr. Spaulding assured him to the contrary; but there was certainly *some* dissatisfaction, and perhaps sufficient to defeat all his efforts.

Had Mr. Stanly been older in the ministry he might have anticipated such exhibitions, and been unmoved by them. As it was, he was in doubt what to do. Possibly he had given offense to the brethren who had called on him, by the nature of his answers, and his refusal to adopt their plans; and from their dissatisfaction, disastrous results would follow. Others, doubtless, would coincide with them, and perhaps an alienation ensue, that might render the whole church powerless for good. Agitated by these fears, and depressed with a sense of the uncertainties of the case, he waited with intense anxiety for the disclosures of the coming Sabbath.

Upon that holy day, the pastor repaired to the house of God with a burdened heart. He almost expected to see signs of disaffection, among those with whom he had been wont to take counsel, but, from the first, was happily disappointed. There was the same serious and attentive congregation, and he rejoiced to witness their increasingly spiritual devotions. Even Brother Cary and his fellows appeared the same as before. They were little aware of the wounds which their unguarded words had inflicted, as in their mistaken zeal they had sought to give direction to the affairs of the church.

Though foiled in their favorite plan of "getting up a revival," these men were far from content to work on

in the ordinary arrangements of the church. Extra
meetings were appointed at private houses, which
were sometimes held to unreasonable hours, and
though by this means interests which ought to have
been one were somewhat divided, as some were not
able to attend both their meetings and those at the
chapel, yet Mr. Stanly thought proper not to advise
in the matter. In all these meetings much was said
against the pride and popularity of the church, and
the unfaithfulness of believers; as though real success
was predicated on disgracing christians in the eyes
of the wicked, and as if the pastor's objections to a
protracted meeting grew out of a desire to gratify
and please the world. Mr. Stanly could only counteract their influence, by seeking in every possible
way to animate and encourage his brethren.

There was no mistaking the influence exerted, by
these zealots, on the cause of God. Though sincere
in their efforts for a revival, they did more than all
others to hinder its occurrence. Even their extra
meetings, established as they were with the best of
designs, were really an embarrassment to the pastor.
The attention of the church was diverted, the efforts
of the people divided, and the strong ties of christian
confidence weakened. Still, if any of the members
expressed a doubt of the propriety of this course, they
were at once charged with want of interest, and
held up as persons for whom special prayers should
be made.

To an intelligent and thinking observer, it was no
wonder there was not a revival. Yet as the majority
were actuated by noble principles, the ill-advised

steps of Mr. Cary and his companions were not as disastrous as might have been feared. A measure of success crowned the efforts of such as were diligent in the Master's vineyard, and labored in accordance with the Divine will.

CHAPTER XVII.

MAKING CALLS.

As the Lyndon Society was comparatively small, Mr. Stanly was not long in becoming personally acquainted with all its members. Many of them, however, he had only seen at church, and he now determined to visit them at their houses, and hold with each of his stated hearers personal interviews on the subject of religion. It was true, this was imposing upon himself no ea y task; but the advantages which he hoped might result from its performance, promised to be more than a compensation for the sacrifice required.

The afternoon of each day was accordingly set apart for this work. Had there been no interruptions, a few weeks would have sufficed for its accomplishment; but it was soon found that company at the parsonage, calls to attend funerals, and other extra labors so broke in upon this arrangement, as to greatly extend the time. Still he seized every available opportunity to pursue the plan marked out. It would have been more pleasant in many respects, to have visited as convenience and inclination should dictate, and temptations to do so were often presented; yet as by such a course some would be inevitably passed by, the original plan was strictly adhered to.

Mr. Stanly soon found that his parishioners were not alone in being profited by these visits. The pastor shared most largely of all in the benefits derived. He saw, in the course pursued, a most favorable opportunity for studying human nature, as well as witnessing the triumphs of Divine grace. It may not be uninteresting for the reader to follow him during a portion of his tour, so as to obtain a few illustrations of the great variety of circumstances into which a minister is thus thrown. The cases given are not peculiar to Lyndon Society. Similar ones may be found in every station and circuit in conference.

He began his systematic visiting by a call at Mr. Burton's. After a few commonplace remarks, and the statement of his plan, the pastor entered into a brief conversation with the different members of the family, concerning their religious state. Highly as he had ever esteemed this circle of devoted christians, he felt that till now their worth had not been fully appreciated. The earnestness and depth of their religious convictions far surpassed his expectations; and when he bowed with them in prayer, so sensible were the manifestations of the Divine presence, that it seemed as if heaven was nearer earth than ever before. The blessing of God was upon them all; and the soul of the preacher caught the hallowed fire, and rejoiced in the rich and powerful displays of sovereign grace. He was encouraged to prosecute the work in which he was engaged, and from this hallowed place went joyfully onward in his labor of love.

The next family called upon presented a strong contrast. They were not members of the church,

though identified with the congregation; and Mr.
Stanly found it almost impossible to induce them to
enter into conversation on the subject of his visit.
Though left to do all the talking, he pressed his suit,
and urged the importance of immediate attention to
the welfare of the soul. At length the lady of the
house, who alone, with her children, was present,
confessed her need of Christ, and wept freely in view
of her sins. Before the interview ended, she promised to give her heart to God, and without further
delay seek to become a christian. The children were
also deeply affected, as he presented various inducements to youthful piety, and the visitor felt on taking
his leave that the seed sown would spring up and produce fruit, which should be finally gathered on high.

The next visit was made to one long confined to
her room by sickness. The parents did not enjoy religion, though believers in its authenticity, and the
sick daughter alone was enabled to rejoice in God.
For six years she had been detained from the house
of worship, and had been the subject of unremitted
suffering; yet her faith was unwavering, and her
hope bright and joyous. No word of complaint escaped her lips, and though she spoke of being deprived of the public means of grace in a manner that
attested her love for the institutions of religion, she
was evidently contented and happy. Mr. Stanly
read and expounded a portion of Scripture, and gathering the family around, engaged in prayer. He, at
least, was deeply affected; and when he arose from
his knees, the word of God seemed clothed with new
beauties, as its exceedingly precious promises were

brought to remembrance, and found to be fulfilled in the case before him. In entering into conversation with the different persons present, and ascertaining their views and feelings, he was convinced that she was far happier than they all. The grace of God was sufficient to make that sick chamber quite on the verge of heaven; and while those possessing health and strength were grasping the world, and pursuing its varied pathways, doomed to disappointment and sorrow, its humble occupant communed with the Father of spirits, and drank in the bliss of angels. New faith sprung up in the pastor's heart as he went his way, for he saw the hand of the Lord stretched out to deliver and save his people.

Mr. Havens came next in course. Calling at his door, the preacher was greeted with a rough cordiality, and invited in with an air of haughty independence that seemed to say, " we are as good as anybody."

"Then you have got round to see *us*, have you?" bawled out Mr. Havens. " I had about given up your calling here at all. Did'nt know but you were going to make all your visits at Brother Burton's, or some where else, where it's more popular to go than here.'

Mr. Stanly was half inclined to answer him as he deserved; but remembering that he was a man of but little information, and probably intended no harm, he concluded to take no notice of the ungenerous thrust, and proceeded to unfold the object of his visit. Mr. Havens was a great talker, and stood ready to discuss in any form the affairs of the church, and the character of its members, upon which subjects he considered himself an oracle; but he manifested a great unwillingness to enter into conversation concerning his own spiritual state. He had no relish for such personal work, and therefore resisted all attempts to reach the object which was had in view by his minister. Failing here, Mr. Stanly turned his attention to the other members of the family, but with no better success.

The old matter of the protracted meeting was not yet forgotten, and Mr. Havens several times alluded to the loss they had suffered in not sending for Brother Bacon and " getting up a revival." He was sure the members were generally backsliding, and they should never see " old times" again. Thus occupying nearly all the time, he ran on until Mr. Stanly proposed a season of prayer. This of course was assented to, though without any real sympathy for the proposition. As they all knelt in an attitude of devotion, Mr. Stanly attempted to pray, but was far from enjoying his usual liberty. A burden was upon his heart, and his struggles to throw it off were altogether in vain.

The prayer ended, the pastor arose to depart. " What! you don't call this a visit, I hope," said the brother.

" I seldom make longer calls when engaged in pastoral duties," answered Mr. Stanly.

" Well, now; this just running in and out is'nt worth a thank-ye. I want you to come and bring your wife, and make an afternoon's visit."

" I fear I should hardly get round at that rate," replied the pastor. " I will endeavor to call again. Good day."

So saying, Mr. Stanly stepped quickly into the street, without waiting for a reply. He had no desire to hear what might be said by one so destitute of a sense of propriety as to grossly insult the feelings of his friends, and so filled with conceit as to be beyond the reach of admonition. Though the afternoon was not yet spent, he bent his steps homeward, being in no mood for the further prosecution of his work. Arriving at the parsonage, he recounted to Emily the events of his tour. She very naturally entered into his feelings, and expressed herself warmly as to the unkind and unchristian spirit manifested by Mr. Havens.

"We must not blame him too much," said Mr. Stanly. "He has had no cultivation, and, as can be readily seen, is extremely ignorant."

"Then let him not assume so much," said she.

"That is the very reason why he is so assuming," was the answer. "It is a common ruse for the ignorant to put on important airs, in hopes thus to hide their deficiencies."

"It is strange that Brother Havens cannot see how ridiculous he makes himself appear," said Emily. "How inconsistent his demands in requiring you to spend the whole day with him."

"Brother Havens no doubt feels a desire to be on good terms with his minister, and thinks in this fault-finding and scolding way to secure attention."

"Let him make himself agreeable if he wants to be visited," said Mrs. Stanly. "I am sure I shall not spend an afternoon in a place where there is neither sympathy nor friendship exhibited. People may be jealous or not, because I go to Brother Burton's oftener than elsewhere, I cannot go into families where I am not treated with cordiality."

"Ah, but you are a minister's wife, and must not be particular. *You* can't be expected to share in the feelings and wishes of human beings in general," said her husband, with a peculiar tone which did not fail to unfold his meaning.

"I am thankful to find that but few of our people indulge in such notions," said she.

Mr. Havens was soon dismissed, and the events connected with the other calls were made the subject of grateful remarks; while the promises of the unconverted mother and her children afforded encouragement, and led to earnest pleadings at the throne of grace.

The plan thus adopted and begun, was faithfully carried out. Mr. Stanly saw that he was engaged in a most interesting and useful, as well as laborious work. By steadily pursuing it, he was enabled to reach the humble and the poor, and form conceptions of the real worth of many whose appearance in public was far from representing their true character. Take the following case for an example: Soon after his settlement at Lyndon, a lady somewhat past middle life presented her church letter, and became enrolled among his parishioners. He saw her but seldom afterward, and as she was an entire stranger, very retiring in her manners and humble in her appearance, but few had formed her acquaintance. One day while passing some dilapidated buildings in the outskirts of the town, he unexpectedly came to her door. As

he entered with the usual salutations, he observed
that every household article which met his eye be-
spoke the poverty of those around him. And yet in
that humble room there was an air of neatness and
taste which gave it an inviting and pleasant appearance, not often found even in the parlors of the rich,
or the halls of the great.

From a few moments' conversation, the pastor
learned that this poor woman had been in affluent
circumstances; but that for several years past the
tides of adversity were strongly set against her. In
early childhood she had become a christian, and had
ever since been actively connected with the church.
About five years before her removal to Lyndon, her
husband had sickened and died, leaving her with
three children, and as the result proved on the settlement of his estate, without means for their support.
A few months later, her little " Willie," the darling
of her heart, followed his father to the grave, and the
poor widow, bereft of her principal hope as regards
this world, was reduced lower than ever. Then again
had death visited her humble dwelling, and a daughter was stricken down in the midst of blooming health,
and hurried the way of all the earth. Thrice had the
bitter cup been pressed to her lips, and she had drank
it to the dregs. An only daughter remained, and
with her, she was buffeting the storms of life in penury and want. No one at Lyndon knew or had
sought her history.

Mr. Stanly was deeply affected by the recital
which he drew from the sister before him. When he
pointed her to the God of the widow and the father-

less, he found her possessed of a hallowed piety that shed a luster on the scene. She recognized the hand of God in all her afflictions, and meekly bowed before Him who doeth all things well. A tribute of praise was on her lips as she looked forward to a land of rest. There she saw her loved ones safely sheltered from the stormy blast, beckoning her to their home in the skies; and her faith lifted up its tearless eye and read her title to a mansion with the blessed.

The widow and her daughter bowed with their pastor in prayer. O what a privilege to call on God in such a place. How sweet the promises, how glorious their fulfillment. The gilded temples of earth have no charms to be compared with those that cluster around an altar like this.

When Mr. Stanly returned that evening and related what he had seen and heard, and how he had been blessed in that visit, Emily, like himself, was deeply affected. She resolved to visit often at that house, and smooth if possible the rugged path which the poor sufferer had been called to travel. The resolution was not in vain; and while they remained at Lyndon she derived great consolation in ministering to the wants of the widow and orphan.

Widely different were the results of another day devoted to this work. Mr. Spaulding, who lived at some distance, sent his carriage for the pastor and his wife, both of whom were glad of an opportunity to visit in the country. Arriving at an early hour of the day, for fashionable restraints were now thrown off, it was ascertained that a number of friends had been invited, and that a large company was in anticipation.

They were all, however, members of the church, and the gathering proved exceedingly pleasant. Mr. and Mrs. Burton were present from the village, together with a number of the neighboring farmers, and to Emily it seemed, for all the world, like one of those memorable occasions in childhood, when on a Thanksgiving or New Year's day, the old homestead was crowded with its merry occupants, as they came together with happy greetings, and mingled, for the time being, like members of a single household. Again and again she thought of the past, and her heart was so inspired by its recollections and by the unaffected friendship around her, that she could but be happy. She felt a burden removed from her spirits, and almost forgetful that she was a minister's wife, she talked and laughed as in the days of her girlhood. Those around her were equally joyous, and none chanced to be present, who would dampen the ardor of her spirits or suppress the rising emotions to which her soul gave utterance.

Mr. and Mrs. Stanly had enjoyed no similar occasion since their marriage. Heretofore, everybody had seemed to say, by look and action, that it was a great part of their business to maintain the dignity of their position. This uncalled for and unscriptural restraint was now thrown off, and the company were possessed of too much sense to suppose them out of place, in thus giving vent to their pent up feelings. Happy would it be for the care-worn and weary spirit of many a christian minister if similar occasions were more frequently enjoyed.

When the time to separate had come, the whole

company looked to God for his blessing. Mr. Stanly led in prayer; and the frequent responses to his supplications told the feelings and emotions of those around him. They were in harmony with his own.

One more case, and we will leave this department of our minister's work. He is at the door of Mr. Cary, has rung the bell, and is waiting for admittance. Mrs. Cary seeks to be a fashionable woman, and accordingly allows him to wait from five to ten minutes before she is prepared to receive him. He is then ushered into the parlor—a cold and cheerless room—presented the great rocking chair, and at the same time urged to sit in it with as much earnestness as though his comfort and ease were being really consulted. The preliminaries over, conversation is attempted, but every word is so exact in its place, and every sentence marked with such studied precision, that it is carried on with the greatest difficulty. A chill rests upon the pastor, but for appearance' sake, he struggles on until a reasonable time is gone by. He sees a heartlessness in the whole affair, and is glad to escape and mingle in more congenial scenes. With profound and lofty expressions of regard, and abundant wishes for the happiness and prosperity of himself and lady, Mrs. Cary allows him to depart. She no doubt thinks she has exerted herself to the utmost in giving her pastor a proper reception, and showing a decided interest in his welfare. On the other hand, Mr. Stanly has to undergo a struggle to throw off the chills brought upon him by such fashionable entertainment.

CHAPTER XVIII.

THE DONATION VISIT.

Thus passed the first summer and autumn of Mr. Stanly's pastorate at Lyndon. His studying, preaching, and visiting, kept him steadily at work, and the winter with its frosts and snows, while it allowed most men a respite from their labors, only increased the range of his duties and enlarged the responsibilities connected with his sacred office. He was now frequently invited to preach in neglected neighborhoods round about, and the prospect of doing good led him cheerfully to sacrifice personal ease and comfort, that he might respond to these calls and scatter the good seed upon the fruitful soil before him. He was already strongly intrenched in the affections of his people, and notwithstanding a few murmurings from those whose tastes it was impossible to gratify, both himself and his companion were highly respected by the entire community.

The time for the usual donation party had now come, and it was already the theme for earnest and excited conversation. Though an established custom in the Lyndon society, it was never held without encountering opposition. Some objected to it for one reason, and some for another, yet in the end most of the objections were waived, and nearly all classes yielded it a hearty and cordial support. At this time

G   10

it was opposed with uncommon earnestness, though
every thinking man knew the preacher could not live
on his salary without its avails. Indeed when the
allowance was made out, the matter was freely talked
over by the official board, and the salary fixed in expectation of a visit of this character. Had this not
been the case, at least another hundred dollars would
have been given; so that, all things considered, the
donation was practically to benefit the society instead of the preacher. It was simply a plan by which
they were to pay him a portion of what was his just
due, in this public and formal manner. Though
not counted on the salary, many of the members
looked upon it in this light, and saw that under these
circumstances, to withhold it would be little short of
open repudiation.

Nevertheless, objections must be made. Mr. Cary
was opposed to it because it looked like making the
preacher an object of charity; and yet it was borne in
mind that this very brother strongly objected to an
increase of the pastor's salary at the beginning of the
year. He did not consider, that by this act the so
much dreaded deed was already done.

Mrs. Blakie thought it was not right to *give* the
minister so much, when the really poor were so numerous. She could think of a great number who
were poorer than Brother Stanly. Still none of them
had been known to share in her offerings. As an
illiterate sister said, in attempting to quote the scriptures in her justification, "her left hand never knew
a charity which her right hand bestowed."

Mr. Steele did not believe in getting up parties, and

as for his donation, he could make it just as well at
some other time.   And so he could, for the arrival of
his gift at the parsonage was not within the remembrance of "the oldest inhabitant," and no one had
any confidence in the sincerity of the reason which
he assigned as an objection.   He had frequently been
known to attend meetings for the advancement of his
political party, and mingle in gatherings quite as dis-
orderly as those enjoyed at the minister's house.   Those
who knew him best, shrewdly suspected that the principal difference between these two classes was that at
the one there was a call for money, at the other not.

Numerous others also regretted the necessity for
donation visits, but while that necessity existed, were
not disposed to shun its responsibility.   Doubtless
none were more willing that they should be laid aside
than Mr. Stanly himself.   That such is the general
wish of the preachers is equally certain.   The only
remedy, however, is with the people, and when they
shall generously and promptly support their ministers, that remedy will be supplied.   Until then, they
cannot well be avoided.

The appointed day soon came round, and at an early hour the parsonage was fully astir.   The committee were at work providing chairs, crockery, and provisions for the company, which was expected to be
large, and they were certainly disposed to magnify
their office.   The whole arrangement was taken into
their hands, and when Emily proposed to engage in
the work going on, Mrs. Burton came up, and, in a
a confidential tone, remarked, "You are to give up
everything to us.   We will make the plans and do the

work; you will be tired enough before it is over." So
saying, she hurried back to the company, and busied
herself as before.

At an early hour in the afternoon the guests began
to arrive. The first sleigh load was from the country.
It was Mr. Spaulding with his large heart and liberal
hands. He brought with him a number of his neighbors, who could not have otherwise attended, and as
some of them were comparatively strangers, Emily
was a little surprised to see how readily they made
themselves at home. Without saying a word on the
subject, they proceeded to deposit their various gifts,
each in its appropriate place; one finding his way into
the cellar, another looking up the pantry, and all acting on the principle already laid down by Mrs. Burton. This was a great relief to the feelings of the
young pastor and his wife, who had never before received a visit of this character.

It was not long before others began to make their
appearance. The crowd continued to increase, until
Mr. Stanly found it impossible to give all the guests
a personal reception. He therefore left the door to
others, and freely mingled with the company, thus
forming the acquaintance of those who were heretofore strangers.

Notwithstanding the excellent arrangements of the
committee, Emily's attention was now constantly demanded. Many of the ladies brought gifts expressly
for her, and each must have an opportunity to explain
the nature and object of her offering. Thus she was
called into the kitchen to take a look at the cake,
when perhaps a dozen strangers were waiting for an

introduction. By the time she had shaken hands with these, (for Methodists always shake hands,) another company would make their appearance, and another call be issued for the minister's wife. Before reaching the place where she was wanted, she would several times be taken aside to listen to some explanation, and in this manner was kept in constant excitement. Mr. Stanly was scarcely less busy. To both, the scene was new, and in view of their straitened circumstances, could not fail to be interesting.

In the meantime, the talking goes on with increased earnestness. The hum of voices is heard from every part of the house. Groups gathered here and there discuss the various topics of the day, without fear of interrupting other groups equally intent on the indulgence of their loquacity. It is easy to be discovered, that this is an occasion of no ordinary interest. Only at such annual gatherings do all these come together, and they seem now determined to improve the opportunity to the best advantage. No wonder that the donation party was highly prized at Lyndon.

The evening, more particularly reserved for the young folks, was bright and beautiful. These turned out in great numbers, and it was exceedingly interesting to see how many belonged to this honored class. Some, whose locks were beginning to grow gray, just then were young again, and gladly mingled with the throng. All seemed joyous and happy as they ministered to the wants of the servant of God.

The gifts of the evening differed somewhat from those in the afternoon. They included several dresses for Mrs. Stanly, with numerous fancy articles, while

George also received additions to his wardrobe and library. The greater part however was in small sums of money, which were paid in to the treasurer, who kept an exact account of the amount presented by the various donors.

The guests had not all yet arrived, when supper was announced, and a call made for a sufficient number to fill the tables. After much urging on the part of the committee, for nearly all preferred to wait, the number was made out, and the work of demolition begun in good earnest. Thus, table after table was set and filled, and Emily began to fear that the stock of provisions would prove insufficient for so great a multitude. She expresssed her fear to Mrs. Burton, but was told there was no danger. "We knew," said that good woman, "with whom we had to deal, and prepared for the worst."

During all this time the merriment continued to increase. Everybody seemed in good spirits, and yet all was conducted in a manner far from trenching on the strictest principles of morality and religion. It would have proved a blessing to many a long-faced moping christian, to have mingled in the scene, and shared the hilarity of the occasion.

Among the friends to whom Mrs. Stanly had been introduced in the course of the evening, was Mr. and Mrs. Tyler and their two daughters, from the country. They were a family of what might be called back-wood's farmers, and presented on this occasion, a rather ludicrous appearance. Dressed in coarse apparel, made up in most antique style, they provoked many a smile from the younger and gayer portion of

the company, and Emily was fearful they would discover the disposition manifested by those about them,
and be grieved by what they might consider disrespectful treatment. To avoid this, she took especial
pains to entertain and interest them, by giving them
a large share of her personal attention, and throwing
around them the most favorable influences under her
control. She flattered herself that she had not been
unsuccessful in accomplishing her design.

A little before the company broke up, Sister Spaulding came to Emily, and whispered in her ear:

"How ridiculous Mr. Tyler's people do act?"

"In what respect?" asked Mrs. Stanly.

"Why, they are finding fault with everything they
set their eyes upon. Mrs. Tyler just remarked, in the
presence of a number of ladies, that she was sorry she
had come to the donation, when the minister's wife
was so gay and expensive in her dress. She said the
dress you had on was better than any she had of her
own, and it was ridiculous to make donations to such
people."

"And this dress," said Emily, "was a donation
from Sister Burton. It is the only decent one I have."

"It is strange that some people will expose their
ignorance to everybody," added Mrs. Spaulding. "I
persuaded the Tylers to come out to-night, in hopes
it would do them some good to go occasionally into
society; but I am satisfied it's of no use. They have
always staid at home, and they may hereafter, for all
me. I see they keep up their complaints yet, pouring them into the ears of all that will consent to
listen."

"Yes," said another, "the old lady was just wishing she had her donation back; she was sure she should never bring another here."

"How much is it?" asked Emily.

"A bushel and a half of apples for four of them," answered Mrs. Spaulding. "They are worth about fifty cents."

"Tell them," said another, "if they will pay for their suppers, we will get the apples for them."

"I fear they would have the worst of the bargain at that rate," said Emily.

"Yes," said Mrs. Spaulding. "They have not brought half enough to pay for what they eat, and yet they are sorry they have *given* so much."

The group dispersed, and Mrs. Stanly was for the moment left alone. She was a little afflicted to know that she was the subject of the earnest conversation carried on in the other corner of the room, in which censures were undoubtedly more free than compliments, but after a moment's reflection wisely concluded to give the affair no further thought.

Supper being ended, the company joined in singing one of those sweet songs of Zion so familiar to the thousands of our Israel. Then followed a few remarks from the pastor, in which he thanked the friends for the kindness exhibited in the substantial tokens which the day had furnished, and expressed a lively interest in their religious welfare. A prayer came next, and the rich blessings of Heaven were invoked on all present. No part of the exercises had been more interesting than this. Even the church service could not be more solemn in its influences and results.

Then came another universal buzz as the company prepared to disperse. The friends soon separated, the merry sleigh bells gave out their evening music, and the minister's house was again in the possession of quiet. A portion of the committee alone remained. The treasurer placed the bundle of money in Mr. Stanly's hands, remarking at the same time, that it amounted to just sixty dollars. He also pointed to a pile of packages, and named various other articles that had been stowed away, the whole reaching, according to the minutes, the respectable sum of one hundred and twenty dollars.

Before leaving, Mrs. Burton took Emily into the pantry, and pointed her to several nice pyramids of cake, together with other provisions that had been carefully put by on the top shelf, remarking, "These are for you. They were brought in for the supper, but I saw there was sufficient without them, and accordingly laid them aside. If they had been left on the table they would have been all cut up whether wanted or not." So saying, she bade them "good night" and returned home.

It was not until a late hour on the following morning that signs of life became apparent at the parsonage. The tired inmates needed rest after the exciting and wearisome duties of the previous day. At length the blue smoke issued from the chimney, and George and Emily began the work of inspection. Mrs. Stanly declared as she passed from room to room that it was a sight to behold. Everything was in confusion. The

G*

carpets were covered with dirt and particles from the
table, chairs and benches in promiscuous juxtaposition
occupied the floors, and on every side were unmistak-
able evidences of the freedom enjoyed in the scene
that was past.

While getting ready for cleaning and arranging
matters, the members of the ever stirring committee,
who considered their work not yet done, made their
appearance. They insisted that Mr. and Mrs. Stanly
should not intermeddle as yet with the affairs of the
household. The work was claimed to be their own,
and with strong hands and willing hearts they soon
brought the dominion of old chaos to an end. By
twelve o'clock everything was restored to its proper
place, and the Lyndon parsonage looked again like
home.

The company then sat down and enjoyed a familiar
chat concerning the affair of the previous day and
evening. All agreed it was one of the very best donation visits ever enjoyed at Lyndon. Of the amount
received, about ninety dollars was as good as cash.
The remainder, though highly prized by the recipients
as mementoes of friendship, was not of the character
to be made available in meeting the wants of a
family.

No sooner was this well-timed visit over, than it
was again made the subject of severe criticism. The
class of persons already referred to, had not been idle.
They had refrained from presenting their gifts with
the others, and as if to cover their deficiencies, now
engaged in bitter fault-finding. Some thought the
company too rude, and were greatly afraid the in-

fluence would be deleterious to the religious interests of the society. Others thought it too bad that so many should go and eat and drink at the minister's house, and congratulated themselves that they were not of the number. Still others said it was giving him too much. He did not need it. *Our charities,* they argued, ought to be more appropriately applied, than was done in bestowing them all on a single individual. Various other reasons were adduced, though it was distinctly observed that they existed only in the minds of those generally suspected of penuriousness, which now as ever seemed to cloud their logic.

CHAPTER XIX.

ECONOMY.

NOTHING could have been more timely for Mr. Stanly, than the donation visit with which his friends had recently favored him. Besides the use of the parsonage, his salary was only three hundred dollars, and thus far but a small proportion of even this sum had been paid. Since his settlement at Lyndon, he had contracted some small debts in reliance upon his quarterage when it should become due, and to meet these and his other obligations was now his first and paramount wish. The money in hand would barely enable him to do this; and though he knew not how to provide for some wants immediately pressing upon him, he determined at all hazards to free himself from debt. No one at Lyndon was aware of his deficiency on his former charge, and he wisely concluded not to let his people know that he was compelled to use their gift for such a purpose. Had they understood this, they might have justly complained. In their weakness, it was enough for them to support their own pastor, without paying the arrearages of other stations. But for Mr. Stanly, situated as he was, there was no other course.

Arrangements were accordingly made to visit Eaton, and Mrs. Stanly chose to accompany her hus-

band to the scene of his earlier labors. Ostensibly
the journey was undertaken for the purpose of min-
gling with former friends, but really to attend to this
business. It was indeed pleasant to meet with the
loved ones of other days, and both George and Emily
highly appreciated the opportunity; but they were
still better pleased with the privilege of removing
their only cause of embarrassment and reproach.
Before leaving Eaton this was entirely taken away.

Our minister and his wife next visited Embury.
Here they found much to cheer and at the same time
sadden their hearts. During the brief year, great
and important changes had taken place. Death had
been busy in the cherished circles of their childhood,
and many of their former companions and friends
had fallen victims to his power. Even among the
living, disappointment and sorrow had more than
their usual place. Business failures had occurred
which affected the entire community, and none more
severely than Emily's father. Amid the general
wreck, Esquire Porter had been reduced from afflu-
ence to a position which barely afforded him the
comforts and conveniences of life; and his plans to
render aid to his daughter as she might need it were
entirely frustrated. Emily did not mourn on this
account; but was greatly grieved to look upon her
parents in the decline of life, thus bereft of what
they had accumulated by the labor of earlier years.

It was nevertheless a cause of gratitude to be once
more at the old homestead. There was the same
running brook and towering elm, by the side of
which, and under whose spreading branches, she had

gamboled in childhood, while every knoll and every nook had something to remind her of the past, and call up those fond recollections with which the thoughtful mind is ever delighted. Then, too, there was the familiar greeting, the inspiring welcome, and the warm kiss of affection on the part of those from whom she had been separated. The years of her absence seemed like a dream, so life-like and real was the occasion enjoyed.

Mr. Stanly was also highly pleased in obtaining temporary relief from the excitement and responsibility of his charge. He was not weary of his work, and had no desire to give up his profession, but after all, was glad to escape, for the time being, the anxiety and care so intimately connected with the life of a pastor. He felt that he should thereby gain renewed strength for the labor yet to be done, and in this he was not disappointed.

After an absence of nearly two weeks, Mr. Stanly returned to Lyndon and resumed his labors. There was much in the condition of his people to interest his feelings and encourage his heart. They had cheerfully ministered to his wants, and were rallying around him so as to strengthen the strong cords of christian love, and animate his powers to their utmost exertion for the spiritual good of those he served. Hope was again triumphant, and the prospect became bright and cheering.

Profiting by his brief experience, and earnestly desiring to avoid the embarrassments to which he had been heretofore subject, Mr. Stanly once more resolved, in the management of his affairs, to study the closest economy. Now that he was out of debt, he hoped to remain unentangled. But he soon found that his difficulties were not at an end. He had expended every dollar of his cash receipts from the donation, and as the congregation relied on what they had so recently given as sufficient for his immediate wants, nothing was being paid in, and he was again obliged to open an account at the store. It was intended to be only temporary, and for a limited amount, but for the reason just named, it was continued for some months. By this time he found himself almost as deeply involved as before, and in spite of his resolution, saw no way but to continue sinking deeper and still deeper in debt. While thus yielding to the mandates of stern necessity, the pastor's spirits became depressed, and his exercises in the pulpit and at the altar lost their accustomed vivacity and power. How could he be expected to preach when his mind was harassed by these things? Though unconscious of the fact, the whole church suffered as well as the preacher, on account of this embarrassment.

Mrs. Stanly was equally troubled. She shared the feelings of her husband in his desire for usefulness, and was deeply pained at the unnecessary hindrances thrown in his way. Her Ladies' Repository was already given up, and other sacrifices made, that she might do her part in bringing their family expenses within the limits of his income. She watched their expenditures for the table and wardrobe with closest scrutiny, and had it not been for the frequent and bountiful gifts of Mr. Spaulding, Mrs. Burton, and a few others, would have enjoyed none of the luxuries which the market supplied.

Spring came, and matters grew worse than ever. The debt at the store was constantly increasing. Various small sums of money which had been borrowed from different brethren began to present an alarming aggregate, and it became plain that the difficulty must be speedily met.

"We shall be obliged to economize more closely than ever," said Mr. Stanly, on one occasion, as he was conversing with Emily on the subject.

"I wish we could," said she; "but I don't see where we can begin."

"We have *begun* already," was the answer. "I think I shall have to stop the Quarterly Review, and give up Zion's Herald," he continued, after a slight pause.

"But you need those."

"To be sure I do. But I don't see as I can have them. And then there is Brother Baldwin, who wishes to purchase Watson's Theological Dictionary. I will let him have that, though it is one of the best books in my library."

"I hope you will not be obliged to break in upon your limited library," said Emily. "Let us see if we can't economize better somewhere else."

"Well, where?"

"Can't we begin with our table?"

"Not without we live on rations. Our food, as you know, is very simple and plain, especially when we are alone."

"Yes," said Emily, "but that is not often. We

must continue to entertain our company respectfully."

"Then we cannot save anything in that department. I agree with you that we must be prepared
to treat company well, and we may as well dismiss
the question of table expenses at once. How is it,
Emily, about our apparel?" inquired Mr. Stanly.
"Can we economize by cheapening that?"

"Perhaps I can," said she, with a sly laugh.
"Your salary, has never yet been touched for me,
even in purchasing a single dress. With the stock I
had on hand when we were married, and those that
have been presented me since, I have got along till
now."

"I am sure I can do no better here than I have
done," said Mr. Stanly. "I shall be obliged to lay
out quite an amount for summer clothing soon."

"It seems that we are obliged to economize," added
Emily. "The only question is, where shall we begin?"

Mr. Stanly attempted no further answer. He saw
that the effort to live on less than heretofore was ut-
terly hopeless. He simply resolved to stop his peri-
odicals and church papers, with the exception of the
Christian Advocate, and by guarding every avenue,
do the best he could.

"Had you not better state your circumstances to
the stewards?" inquired Emily.

"They know I need money, and if they were disposed to relieve me, would have done so before this,"
said he, with a tone more bitter than was accustomed
to fall from his lips.

"I am sure some of our brethren would take hold

11

of the matter, if they knew our circumstances," said
Mrs. Stanly.

"They do know them. There isn't a member of
the church but knows that a hundred dollars is now
my due."

"But they cannot know how much we need it."

"I cannot consent to go before them in the attitude
of a beggar," said Mr. Stanly. "If I must plead
poverty, expose all my family affairs to the public,
and work on the sympathies of the benevolent before
getting what is justly my due, I shall suffer on. I
can never play such a part, let what will come."

Just then a rap was heard at the door, and Mr.
Spaulding came in with his usual good nature, and
remarked to Mr. Stanly that he had brought him a
bushel of apples, and wished him to accept them. The
brother was in a hurry, and having done his errand,
immediately left.

This little incident gave a new turn to the conversation. It reminded the preacher and his wife that
the people were kind, and disposed to aid and encourage their minister according to the best of their
ability. Many similar acts were brought to remembrance, and Mr. Stanly was almost ashamed that he
had uttered a word of complaint. He decided by
the help of the Lord to suppress his murmurings,
and go forward in his chosen work.

The reader may perhaps think that this anxiety on
the part of the preacher was unwise and altogether
uncalled for, as what was due on the salary was sufficient to meet the obligations that troubled him. In
most cases it is true such a state of things might be

satisfactory. But a Methodist preacher's position in
relation to salary is altogether anomalous. He has
no legal claim whatever. There is no power by
which he can collect a farthing of what is his due.
His support is entirely voluntary. Other clergymen
enter into a contract with their people, by which they
are guaranteed the sum agreed upon, but according
to the Itinerant system this can never be done. The
people estimate what ought to be paid, and then pay
it, if they choose. Quite frequently there is a deficiency at the end of the year, and when it occurs
the preacher suffers the loss, and there is no remedy.
Thus viewed, he is certain of no more than he has
actually received, as he can make no bargain and secure no pledges.

It is no wonder, then, that Mr. Stanly was concerned at his situation, and sought to escape results
which he saw before him. His efforts to "economize"
met with but limited success. Company continued
to increase as his acquaintance extended, and various
other items grew on his hands. Not the least of
these consisted in the fact that a daughter, now the
light and joy of the parsonage, demanded the attention and care of its inmates. Help in the family
could no longer be dispensed with, and at the session
of conference he found himself situated much as at
the close of the previous year.

CHAPTER XX.

THE REVIVAL.

PASSING over a period of several months, we find the
Lyndon church in the enjoyment of a powerful and
extensive religious revival. It is in the midst of Mr.
Stanly's second year, and on every hand the results
of his arduous labors are becoming manifest. Evening after evening the house of worship is crowded
with serious and attentive listeners, many of whom
are also seekers of that grace which alone bringeth
salvation. Large numbers are already rejoicing in
the knowledge of sins forgiven. Others are pressing
to the attainment of a similar blessing. The scene
is well calculated to gladden the pastor's heart, and
inspire with new zeal such as labor in the Master's
vineyard.

This work of grace had begun in a quiet and unobtrusive manner, soon after the late session of conference, and had been gradually increasing in interest to the present time. The youth connected with
the Sabbath school were among its earliest fruits.
These had been followed by others of different stations, until at almost every meeting some would be
present who desired the prayers of God's people.
To meet the wants of these, it was found necessary
to increase the services of the church, and they had

been accordingly multiplied. For several weeks Mr. Stanly had preached nearly every evening, and had felt richly rewarded for his arduous labors, in witnessing the conversion of souls. At present, one of the neighboring preachers assisted him, leaving the pastor free to attend to the other departments of the work.

This season of spiritual refreshing, so ardently longed for and earnestly sought, brought with it a multiplicity of cares, and at times greatly increased the perplexity of Mr. Stanly's position. In addition to his public labors, he found it necessary to visit such as were awakened, to pray with the penitent, and point the seeker to the path of life. Thus he went from house to house, in the fulfillment of his mission, until he found himself worn down, and his physical strength nearly exhausted. Long before the revival ceased, he became scarcely able to attend to the duties devolving upon him. Still he could not consent to be idle. A great work was being accomplished, and as a leader in the sacramental host, he must press forward, leaving the results in the hand of God.

At this juncture, Mr. Burton interposed, and advised his pastor to seek the rest he so much needed. To enable him to do this, that good man proposed to leave his business, and devote his own time to making calls, and performing duties which ordinarily fall to the minister. This plan was agreed to, and partially carried out; but such was Mr. Stanly's anxiety, that he could not wholly refrain. In the public congregations his labors were in no wise diminished.

It may be interesting to know what has become of Mr. Carey and his associates, who, a year since, were such earnest advocates of a protracted meeting. And surely, it will not do to lose sight of them. They are yet at Lyndon, and somewhat interested in the meetings going on, though their old propensities are painfully apparent. They are still dissatisfied. The arrangements are not according to their mind, and though actively engaging in the services of the sanctuary, they frequently express their fears that the work will not be genuine, nor the results lasting in their influence upon those who profess to be converted. According to their theory, the revival did not begin right. There was not a sufficient breaking down of the church. Brother Bacon should have been sent for, and allowed, in his usual way, to displace the pastor and take the sole charge of the meeting. The members were not sufficiently humbled. Some one was needed to ferret out their misdeeds, and hold them up to the public gaze, that the church might be purified before sinners were urged to come to Christ, and be saved through faith in his name.

Such were the hints thrown out both in public and private, by which the influence of these men for good was more than counterbalanced. Though unconscious of the fact, they made themselves great hinderances to the success of the gospel.

But by far the greatest drawback to the pastor's success, was found in his domestic affairs. His ef-

forts to so economize as to live within his means,
had heretofore been a failure, and he was now more
seriously embarrassed than ever. In their great
anxiety to save sinners, the church had overlooked
their minister, and really left him to suffer. Not a
day passed, in which the parsonage was not thronged
with company. Preachers who came to assist him
in his work, and members and others living at a
distance, who remained from the afternoon to the
evening service, were being entertained, and Mrs.
Stanly, as well as her husband, was greatly overtaxed. More than this : they were plunging into
debt for nearly the whole of their present expenses.
Quarterage was not to be thought of, in the midst of
a revival.

No one suspected that his pastor's cares were being greatly augmented by this state of things, and
yet all might have known it to be true. Had it not
been for the kindness of the few whose frequent
calls at the parsonage were accompanied by substantial offerings, this season of triumph to the church
would have been one of utter despondency to its
minister. As it was, those were days of trial and
suffering.

The spring opened, and Mr. Stanly was entirely
prostrate. His nervous system gave way, and he
was obliged for a season to suspend his labors.
The physician recommended traveling, but he was
unable to undertake it, for the want of means. As
a substitute, he spent some little time with Mr.
Spaulding, and several other farmers connected with
his station, and from this relaxation from his pasto-

ral duties, derived substantial benefit. As soon as possible he resumed his work, which was still arduous, there being more than a hundred young converts who looked to him for instruction, and were in need of his care.

CHAPTER XXI.

ANOTHER REMOVAL.

As the summer months came on, thoughts of another removal began to find a place in the minds of our minister and his people. The accustomed term of a Methodist preacher's service in a single appointment, was about to expire, and Mr. Stanly accordingly made his plans and bent his energies to arrange the affairs of the station in proper order for his successor. As is well known, this is a matter of no small importance. Many things that might be deferred to a more favorable opportunity, were the same pastor to remain, have, under these circumstances, to be attended to in a hurried and often imperfect manner. Thus it proved on this occasion. A large number of probationers were to be baptized and received into full connection; the various benevolent and financial enterprises looked after; the church record revised and re-written; besides the usual amount of visiting with the kind friends that had been raised up, whose love for their minister had never appeared so ardent and cheering as in the parting hour, now near at hand.

These labors, joined to the uncertainties connected with the appointments for the future, awakened in Mr. Stanly an excited state of feeling, which Emily,

H

as the partner of his toils, fully shared. They were both strongly attached to the Lyndon society, and sincerely regretted the necessity of the separation, which the uniform-practice of the church forced upon them. The sorrow of the people was at least equal to their own; and some were almost inclined to murmur against the rule which required the change. The young converts, especially, indulged in these regrets. They had not yet yet taken those comprehensive views of the general interests of the church, which enabled them to see the propriety of such personal sacrifices for the public good. Inexperienced, and unacquainted with the workings of the Itinerant system, it was very natural for them to suppose that no minister who should be sent them, would be able to supply the place of the one through whose instrumentality they had been converted. All the wisdom and ingenuity of the retiring pastor were required to reconcile his friends to the change demanded by the discipline, to which they had mutually subscribed.

It is doubtless true, that the permanence and stability of the congregations are in some degree affected by the frequent changes to which they are subject. On the other hand, there are advantages which more than counterbalance these evils, to which the system is mainly indebted for its perpetuity. The practical results are everywhere apparent in the rapid growth of the church, and the unequaled triumphs which it has secured. These are sufficient to refute the objections so frequently urged, and show the wisdom of those who, under God, were the founders and supporters of this branch of Zion.

THe last quarterly meeting was held but a single Sabbath before the session of conference, and while Mr. Stanly had succeeded in his plans for the good of his people to their entire satisfaction, they had not been wholly unmindful of his interests. By great effort, the stewards secured the remainder of his salary, and settled with him by paying the entire amount of his allowance. It was acknowledged to be insufficient, and yet was the best they were able to do. Had he come among them unembarrassed, it might have met his expenses. As it was, he had been obliged to make most of his purchases on credit, without being able to take advantage of the market, and as a result, it proved insufficient to meet the demands against him. A small addition was therefore made to the amount of his indebtedness when he came from Eaton.

Mr. Stanly keenly felt the embarrassment to which he was thus subjected, but was still more deeply pained by the fact that his straitened circumstances also involved his reputation. It was known that other ministers had lived on the salary allowed and paid him, and when the community were apprised of his account at the stores—for the affairs of a preacher are always considered public property—many wondered why he could not get along as well as those who had preceded him. They knew nothing of his deficiency on his former charge, and it began to be whispered that the difficulty was in a want of proper management.

Mrs. Cary was quite sure that there had been extravagance at the parsonage. The fault must cer-

tainly be in the preacher's wife. For one, she really
pitied Brother Stanly, but saw no way of relief except by a change in his household economy. This
view of the subject was soon spread abroad, and
though no one had suspected it before, it was now
generally conceded that it must be correct. Thus
poor Emily, who had planned, and contrived, and
wept over her husband's difficulties, was made to
bear the responsibility. It was well for her that she
did not hear these surmisings. The sufferings which
she already endured were of no trifling character,
and the heartlessness of such complaints would have
filled her cup to overflowing.

Perhaps it would have been better, had Mr. Stanly
given the public a statement of his financial affairs;
but he very justly concluded to spare himself the hu-
miliating task. The persons responsible for the whole
difficulty were the official members at Eaton, and the
fact of his becoming embarrassed there, might be as
easily construed into extravagance and indiscretion,
as though it was supposed to have occured at Lyndon.

Though it was not known at the parsonage that the
opinion referred to prevailed to any considerable extent, enough had been said to convince the young
preacher and his wife that views derogatory to their
character were being entertained. To them it was
indeed painful to go away, with these impressions in
the minds of their brethren. But there was no remedy. Certain members found it more agreeable to
throw the responsibility of their pastor's trouble upon
his wife, than allow it to rest upon themselves. It
was evident, however, to the candid observer, that

this cry of extravagance in the minister's family, was simply raised to preserve the credit of the station, which was supposed to be jeopardized. Many knew it to be false, and gave it no countenance. Brothers Burton, Spaulding, and others sought to suppress it, but their co-laborers, Cary, Havens, and Smith, who did comparatively little for the financial interests of the station, persisted in efforts to deepen the impression, as if in this manner to justify their personal delinquencies. It would be well for the church had these men no imitators in other parts of the general work.

The conference was no sooner over, and Mr. Stanly's location fixed for another year, than arrangements were made for an immediate removal. Colombia, to which he was now appointed, was but a few miles distant. He was highly gratified with the arrangement, as it promised relief from his temporal perplexities—that church having the reputation of being more than usually liberal in the support of its ministers.

There was also another pleasing thought connected with this appointment. It was near Lyndon, and the friendships formed there need not be interrupted by the removal. Mrs. Stanly was especially pleased to know that she could often visit the kind friends with whom she had been associated during the past two years. This reflection did much toward reconciling her feelings to the required change.

A brief time was sufficient for the preacher to become established in his new home. The parsonage was comfortable and inviting, and the people kind

and considerate, though less familiar in their introductory greetings than those at Lyndon. From the
first, they appeared highly pleased with their preacher, and seemed to vie with each other in making his
stay with them pleasant and agreeable.

These little attentions were not without their favorable influence. They cheered the pastor and his
wife, who came as strangers among the people, and
who, at this time, were in special need of encouragement. Had the brethren and sisters known the full
influence of such acts of kindness at these particular
periods of a minister's history, they would have been
still more abundant. Nothing can do more toward
giving a preacher a favorable introduction to a new
congregation, than to cause him to feel that he is
among friends, and allow him to see that they are interesting themselves in his favor.

CHAPTER XXII.

THERE was more of a fashionable air about the congregation at Colombia, than Mr. Stanly had heretofore witnessed in his people. The house of worship was large and elegant, and everything connected with it presented evidences of worldly thrift and enterprise, above what he had usually seen. For the first time in his ministry, he found himself in charge of the most prominent church in the place where he lived; and his fears were awakened that the humility and meekness, which so beautifully adorn the christian character, would be found wanting among those thus signally favored. Still, nothing of the kind was apparent, and though the triumphs of the church have often led to its corruption, he rejoiced to know that such were not the necessary results of its prosperity.

As Mr. Stanly was becoming settled in the parsonage, he was pleased to learn that one of the oldest and most respected superannuated preachers in the conference, was residing in his immediate neighborhood. This Brother Tompkins cordially welcomed him to his new home, and did much by his influence, to prepare the way for his favorable reception and successful labors.

In such a friend and counselor, the preacher felt at

once to confide. The presiding elder of the district also had his home in the same village, and both himself and family extended a prompt and cordial greeting. These circumstances were regarded with great favor.

From the numerous calls made at the parsonage during the first few weeks, Mr. and Mr. Stanly mostly formed their early impressions of the people with whom they were now associated. As these calls may be presumed to give a fair representation of the whole charge, we will briefly notice a few among the many, and leave the reader to his own reflections.

Among the foremost that visited the preacher's house, was a Brother Roberts, who introduced himself as one of the stewards. He came, as he said, to make inquiry if anything was needed to defray the expenses of moving and becoming settled; and if so, to furnish the amount required. Though from a feeling of delicacy, an affirmative answer was not given, and though the allowance was not yet made out, he insisted on paying at least his own quarterage for the year. He accordingly placed twenty-five dollars in the preacher's hands and withdrew; at the same time requesting Mr. Stanly, if at any period the salary was not paid with sufficient promptness, to give him notice, and he would see that the lack was at once supplied.

To the new comers, this was an unusual, but most agreeable introduction. They were inspired with the hope that their pecuniary obligations should now be met, and relief afforded from further embarrassment.

"If this could be accomplished," said Mr. Stanly,

"how much better I could study and preach than otherwise."

"I have often thought," said Emily, "that our indebtedness has been a great hinderance to your usefulness. It is really too bad that such a matter should interfere with a minister's labors."

"I confess it should not;" said Mr. Stanly, "and the church is recreant to her duty when she allows such to be the case. I presume some persons think a preacher should not be troubled about these things, but they must certainly forget that we are human beings. I have frequently suffered to such an extent under this influence, that I was almost wholly unfitted for the duties of my calling."

"We may look for better times now," said Emily, casting her eye toward the money still lying on the table.

"I have never dared to say, even to you, all that has been in my mind on this subject," said her husband. "You have known my efforts, joined with yours, to so economize as to live within my means, and the sacrifices that have been made; but you have had no intimation that my failure has presented strong temptations to leave the ministry, and enter some business where I can earn and receive an honest living."

"I beg of you, never listen to such a temptation," said the devoted wife.

"I would not, if I could help it," was the quick response. "I know it is my duty to preach, but I am satisfied I can never do it successfully, with such drawbacks as have thus far harassed me."

H*   12

"But your labors have been blessed to the conversion of many souls."

"I know it, and this alone has kept me up. I have been living in hope, and did I not now look forward with the expectation of a different state of things, I should have no heart to commence the work on this station. If for another two years I continue to fall behind, I shall take it for granted that Providence indicates a withdrawal from the work."

"Don't be too hasty in coming to so important a conclusion," said Emily. "Let us be encouraged by the better prospect."

"I hope to be able to suppress all disposition to murmur, but I can never be at ease while this state of things continues. I can never be what a minister should be—a man of one work—while compelled to contrive and plan to make up for the deficiencies of my brethren."

"I admit the difficulty, but let me ask you again to never think of locating."

"I will not," said he, "unless driven to it by the sternest necessity. I confess, this visit of Brother Roberts, with its promising indications, has greatly encouraged me."

Such were the feelings awakened by the brief call of the financial agent of the new station. Little did the good brother think that he was driving away so dark a cloud from the heart of his pastor. He had come, in fact, as a messenger of mercy to that doubting and almost desponding mind, and through his ministering, hope was once more enabled to triumph, and faith seized, with a firmer grasp than ever, the unyielding promises of God.

A few days later, a farmer in coarse and homely attire presented himself at the parsonage, remarking that he had come to the village on business, and having a little unoccupied time, had concluded to drop in and get acquainted with the new preacher. In his hand he brought a gift, which was unostentatiously presented, and which by its influence did more to encourage, than otherwise benefit those for whom it was designed. He introduced himself as Brother Bennett, and the kind, christian spirit which he manifested during his brief stay, did not fail to win the respect of those on whom he called.

From this interview, Mr. Stanly learned much of the history and state of the church at Colombia. On the whole, the information received was of the most encouraging character, though he obtained a knowledge of the existence of some difficulties between brethren, of which he had, until now, no intimation. "Go straight ahead," said Brother Bennett, "and you will be cordially sustained. The members here always rally round their preacher with a hearty good will."

This gentleman was not alone in these expressions of kindness. Many others exhibited the same spirit, and the pastor's heart was greatly cheered by the place which he was allowed to occupy in the sympathies of the people.

George and Emily were one morning conversing on the favorable indications connected with the new

station, when they saw a man, dressed almost in the
Quaker costume, turning in at their gate.

"Do you know him?" asked Emily.

"No, but I recollect seeing him in church on Sabbath," said Mr. Stanly.

"I wonder if he is one of our people?"

"I presume so. I confess I was not pleased with
his appearance, as he sat in the gallery and listened
to the preaching. There seemed to be a great deal
of self-conceit about him."

Just then the stranger rapped at the door, and was
admitted. "Good morning, Brother Stanly. My name
is Pindar. I wanted to get acquainted with our
preacher, and so have called round to see him."

"Thank you, Brother Pindar. I feel it a privilege
to become acquainted with my members. Do you
live in the village."

"Not exactly. I am a plain farmer; a little out. I
have lived there about twenty years, during all of
which I have been a member of this society. For
fifteen years I was class-leader, and am now an exhorter. How do you like it here?"

"Very well, indeed," said Mr. Stanly.

"This used to be one of the best societies in this
section, but times have sadly changed," remarked the
visitor.

"From what I have seen," was the answer, "I think
it very good now."

"We have got too much pride and popularity
among us to prosper. We used to be a plain and
humble people. I can remember when one could

tell a Methodist as soon as he saw him, but now they are all conformed to the world."

"I hope they can yet be distinguished by their good works, if not by their clothes," said the preacher.

"The scriptures require us to be a peculiar people, you know, and this we can never be while we dress like other folks;" and the speaker gave a look of satisfaction to his straight-sided coat.

"Yes," said Mr. Stanly, "but does not this peculiarity consist rather in their being 'zealous of good works ?'"

"Shouldn't we come out from the world and be separate ?" asked Mr. Pindar, without noticing the pastor's remark.

"Undoubledly ; but I never supposed that passage in the bible referred to any peculiarity in the shape of our garments. I admire plain dress, but have never thought entire uniformity in our apparel to be imperative, or even desirable."

"I think it is," said the brother. "For one, I have never changed since I became a Methodist."

"Do you think there is any scripture requiring that particular form ?"

"O, no, only we should all dress alike."

"Suppose you change, then, Brother Pindar, and dress like the rest of us," said Mr. Stanly, with a sort of roguish laugh.

"I could never do that, let what would come. While I live, I mean to keep up a testimony in favor of old fashioned Methodism. I often call myself the old fashioned disciple, and wish to be known as one that has never turned aside from the old paths."

"To whose class do you belong, Brother Pindar?" inquired Mr. Stanly, changing the topic of conversation.

"Brother Bennett's; but I don't attend much. I can't enjoy myself at meeting as I used to, when we met in log houses and barns."

"You come to the prayer meeting, do you not?"

"Only once in a while. I am not very often at the preaching. Sometimes I hold meetings myself, in the back neighborhoods on Sundays."

"I saw you in the gallery, I believe, last Sabbath," said Mr. Stanly.

"Yes; I choose to sit up stairs since the pews are rented below. They wanted me to pay ten dollars a year for a seat, but I never believed in so much extravagance. After helping build the meeting house, I think I ought to sit in it for nothing."

"But what is paid is simply the sum necessary to support the gospel in your midst, is it not?" asked Mr. Stanly.

"Yes, but they wanted too much. I never pay but a dollar a quarter. That was all that was required when I first joined society."

"As I am a stranger," said Mr. Stanly, "I know nothing of the finances of the station, nor of your ability to pay. But I believe the Lord requires a faithful use of our means for the advancement of his cause. If there is no need of it in one direcrection, there are always calls from other sources."

"Calls! I guess there is. You can't hardly go to meeting but what there is a collection for something. It is impossible to give to all, so I don't trouble myself about any of them. I sometimes give however."

"And the Lord loveth a cheerful giver," quoted the preacher.

"Some folks think giving is a part of religion, but I don't subscribe to that. All I want is the Holy Ghost in the heart."

"That is the essential thing, no doubt. But, Brother Pindar, does not the religion of the heart lead to liberality in the use of this world's goods?"

"I suppose it does," he answered. "It will lead us also to lay aside all superfluity of apparel. I wish you and Sister Stanly would set an example for us to follow, while you are with us."

"We will try, Brother Pindar."

"I mean in respect to dress."

"I think no body will complain of *me*," said Emily, speaking for the first time since he had come in. "I have always been *obliged* to dress plain as well as cheap."

"I find no fault in that respect," replied Brother Pindar; "but it is not in Methodist style, after all."

"I did not know that we had a denominational style," said Mrs. Stanly. "So you see my ignorance must be my excuse."

"Isn't it possible that you lay too much stress on these matters?" asked Mr. Stanly. "It seems from your own account that you neglect much weightier matters, and violate much plainer commandments. In searching for a mote is it not well to look out for the beam? It seems to me that the caution which our Saviour gave to the Jews would do you no harm."

"I see: all the preachers favor the new state of things. I expect God will cast us off and raise up another people, unless we repent and do our first works over."

"You will, of course, take no offense at my plainness of speech," said the pastor.

"O, no; but I am sorry to hear you talk so," said the old gentleman.

"Well, Brother Pindar," said Mr. Stanly, "let us try to get more religion, and live it daily, and all will be well."

"It's of no use while we indulge in so much superfluity." So saying, he rose to go, and though in no very pleasant mood, promised, in reply to the invitation extended, to call again.

"Another specimen of a one idea man," said George, as soon as he was gone. "I presume, from his remarks, he is as covetous in his practice as illiberal in his creed."

"I wish he knew," said Emily, "how little I have laid out for dress during the last four years, and how many times I have fitted old garments over, and made them into new ones to save expense."

"That would be nothing to him. It is the peculiar cut that he is after," answered her husband.

"What a slander on primitive Methodism for such a man as he to pretend to represent it. I hope we shall not find many like him," continued Emily.

"You need have no fears of that. He is, and must

necessarily be, a man by himself. If others were like him, his philosophy would drive him somewhere else. Such is his reasoning, that if every body around him should dress as he does, he would necessarily change in order to be '*peculiar.*'"

"He is almost a match for old Mrs. Blakie."

"Not quite so bad as she, I should judge," replied Mr. Stanly. "Mrs. Blakie made war with all the brethren—while this Brother Pindar only quarrels with their clothes."

"It looks to me almost like ancient Phariseeism."

"It is, precisely. And while we are pained for him as an individual, we may congratulate ourselves that such men are always destitute of influence. Their absurdity is so great that no one feels bound to respect their opinions."

As we shall hear from this Mr. Pindar again, we will here take our leave of him by saying, that the pastor was right in his estimate of the character and standing of his parishioner. He was a man not inaptly described by our Savior, as straining at a gnat and swallowing a camel. Having become all absorbed with his favorite idea, he forgot the plainest precepts, and neglected the most important duties.

Mrs. Stanly saw also the usual diversity of temperament and feeling in the sisters, who came from time to time and paid their respects at the parsonage. With most of them she was highly pleased. They furnished numerous evidences of kind feeling and christian friendship, that caused her, though among strangers, to feel once more at home.

Occasionally some one would call and attempt to

play the lady, by assuming that awkward stiffness, so intimately connected with the cold and heartless forms of worldly politeness. On such occasions, Emily was easily embarrassed. The avenues to a free and easy conversation with persons of this character, could not be reached by one naturally so diffident and confiding.

CHAPTER XXIII.

At the close of the Saturday service of the first quarterly meeting, the quarterly conference convened as usual for the transaction of business. This body is composed, according to Methodist usage and discipline, of the preachers, exhorters, stewards, and class-leaders connected with the station. Having the oversight of the affairs of the congregation, they meet once in three months, to take into consideration the interests submitted to them, and decide on the policy to be pursued. The present being the first and most important meeting for the year, the attendance was unusually large, embracing nearly every member.

The list having been called, the presiding elder presented various topics for consideration, which were attended to without much discussion, or the manifestation of any very especial interest. At length the report of the committee to estimate the preacher's salary was called for, when a difference of opinion was at once apparent. Mr. Dickson, the chairman, made a majority report, allowing him five hundred dollars, which was an addition of fifty dollars to the sum usually paid. This brother argued that the expense of living was constantly increasing; that the church was abundantly able to pay that sum; that

many ministers were actually suffering for want of
a competent support, while some were being driven
from the work altogether ; and that it was due Mr.
Stanly to make him a respectable allowance, which
the committee claimed was no more than done in the
estimate presented.

This view of the subject was met by the arguments
usually employed on such occasions. Mr. Jones, a
local preacher, insisted that it was wrong to allow a
minister to get rich out of preaching the gospel, and
he was sure Mr. Stanly could live on less than
five hundred a year. As for himself, he preached
for nothing, and did not believe in making so much
difference betwen laborers in the same field. Besides, many other charges paid less, and got along
just as well. For one, he should vote against the
report.

Mr. Bennett thought the old allowance quite sufficient. He was sure it did not cost *him* so much to
live, and he did not see why it should a preacher.
Still, if the brethren thought best, he should acqui-
esce in the arrangement, and increase his subscription
accordingly.

Mr. Pindar was greatly displeased at the proposition. In his view it was another departure from old
fashioned Methodism. He remembered the time
when the preachers received less than half the sum
now proposed, and yet were satisfied. In those days
they worked hard, traveling large circuits, and enduring great hardships, but were never heard to complain of the want of pay. " I don't believe," said he,
" in these hireling ministers. You may depend upon

it; if the Lord calls a man to preach, he will take
care of him and not allow him to starve. Let the
preachers learn to trust more in Providence, and we
shall see better times."

"That's it," ejaculated one of the stewards.

"Brethren," said Mr. Roberts, another of the stewards, "I was not a member of the committee, but am
highly pleased with the report. I think we pursue a
mistaken policy when we suffer our preachers to be
embarrassed by an incompetent support. 'The laborer
is worthy of his hire.' If a man devotes all his time,
week days and Sundays, to the service of the church,
he is entitled to a living from the church ; religion,
justice, and fair, honorable dealing, require such a return. The distinction referred to between traveling
and local preachers is altogether proper. Our local
preachers are engaged in business, like other men.
They sacrifice but little time to the duties of their
office. The traveling preachers have no other business. They are allowed to have none. We give
them enough to do to occupy all their time and talents, and they are desecrating the sacred office when
they turn aside to serve tables.

"Brother Bennett compares a preacher's expenses to
his own, and from the comparison draws his infer-
ence. Now, as matters are, he can come to no safe
conclusion by such reasoning. Brother Bennett is a
farmer, and one half the items for which a preacher
pays cash, he counts nothing. Generally, farmers
have no idea what it costs to live, where every article,
great and small, comes from the market."

"I presume Brother Roberts is about right," interrupted the honest old farmer. "I have been counting up a little, and have come to the conclusion that the report is not far out of the way."

"And I want to say a word or two," said Mr. Dickson, in reply to Brother Pindar. "He seems to judge the present by the past, and argues that because a man could live on two hundred dollars when everything could be bought for half the present prices, he can do so now. I would like to ask Brother Pindar if he will supply Brother Stanly with the necessaries of life at the prices they brought at the time of which he speaks. He has a large farm, and raises produce of all kinds to sell. Let him now show his faith in his reasoning by making the proposition."

"Brother Pindar will be far from doing that," said Mr. Roberts. "He thinks Providence will take care of preachers. What are we to understand by Providence? Is it feeding the hungry by miracles, or clothing the naked without human agencies? Far from it. I believe Providence calls upon us to do what is here proposed."

"I agree with Brother Roberts," said Mr. Anderson, one of the leaders, "but it seems to me, five hundred is more than is necessary. I am a mechanic, and have everything to buy, but it don't cost me as much as that to support *my* family."

"About how much does it cost you?" asked Mr. Dickson.

"Not more than three hundred and fifty dollars?"

"Well, let us take that for the basis, and see how we shall come out. A preacher has some expenses which you do not. You have no help in the family,

Brother Stanly is obliged to keep a girl.   And then there are other items.   Let us see,

Assumed expenses,	$350,00
Wages and board of a hired girl,	120,00
Moving expenses,	30,00
Additions to Library, and Periodicals, say,	40,00
Company and traveling expenses, say,	50,00
Total,	$590,00

It is clear, Brother Anderson, that your experience will not help the case."

" I will give it up," answered the brother, looking a little puzzled by the result.

" But you have not included all," said Mr. Roberts. "There is the extra expense for clothing. We should not be willing to have our minister go about in the community making pastoral visits, with just such clothes as we wear in our shops and on our farms. We would not go thus ourselves. The same is true of his wife. And this makes quite an addition to your figures."

"And then," put in Mr. Bennett, "he has more calls for benevolent objects than we have."

"Yes, and generally responds more liberally than do some of us," said Mr. Anderson, looking toward Brother Pindar.

"It is all for pride and popularity," added the latter.

"I have no doubt," said an elderly man who spoke for the first time, "that all are willing Brother Stanly should have all he can get, but I don't see how we can obligate ourselves to pay so much. Tell us where the money is to come from before you ask us to adopt this report. If you will clear that up, I will go for it."

"From our pockets," answered Mr. Dickson. "We are *able* to pay twice as much. All we lack is the disposition."

"I was opposed to this move when it was first introduced," said Mr. Bennett, "but can't see how in justice we can agree on less than five hundred dollars. The facts and figures are all against us. I think we should adopt the report as it is."

"And then there is the donation," said Mr. Jones.

"And the wedding fees," said another.

This started a new train of remark. The donation generally netted about one hundred dollars, and several now proposed to reckon it on the salary. As will be seen, this would cut down the allowance, and make it less than ever before. The proposition was looked upon with contempt by every member who had a spark of liberal feeling, and yet it was pressed by a few with much earnestness.

"The donation, if one should be made, don't belong to the quarterly conference," said Mr. Dickson. "We had better wait until *we* have a donation, before deciding what to do with it. If the people make one to the preacher, it is his and not ours, and we should be in pretty business to take it from him to pay our debts."

"I hope we will never make another donation visit," said Mr. Pindar.

"*We* never did make one yet," said Mr. Roberts with a sarcastic tone.

The donation was soon disposed of. The conclusion was reached that the quarterly conference had nothing to do with Mr. Stanly's gifts, and the matter was dropped by mutual consent. The vote on the committee's report was taken, and it was adopted by a large majority. With the exception of Brothers Jones and Pindar, all were gratified with the result. *They* were never satisfied, and their murmurings awakened no surprise.

The reader may wish to know if this is the usual way of making out a Methodist preacher's salary; and if he himself has no voice in the matter. Let him not be surprised to learn that it is. The discipline of the church fixes the basis, by enumerating items of expense which are to be estimated in the manner above represented. To the contract, the minister is not a party. And then in many cases, the sum agreed upon is never paid. No claim is allowed which could be collected by a process of law. For deficiencies there is no remedy. If the sum is not made up on the charge, the preacher suffers the loss, and generally without uttering a word of complaint. The world, probably, does not furnish a parallel, where men go forth and devote their lives to a calling, without a voice as to the amount of compensation to be received, or power to collect that which the other party from time to time sees fit to promise.

This system of the voluntary support of the ministry, though sometimes creating hardships, is nevertheless so scriptural and practically successful, that

I   13

no effort has ever been made to change it. It was adopted and is perpetuated by the ministers themselves. Where the membership is governed by an enlightened and consistent piety, there is but little difficulty in carrying it out.

CHAPTER XXIV.

OUT OF DEBT.

THE prospect of a more comfortable support, enabled Mr. Stanly to engage in his work with a buoyancy of spirits to which he had been for some time past a stranger. He was not only well received by the brethren with whom he was appointed to labor, but was also permitted to share largely in their sympathies and prayers. Such was the kindness shown him, that all thoughts of his being a stranger were quickly driven away. Already he looked upon those around him as tried and familiar friends, and had reason to be assured that himself and companion were loved and respected in return.

This kind reception and hearty coöperation could not fail to exert a favorable influence on the young minister's mind and heart. He could now be a man of one work. The disagreeable subjects, that had engrossed his thoughts, were dismissed in view of the quarterly conference action, which seemed the pledge of immediate and permanent relief. Whether in the study, the social circle, or the pulpit, he was a new man. No longer harassed by doubts and fears as to his temporal support, he could devote all his energies to the work of the Lord.

Still the same rigid economy was pursued as before in all the expenditures of the parsonage. At best,

Mr. Stanly could only hope to meet existing obligations from the salary given. The necessity of keeping hired help in his family, and the increase in the price of provisions which had just now taken place, prevented various little outlays that would have been otherwise m de.

In matters of dress, neither George nor Emily for the last two years, had appeared in a manner becoming their station. With all their arranging and planning, they had found no means of properly supplying their wardrobe. While in debt, they had not felt at liberty to pay out for any object more than was demanded by the sternest necessity.

Fortunately, Mrs. Stanly had a peculiar tact in this department, for practicing economy. By her ingenuity and skill, garments worn and soiled until they would have been thrown aside as worthless by those more highly favored, were often turned, and in her expressive language, made "as good as new." A winter hat, which had been purchased several years before her marriage, had been thus fitted and refitted, so as to answer to the present. Since their settlement at Colombia, it had been once again submitted to the remodeling process. Her cloak was for the third time shaped to the style demanded by the times, while the little one of the household shared in a bounteous manner of such articles as could be put to no other use.

Notwithstanding all this, there was a neatness and tidiness seldom surpassed, in the arrangements of our minister's family. Scores of ladies associated with Mrs. Stanly, who expended large sums in the purchase of beautiful and costly apparel, did not appear to as good advantage as she. Her fine taste, and persevering labors, made up in a great measure for the limited amount of her husband's means.

The thoughtless manner in which preachers' wives are sometimes criticised, may be seen in the fact, that the identical hat and cloak referred to, were on several occasions made the subject of disparaging remarks. Thus, Mrs. Miles at Eaton, and Mrs. Cary at Lyndon, among others, had charged Emily with great extravagance on their rejuvenated appearance, when in fact not a single dollar had been expended in making them what they were.

A laughable circumstance of this character just now came to Mrs. Stanly's knowledge. Early in the spring, she had been visiting at Brother Dickson's, and while there, had seen an old straw bonnet, which one of the daughters had thrown aside a year or two since as worn out and useless ; and it occurred to her that she might take the material and work it over, and make a suitable summer hat for her little girl. Knowing that Mrs. Dickson could have no further use for it, Emily asked the privilege of trying the experiment, which was of course readily granted.

She accordingly took the old straw, ripped up the braids, and sewed them anew, so that after a great deal of perplexity, her effort proved successful. The trimming cost just twenty-five cents, which amount covered the entire expense. And yet by her ingenuity, a very neat and appropriate child's bonnet was procured.

Not long after, Mrs. Dickson called at the parson-

age, and as if highly pleased with something that had
occurred, proceeded at once to rally the minister's
wife on her extravagance.

"I told you better," said the sister, without unfold-
ing her meaning. "I think you had better take my
advice after this, and keep within bounds."

"Please explain yourself," said Emily, not a little
puzzled as well as amused.

"O, it's no use. You are tried and condemned on
the charge of extravagant expenditures. I really
pity you, but so far as I can see, the case is beyond
hope."

"Let it be as it may, you don't seem to feel very
bad," said Mrs. Stanly. "Come now, tell me what
you mean; I don't understand all this."

"Just as well. You'll find out when the time
comes."

"I should think it had come by the way you laugh
and take on."

"Well, to be serious. You remember the old straw
bonnet I gave you?"

"Yes, but what of it?"

"Enough of it, I assure you. You know I advised
you not to take it, because it was so worthless."

"I recollect all that very well. But what do you
keep laughing about?"

"Why, simply this. Your little girl's bonnet is
said to be extravagant. Several of the sisters are
helping Brother Pindar make a fuss over such a useless and extensive expenditure."

"Pray tell. Who are they?"

"Old Mrs. Carruth came to me to-day, and asked

in very solemn tones if I did not think it would hurt
Brother Stanly's influence with the church. I told
her I did not believe any such thing. She then went
on to say that Sister Jones first told her about it, and
since then, she had herself spoken to several concerning the matter, and they all agreed it was too rich
and expensive to look well in a minister's family."

"Did you tell her how I came by it?" interrupted
Emily.

"Not at first. I let her run on as long as she
pleased, and then asked her if she knew how much
Sister Jones paid for the one worn by her daughter
of the same age as yours. She said only twenty
shillings; and added that yours must have come
much higher, as it was altogether a better article.
But, said I, this of Sister Stanly's did not cost more
than half a dollar."

"What did she have to say to that?"

"O, she was sure I must be mistaken. She declared it was the prettiest and best of any in the congregation. I then explained how you came by it,
and I never saw a person so cast down in my life.
She apologized, and begged a thousand pardons for
having mentioned the subject at all."

"For shame on such intermeddling in my affairs,"
said Emily, half pleased and half indignant.

"I should think as much," answered Mrs. Dickson,
" and I told the old lady so in plain terms."

"How did she excuse herself?"

"By calling it a mere mistake. She would not
have cared if she had only known."

"Well, next time I get an old straw, I'll have it given out in church for her benefit."

"Perhaps it would be well."

"It will undoubtedly save excitement on the part of the scandal-mongers."

"Suppose we have a 'society of inquiry' to hang around and pry out all the affairs of the preacher's family," said Mrs. Dickson.

"A capital idea. Just think what excellent material is at hand," answered Emily, fully restored to good nature.

"I am not certain but the organization exists already," added the former.

"They should have power to send for persons and papers, as the lawyers say, and then make daily reports for the benefit of the interested parties," continued Emily.

It was no wonder the ladies were amused by the ludicrous circumstance that had arrested their attention. They will be pardoned for their seeming levity while contemplating so comic a scene. Two or three men and a half dozen women intensely excited over a baby's bonnet, was an affair not to be treated with seriousness.

When Mr. Stanly came in and learned the history of the matter, he laughed as heartily as had the ladies. Mrs. Dickson and a few others were determined that the fault-finders should not hear the last of it, until they gave up their ridiculous habit and consented to attend to their own business. For some time afterward when the apparel of the preacher's family was under criticism, a single allusion to the "old straw" was pretty sure to restore quiet.

Notwithstanding these little perplexities, and the evident wish on the part of some to find fault, Mr. and Mrs. Stanly found themselves most agreeably situated. They were surrounded by a host of friends, who watched over the interests and reputation of their pastor, and ministered greatly to the comfort and happiness of his family. The Pindars, Joneses, and Carruths, constituted the exception and not the rule; and while some would have been grieviously afflicted with their course, the present minister and his wife looked upon it with merited contempt.

Mr. Stanly was especially relieved from his financial embarrassment, by the liberal donations which he received from his friends at Colombia. He had not been settled many months among them, when a visit of this character was announced at the parsonage. According to arrangement a large company came together, enjoyed a social hour, and dispersed, leaving a hundred and fifty dollars as an expression of regard for their preacher. Of this sum nearly one-half was in cash, and most of the remainder was in articles of a substantial character. The congregation had evidently observed the scantiness of the pastor's wardrobe, and decided that it should no longer continue. The young men presented him a valuable suit of clothes, and the ladies were not behind in paying their respects to Emily. In this particular, the wants of both were magnificently supplied. The baby, too, which was rapidly rising into favor, was had in remembrance. To the "wee little thing," just begin-

I*

ning to run alone, the children's offerings were mostly made. Shoes, stockings and various kinds of playthings were presented, almost without number. On the whole, this proved to be the best visit of the kind which Mr. Stanly had yet received.

The hopes of the preacher thus awakened, were not to be disappointed. As the year wore away, each installment of the salary was paid when it became due. The stewards at Colombia saw no reason for putting off the preacher that was not equally valid in withholding the dearly bought earnings of the common day laborer. At each quarterly meeting the cash was in hand and paid over, as the discipline contemplates. They found it much easier, as would all other stewards if they should make the effort, to raise the required amount in this way, than to defer it to the end of the year.

It was a happy day at the parsonage, when it was known that the last debt was canceled. Few persons can be aware of the depressing influence which these temporal embarrassments exert on the mind of a christian minister. Few will be able therefore to appreciate the feelings awakened by this opportune deliverance. Let no one suppose that such a circumstance in the life of a Methodist preacher is an affair of small importance.

From the beginning of his ministry, Mr. Stanly had felt the want of a suitable library ; and the severest self-denial that he had suffered, arose from his paucity of means to procure it. Thus far he had bought such books only as were absolutely required, and he did not yet possess anything like a respectable number.

Under the influence of the encouraging prospect now before him, he ventured a little further than he had hitherto dared; subscribing for the Quarterly, which he had been obliged to discontinue, and adding several standard works to his limited stock.

Taken all in all, a family could scarcely fare better than did that of our preacher at Colombia. It is true there was plenty of hard work to be done, and about the ordinary number of croakers to be found in the church, but these were of little account when it was seen that the interest felt for the charge, was on the whole reciprocated in a corresponding regard for the pastor. Under such circumstances, burdens were easy to be borne, and success in cultivating the moral field was rendered certain. This people had learned that if they would have a good and useful preacher, they must encourage his heart and strengthen his hands by promptly relieving his temporal wants. Hence their success, above what was enjoyed by the surrounding churches.

Mr. Stanly was now advised to make purchase of a house and lot, which was on sale at a very low price, and for which a long credit would be given. It was argued that by so doing, he could occasionally make small payments, and eventually come in possession of a home; so that when laid by from active service, he could have a place to which he might retire and be at rest. This was certainly desirable. The plan also seemed feasible; and after much consultation it was adopted, and the purchase made. Before leaving Colombia, he was enable to pay one hundred and fifty dollars of his receipts to this object. It was just the sum received from his annual donation visit. The people who made the contribution were justly pleased, to know that they were enabled to assist in the accomplishment of so desirable an end.

CHAPTER XXV.

FROM the time of Mr. Stanly's settlement at Colombia, an intimacy of no ordinary character existed between him and his neighbor, the Rev. Mr. Tompkins, to whom allusion has been already made. This gentleman had been for several years on the superannuated list, and was one of the most aged and respected members of the conference. At two or three periods in his long and useful ministry, he had been stationed at the place of his present residence, and was now universally respected in the home he had chosen.

To the stationed preacher, Mr. Tompkins proved an invaluable friend and counselor. Blessed with the wisdom of experience, intimately acquainted with the practical operations of the Itinerancy, and animated by a sincere desire for the public good, he was well calculated to advise and assist a young minister in the prosecution of his work. Mr. Stanly gladly availed himself of his counsel, and had great reason to be thankful for the association enjoyed.

Like many other superannuated preachers, Mr. Tompkins had but very little of this world's goods. He had nobly battled for the church in the days of her feebleness, and by the grace of God had won many victories; but his treasure was in heaven and not on earth. He could still sing,

> "No foot of land do I possess,
> No cottage in this wilderness,
> A poor, wayfaring man."

Trusting in the provision of the discipline for the support of worn out ministers, Mr. Tompkins had not been anxious to accumulate; and had now no other dependence than the annual dividend made by the conference, and the charities which he might receive from those around him. For several years that dividend had been growing less, and as his necessities increased with his infirmities, he was frequently reduced to circumstances of a most distressing character. His income, as many others similarly situated have found to their sorrow, was far from being adequate to his wants. Still no word of complaint was ever heard, and no charge of ingratitude escaped his lips.

Though Mr. Stanly had often observed the evidences of poverty which marked the good man's home, it was some months before he understood the real circumstances of his case. At length, as the ties of friendship were strengthened, and the familiarity of the parties increased, he ventured to inquire into the old gentleman's pecuniary affairs, and ask for a sketch of his personal history. The request was readily granted, and the answer given, nearly as follows:

"I commenced the duties of the Itinerancy when twenty-two years of age. My father was a New

England farmer, and being a member of the Congre-
gational church, was at first greatly opposed to the
choice I made. He was, however, too pious and too
affectionate toward his children to continue his opposition, and after I was fairly enlisted in the work, did
all that he could to give me encouragement and aid.
At his death, which occurred a few years later, my
portion of the estate amounted to about two thousand
dollars, and I was again urged by my friends to retire from the mimistry, and engage in secular pursuits. This I declined to do, and feeling that the sum
now possessed would relieve me from the danger of
pecuniary embarrassment, I continued to travel.

"In those days, our people were comparatively
poor, and in many places were not able to give their
preachers a comfortable support. Many of the brethren who started with me, were obliged to locate ; and
in looking over the old minutes, I have often thought
that the very best of our fathers were driven from the
work to which God had called them. Nearly or quite
one-half our early preachers thus left the conferences to which they belonged. By frequently draw-
ing on what my father had left me, I was enabled to
hold on amid the general sufferings of those times,
and have great reason for thankfulness that I was
never compelled to leave the Itinerant ranks.

"Thus, year by year, my little property was eked
out. I traveled large circuits, was frequently absent
from my home for weeks together, and suffered much
from exposure and toil, but after all, those were glorious days. On every hand the work of God grew
and multiplied ; and I had the pleasure of seeing the

little societies become large and flourishing churches. Still, the wants of the preachers were no better supplied than before. The increased expensiveness of living was greater than the increase in the allowance of quarterage, and so, according to my judgment, it has continued to this day.

"It was generally known that I had some funds, and the report was not unfrequently put in circulation that Brother Tompkins was rich. This was sometimes made an excuse for withholding my just dues, and there were never wanting those to seize upon it as a justification for their penuriousness.

"As my family increased, and my children grew up, there were still greater demands upon my purse. These were to be educated as well as clothed and fed, and no other way way presented itself, but to use the means which I had hoped to keep against the wants and infirmities of age. Long since, that two thousand dollars was entirely gone, and myself and family were thrown upon the income received from my charges as our only reliance. Sometimes this has been sufficient, and sometimes not. At Colombia and a few other places, we were more than supported, but on the whole were only able to keep clear from debt.

"You may imagine our feelings, Brother Stanly, when my health began to fail, and we saw before us the necessity of retiring from the regular work. We had always hoped for some favorable turn in our affairs before that dark day should come, by which we might be placed above want, or else, had desired to cease at once to work and live.

"Unexpectedly I was prostrated in the midst of my labors. I had a multitude of friends. These rallied around me, and ministered to my necessities, until I was partially restored. The congregation then raised means for me to travel, that the effects of the sea air might be tried, from which I received some benefit. My quarterage was allowed to go on for the year, and on the whole we fared much better than we expected.

"At conference it was thought advisable for me to retire, at least for the present, and seek the restoration of health. I did so. My necessities were known, and an appeal was made to some of my former stations, where kind friends contributed freely. From that day I have not been able to resume the duties of the ministerial office, and am now past the age to hope again to stand on the walls of Zion.

"As I said, for a year or two I had no lack. But as must ever be the case, this flow of active sympathy soon ceased. Others were as needy as I, and the church must also care for them. Friends became weary of contributing, and for several years my only receipts have been from the conference collections, and the profit on a few books which I have been able to sell. You judge rightly, my brother, in supposing that we are sorely embarrassed by our present circumstances. I sometimes wonder how we have lived at all for the last five years. But God in his mercy has provided for us, and in Him is our only trust.

"I would not have you, from this recital of the matters concerning which you inquire, suppose that

14

I have ever regretted my connection with the Itinerant ministry. Far from it. It has wrought wonders, and myself and aged companion would devote a thousand lives, had we them to give, to this blessed work. God has favored us above measure. We have a treasure in heaven, and ere long shall go up and possess our inheritance on high. Amid all our conflicts, our triumphs have been great and glorious. Our faith is still in God. He will provide."

Mr. Stanly was at a loss what to say, as the venerable preacher paused in his narrative, and wiped a falling tear from his wrinkled cheek. He saw before him the true model of a christian minister, and could but sympathize with him, in view of what he had heard and seen. With a few words of encouragement, and the proffer of such help as he could command, the young preacher turned away with saddened feelings, and sought the retirement of his own study.

When an opportunity presented, he stated the case of Brother Tompkins to Emily, and consulted with her as to the best means of affording him relief. Plans were at once formed, which were in due time executed with the happiest results. But there were other interests awakened, which came nearer home. The question involuntarily arose as to the probability of their eventually occupying in person a similar. position.

" Are not the same results before us ? " inquired Mr. Stanly. "Thus far, our experience has been similar to that of Brother Tompkins, and are we not to expect a similar conclusion ? "

" I see no material difference, I confess," answered Emily. " But we must hope for better things.''

" If I did not, I am sure I should not feel it my duty to continue in the ministry. And yet, I do not know of any substantial reasons for such an expectation," said he, thoughtfully.

" You know, George, the churches support their preachers better now than formerly," said Mrs. Stanly.

" They pay more, it is true ; and so, also, it costs more to live," was the reply. " Many of our elder brethren think that in proportion to the expensiveness of the times, our salaries are not larger now than then."

" I have no fears," said the devoted Emily, " but what our stations and circuits will furnish us the necessaries of life, while we give ourselves to their service."

" Yes, that is it, too truly," answered Mr. Stanly. " While we devote ourselves to their interests, we shall have just enough to keep us along ; but when we sicken and are laid by, what then? According to the theory of our brethren, we must not be allowed to lay up anything for a rainy day. Everybody else supposes it a solemn duty to provide as far as possible for the contingencies of the future, but most people seem to think that Methodist preachers form exceptions to the general rule."

We will not pursue the conversation. The reader may imagine the reflections of a husband and parent in thus looking forward. Before him was a living illustration, and the lesson sunk deep in the heart of the young pastor. For a time his mind balanced between hope and fear. At length faith triumphed, and the offering was renewedly laid upon the altar.

CHAPTER XXVI.

BOOKS AND STUDY.

FROM early youth, Mr. Stanly had been a great lover of books. He had entered the ministry with a degree of reluctance, on account of a conscious want of preparation, but with a full purpose of pursuing his studies with the same earnestness as though in the seminary or college. This he was assured he could do, or he would have delayed his connection with the conference for a few years, and improved the advantageous circumstances with which he was then favored.

Thus far, his want of means had prevented the accumulation of such a library as he desired, though, one by one, a respectable number of volumes were now being picked up and brought into use. From the first, insurmountable difficulties had arisen in the way of the successful prosecution of his plan. So extensive and exacting was the work of the pastorate, and so numerous the interruptions when he attempted to employ his time in this manner, that comparatively little had been accomplished. None of the hardships of the Itinerancy bore so heavily on his mind and feelings, as this inability to cultivate, as he wished, his intellectual faculties. Though not disposed to find fault, yet on this score he sometimes complained. Let the following history of two weeks' especial effort give the reader a view of the embarrassment connected with this department of a minister's work.

"I declare," said Mr. Stanly while sitting at the tea table, "I have scarcely spent an hour in my study this week; only as I have been engaged in writing letters, and the like. I begin to feel that this will never do."

"It is too late to make up a week's work, now that Saturday night has come," said Emily with a smile.

"I don't propose to do that, my dear; but I must turn over a new leaf for the future. I never intended to live in this way, I assure you."

"You don't seem to idle away much time," said the wife. "I am sure you are not often with *me*."

"I ought to economize and use it to better advantage," answered Mr. Stanly, without noticing the sly hint just given. "I must be less abroad among the people and more at home in the study."

"Some of our friends complain now that you don't visit enough," said Emily.

"And so they would if I was upon the run all the time. I tell you, I have about made up my mind to consult my own opinions hereafter, as well as those of other people."

"Haven't you done so heretofore?"

"Scarcely. Ever since I joined the conference I have run at every man's beck, neglecting my studies and even my family, in my anxiety to do good. I don't believe it is my duty to do so any longer."

"Be careful not to make too fierce resolutions now."

"No fear of that. The danger lies on the other side," said Mr. Stanly. "But I am fixed in my purpose to begin with next week, and prosecute my studies in a consecutive and systematic manner. And I want you to help me."

"Help you! What have I to do with your studies?"

"Very much indeed. We must rise earlier, have our meals more regularly, and you must receive calls and wait on the visitors."

"Quite a programme."

"Will you help me carry it out?"

"I don't see," answered Emily, "as it needs any help from me. I think I can carry it out, though, as it nearly all relates to my department."

The plan was easily adopted. Mrs. Stanly was equally interested with her husband in seeking to promote the desired end. She therefore gladly took upon herself an increase of burdens and responsibilities, that he might have more leisure to devote to his books. An early hour was agreed upon for rising, and the work of the day regularly planned. Each forenoon was to be devoted exclusively to study—the afternoons to pastoral visiting, and the incidentals of a minister's work. This arrangement was to be carried out, as Mr. Stanly expressed it, to the very letter. Things had gone hap-hazard long enough. Occasions of insignificant importance had been allowed to occupy valuable time, and circumscribe the zeal and usefulness of the minister, until he began to be alarmed at the prospect.

With these purposes uppermost in the mind of Mr. Stanly, when he thought of the coming week, the Sabbath passed, and Monday, the appointed time to begin his new mode of life, was at hand. He did not

go immediately into the study, as his services were
needed for a little while below, it being washing day,
and when he found himself shut in with his books, the
languor resulting from his recent labors in the pulpit
was so great, that he could do but little execution.
On going to his dinner, and being quizzed as to the
new order of things, he excused himself by declaring
that he never could do much on " blue Monday," and
it was of no use to try. To-morrow, however, the
work was to be fairly begun.

Tuesday found Mr. Stanly early at his books.   He
felt very much more like study than on the previous
day, and was soon absorbed in the subject to which
he gave his attention.   Just as he had reached an
important point in his cogitations, Emily called for
him to come below, as Brother Bennett wished to speak
with him.   Reluctantly he went down, and met the
good brother, who had come in to spend a leisure
hour, and at the same time talk over some matters
connected with the class of which he was leader.   An
 greeable conversation was entered into, and before
it closed, the morning was gone.   Mr. Stanly was
grieved at the loss, but could make no effort to remedy it.   The afternoon had its appropriate work.   He
could only hope for better results in time to come.

On Wednesday morning our preacher was again
at his post.   Before nine o'clock, a sister called, and
asked for a church letter.   She was about moving
west; and though the letter was quickly written and
placed in her hands, she waited an hour, and entertained her pastor with a sketch of her plans when
she reached her new home, and with expressions of

regret that she was compelled to leave the society at Colombia, which she ardently loved, and go among those who were entire strangers. Mr. Stanly several times looked at his watch and almost counted the precious moments, but it was all in vain. She was in no hurry, and did not dream that a minister could have anything at home to occupy his attention.

At length the sister left, and once more the study door was closed on the preacher, as he resumed his work. At the expiration of about twenty minutes, he chanced to look out at the window, and saw a brother minister driving into his yard. Again he hastened down, but this time without any thought of returning. He was glad to greet his fellow laborer in the gospel, and enjoy with him a social hour, notwithstanding the sacrifice which he was required to make.

Thursday came, and with it, a traveling book agent. Mr. Stanly promptly told him that he did not wish at that time to purchase, but the peddler insisted on showing his wares, and at the same time exhibiting the notes of recommendation which ministers and others had given the books he carried. And thus, as if conferring a favor, which he no doubt intended, the various volumes were spread out to view, while the agent grew eloquent in expatiating on their merits. Mr. Stanly did not wish to appear rude or uncivil, and therefore quietly submitted to his fate. Finally, even the book agent was satisfied, and withdrew, and for that day no further interruption was suffered.

J

On Friday a funeral had to be attended at half past ten o'clock; and consequently no effort was made in the study. Saturday was taken up in completing the arrangements for the Sabbath, so that at the week's end but very little had been accomplished. Still, Mr. Stanly had adhered to his resolution. He had no doubt but the week to come would furnish a better result.

The Sabbath was a day of great interest. Large and attentive congregations were in the house of God, and the preacher felt an unusual engagedness as he attempted to preach the word of life. At the termination of the third service he was almost prostrated by the severity of his labors, and Monday was needed, and had to be taken, as a day of rest. Nothing was attempted in the study. In the evening, Mr. Stanly received an invitation to attend a wedding on the following morning at precisely nine o'clock, at a place about two miles distant.

Now ministers are always glad of an opportunity to perform this interesting ceremony, if for no othei reason, because there is a fee connected with it, that often materially aids in furnishing the staff of life. Mr. Stanly had decided to appropriate his wedding fees to the purchase of books for his library, and this call seemed rather to favor his late plans than otherwise. Besides, he did not expect to be delayed more than an hour or two, and therefore congratulated himself, on the whole, that he had received the invitation. Had it been for the afternoon instead of the morning, it would have still more highly gratified him.

Tuesday came, and nine o'clock found the preacher

at the appointed place. He had ever made it a rule
to be prompt in fulfilling his appointments, though
often afflicted with the delays of those with whom it
was his fortune to be associated. On this occasion it
was soon ascertained that the parties were not in
readiness. They were waiting for friends to come
from a distance, and for various arrangements which
were yet incomplete. Mr. Stanly therefore sat down,
and picking up a little book which he found on the
table, attempted to read. The persons present
were all strangers, and as they were hurriedly passing to and fro, cracking their jokes with each other—
many of which were of no edifying character—and
otherwise amusing themselves, he took it for granted
that his course would not be construed into one of
disrespect.

An hour passed and the scene continued much the
same. Additions to the company continued to arrive, but the "wedding" seemed as far off as ever.
Occasionally some one would come along by the
minister's corner, and congratulate "the elder" on
his good fortune in having so many calls of this character, and at the same time throw out a hint as to
the value of such occasions to those who were favored
with the liberal fees usually given. Under these
circumstances, Mr. Stanly maintained as cheerful an
air as possible, though he was far from enjoying the
hilarity with which he was surrounded. He thought
of his books at home, and the needless waste of time
to which he was thus subjected, and saw with pain
that his plan was being frustrated for at least another
day.

At a quarter past eleven, a move was made which indicated the readiness of the parties to have the ceremony performed. The house became suddenly still, and while the service continued, this silence prevailed; but no sooner were the happy pair pronounced one, than came another scene of confusion. Refreshments were now served, and the minister was expected, as a matter of course, to remain and participate with the company. This detained him another hour, as it would seem disrespectful to break away, and his time for study was now entirely gone.

While dinner was being served, the lady of the house inquired of the preacher why Mrs. Stanly did not accompany him. He gave an answer which he saw was not satisfactory, as it seemed the family had really expected her, though no invitation had been extended, and no wish expressed to have her present. They took it for granted that a minister's wife should not wait for the common civilities of life, but as a sort of privileged character, should break over the rules of courtesy, and make herself everywhere at home. For not doing so, she was now indirectly though distinctly censured.

Mr. Stanly returned early in the afternoon, with a fee of one dollar for services rendered. He was almost tempted to go into his study even then, and make up the loss he had so unnecessarily suffered. But there was much to engage him elsewhere, and he accordingly refrained.

On the day following, he suffered no interruptions. His morning hours were wholly devoted to his books, and he was prepared to receive with pleasure a number of friends who visited him from a distance, and spent the afternoon and evening at the parsonage. As some of these remained over night, Thursday found him away from the study, so that during this day nothing was accomplished. Two precious hours were wasted on Friday by the call of a temperance lecturer, who wished to obtain the use of the church for the purpose of presenting the claims of the great reformation in which he was engaged. As Mr. Stanly had been several times imposed upon by this class of men, he had come to exercise great cautiousness in admitting them to his pulpit. The trustees very unwisely left these matters entirely to the minister, and when applications were made for the church, invariably referred them to his decision. This course made a draft upon his time which he could illy afford to meet. He was also frequently exposed to censure, by being thus compelled to assume responsibilities not properly belonging to his office. The loss which he suffered on this occasion was comparatively small to that at other times endured, and yet it practically robbed him of a day which ought to have been devoted to the Master's work.

Saturday only remained. It was also broken in upon, so that but little was accomplished. On the whole, the two weeks' experiment had been a failure; and Mr. Stanly, now that he more clearly saw his situation, was deeply troubled at the result. Heretofore he had supposed his delinquency to be in part voluntary, and had thought himself able to make application, at pleasure, to the studies which demanded his attention. The trial just made convinced him of his mistake. He was surrounded by influences that he could not control, and his long-cherished hopes must be abandoned, or a new mode of labor adopted.

Under these circumstances, he carefully examined the field before him. It was evidently his duty to study, to make himself approved as a minister of the Lord Jesus Christ. He had never even hoped for permanent usefulness without a thorough preparation for his pulpit services. This it was impossible to secure, unless he could command more of his time for this purpose, than he had heretofore taken.

On the whole, he began to suspect that he had spent too many of his hours in social intercourse among his people. A large proportion of his congregations had apparently come to the conclusion that the chief part of a minister's business was to go from house to house, and that everything else was to be made subservient to this great and paramount work. This unreasonable clamor for pastoral visiting had not been without its influence, and while the people were gratified, the minister was suffering serious embarrassment. It was now evident that he could not meet the demands of the pulpit to which he had been called of God, and at the same time comply with the wishes of his brethren, who were making the preaching of the gospel an affair of secondary importance.

With regard to a question of this character, he could not long hesitate. The command to go and preach the gospel was imperative; and if the church issued a call conflicting with the proper performance of this duty, it must be disregarded. He felt bound to obey God rather than men.

Let it not be supposed that Mr. Stanly under-estimated the value of pastoral visiting. While looking upon it as vastly important, he simply came to the conclusion that it was secondary to the preaching of the word, and consequently to the work of making proper preparation for the duties of the pulpit. The resolution was accordingly adopted to take, first of all, the necessary time for study, and devote what remained to the incidental departments of a minister's occupation.

The plan thus formed was faithfully executed, and with the happiest results. The thoughtless complained, as they had ever done, that the preacher did not visit as much as he ought, but the more intelligent and really pious portion of the church approved the pastor's course, and encouraged him in his chosen way. He was soon satisfied that a greater degree of success followed his labors, than if he had yielded to the unscriptural and unreasonable demands made upon his time and attention.

Mr. Stanly was never afterward reputed to be a great visitor. He did not neglect this duty, and was perhaps equal to the average of his brethren in attending to it, but he did not allow it to interfere with the regular and higher branches of the ministerial calling. Among the sick and poor he was frequently to be found; and here no man charged him with delinquency. His efforts in this direction were in no wise lessened, and doubtless many such will rise up in the judgment and call him blessed. But the fashionable ministerial chit-chat of the times, the kind of visiting in so great demand, was almost entirely abandoned, except when indulged in as a recreation from more stern and laborious duties.

CHAPTER XXVII.

HARD TIMES.

Thus far we have followed our friends, the pastor and his wife, from place to place, and seen them under a variety of circumstances, that cannot fail to throw light on the ordinarily unseen phases of ministerial life. We will next take a view of them as they are removing from Colombia to a distant part of the conference. They are once more going among strangers. The kind friends with whom they have been associated for the past two years are left behind, and the experiment is again to be tried, whether or not others will be found to take their place.

As heretofore, the removal occurs in midsummer. Mr. Stanly, his wife, and two children are slowly pursuing their way to Prattsville, the place to which they have been assigned. The worrisome babe which Emily carries in her arms adds much to the anxiety and fatigue of the journey, and causes the mother to earnestly desire the rest and quiet of home. For the week past, the family has been broken up in busy preparation for the removal. Another week of exhausting labor is before them, which, with the excitement usually connected with such occasions, seriously threatens to overtax the energies of Mrs. Stanly, whose health is now comparatively feeble.

"I fear we shall not reach Prattsville to-night," said Mr. Stanly, looking at his watch.

"It will be exceedingly unpleasant to stay at a public house with the children," was the reply.

"We may possibly go through by riding a while in the evening," added Mr. Stanly.

"Do, if you can," answered Emily. "I am anxious to get settled as soon as may be."

"I suppose, too, you want to see the parsonage, and be making up your mind as to the station!"

"I would like to know what kind of a house we are to have," said she. "I wonder if it will be in order, or if we shall be obliged to wait and get it ready for use."

"I presume our brethren will be prepared to receive us. There has been sufficient time since conference to get everything in readiness." So saying, Mr. Stanly quickened the speed of his horse with a flourish of his whip, and drove on in silence.

It was not until after dark that the wished for town was reached. As it was too late to make observations, our travelers rode at once to a Brother Brown's, where they had been directed. Mr. Stanly alighted, and stepping quickly to the door, introduced himself to the family before him.

"You have probably heard," said he, "that I am appointed to your station for the coming year."

"Yes," said Mr. Brown; "but you are not the man we wanted. We petitioned for Brother Fay, and expected him, but it didn't seem to do much good."

"I was not aware of that," answered Mr. Stanly,

somewhat perplexed by the manner of his reception, and scarcely knowing what to say.

"No, I suppose not," was the reply. "Nobody is disposed to blame *you*, that I know of; but we think our presiding elder did not do right by us. Our people had their hearts set on Brother Fay, and nobody else will satisfy them."

"Well, I am sorry for you," said Mr. Stanly, beginning to feel a little afflicted. "As matters are, we must do the best we can."

With this last remark he turned to go out, thinking to find his way to a hotel, where at least he might be courteously entertained. As he reached the door, Mrs. Brown interposed, and inquired if his family were not with him. On being answered affirmatively, she went out, and with a degree of kindness which entirely frustrated his plan to seek a public house, invited Emily in, at the same time taking the children from the carriage. Brother Brown came also with his lantern, and proceeded at once to take care of the horse, so that Mr. Stanly yielded his preference, and accepted the proffered hospitality.

During the remainder of the evening no allusion was made to the subject of the appointments, and but little was said in relation to the affairs of the station. Emily ventured a few inquiries of the ladies, but the feelings of her husband were too deeply wounded to allow him to make further advances. He resolved in his own mind to go to the parsonage early on the following morning, and remain there, and be no greater burden than possible to the people of his charge. Mrs. Stanly knew nothing of the manner of his reception,

and he wisely determined, for the present at least, to
to keep his secret to himself.

The morning came, and as soon as the breakfast
was dispatched and the family devotions attended-
Mr. and Mrs. Stanly set out for the parsonage. They
found it conveniently located and presenting a fair
appearance from the street, but within, everything
was in the wildest disorder. The house remained in
precisely the same condition in which it was left when
the late pastor's goods were taken away. The floors
were strewed with fragments of boxes and the straw
used in packing; the paper on the walls was old,
and in several places hung loose and dangling; the
ceiling was in immediate want of whitewash; the
windows were minus several panes of glass; and,
taken altogether, it presented a sombre and most forbidding appearance. Mr. Stanly, as he looked about,
did not hesitate to speak his mind, while Emily sat
down by herself and wept. She felt that it was altogether too much. Exhausted by the labors which
had thus far attended their removal, it seemed almost impossible for her to endure the wear and tear
of the work to be done. But there was no avoiding
it; and after a long and earnest conversation they
formed their plan, and proceeded to its execution
without delay.

It was agreed that the lower rooms should be
whitewashed and papered, before they would undertake to make use of them. The sitting room was
also to be painted, whether the trustees would bear
the expense or not. Inquiries were accordingly made,
and with much difficulty the workmen employed.

As it would take several days to get the parsonage
ready for use, Mr. Stanly proposed to leave his
present quarters, and go to some public boarding
house. But no sooner was the proposition made,
than every member of the family which had thus far
entertained him, put in a remonstrance. Mrs. Brown
ridiculed the idea that a Methodist preacher should
want for entertainment among so many of his brethren; Mr. Brown and the daughters joined her in
making them welcome where they were, and such
was the hearty good will now manifest, that the
pastor was convinced he had misjudged in his estimate of the brother before him. As he afterward
learned, Brother Brown was one of the very best
members in the station. Aside from his being so
blunt and plain-spoken, no man was better calculated
to minister to a preacher's wants; and though of limited means, no one at Prattsville did more than he
for the pastor's support. He was greatly grieved
that Mr. Fay had not been appointed to their charge,
and hence his abruptness and coolness toward the
present incumbent.

The indifference which he manifested was not long
continued. He now entered heartily into Mr. Stanly's plans, and did all in his power to aid him in their
accomplishment. His business was such that he could
not leave it to assist at the parsonage in person, and
as no one else offered his services, the preacher continued the repairs to his own liking.

Mr. Stanly's goods were one day later than himself in reaching the place of their destination. With
the help of a gentleman who came by invitation, the

boxes were unloaded and stowed promiscuously away in the single room not otherwise in use. Immediately the preacher and his wife commenced unpacking and arranging such articles as were within their reach. Day after day they continued at their task, so that by the time the workmen left, they were nearly settled. A little more than a week was thus occupied, and at its close, Emily's overtaxed constitution gave way, and she was entirely prostrate. The labor and mental anxiety which she had endured, threw her into a violent fever. A physician was called, who pronounced her case exceedingly critical, and all around doubts began to be expressed as to her recovery. Mr. Stanly was now obliged to procure a nurse to take care of her, and a girl to superintend the affairs of the kitchen, though both were obtained with great difficulty and at no little expense.

Several weeks passed before the fever that coursed along the veins of the sufferer was subdued. At times, hope and fear hung in the balance, and the weary watcher, who stood over his companion by night and by day, with none but strangers around him, was himself well-nigh prostrate. Still he struggled on, and nerved by that superior energy which is on such occasions inspired, his strength proved sufficient for his day.

When it was known that the minister's wife was sick, a lively interest was awakened in the whole church. Sister Brown cared for her as tenderly, and stood by her bedside as faithfully, as though it had been her own sister, and many others rendered

substantial aid. A host of friends appeared at the
parsonage, and all was done that well could be, for
the comfort of the afflicted family. The children
were taken away and properly cared for, and there
was no lack of financial assistance.

For these acts of kindness, Mr. and Mrs. Stanly
felt greatly obliged; and though the sick one would
have delighted in being permitted to look into familiar faces among those who stood at her bedside,
she could not fail to recognize true christian friendship in the persons before her. It was a noble ex-
hibition of the principles of the gospel, and called
forth many a sincere expression of thanks.

While so many were sympathizing with the sufferings of the preacher's family, probably not one
would have been willing to confess the true cause
of its existence. It was quite easy for all to say that
Mrs. Stanly had overdone while moving and becoming settled, but not so easy to confess that the necessity for this overdoing grew out of their own neglect. Had the parsonage been ready for use when
it was needed, and all will admit that it should have
been, the probabilities are that she would have been
saved her sickness. There is little room to doubt
but those throbbing pains and exciting cares had
their origin here. Mr. Stanly felt this truth most
keenly, and it did not fail to add greatly to the in-
tensity of his affliction.

Such were the circumstances under which he commenced and prosecuted his labors in the new station.
It is not at all surprising that he failed to make his
usually favorable impression in the pulpit, and that

the people came to the conclusion, that though he was a good man, he was not much of a preacher. For three months scarcely an hour was devoted to his studies, and the work of pastoral visiting was not even undertaken. As a consequence, the congregation dwindled, the church languished, and what was worse than all, many could see no apology for the pastor in the scenes through which he was called to pass.

Toward the latter part of the year, more favorable indications occasionally appeared. A few conversions occurred, but on the whole there was no great advancement. Mr. Stanly felt that the tide was against him, and that, for the first time in his ministry, he was not succeeding in the work to which he was called. Thus he struggled on, with no perceptible improvement, to the end of his term.

Mrs. Stanly was still feeble. Though recovered from her fever, she was far from having been restored to her usual health. Extra help was constantly required in the family, and the pastor's expenses for the year were unusually large. His debts were already equal to the sum he had paid on his little home at Colombia, so that, in fact, he was again without a dollar.

Prattsville was generally considered a good appointment, and, under ordinary circumstances, had paid its preachers enough for their support. It doubtless would have done so on this occasion, had it not been for the facts narrated. As it was, the pastor fell behind full two hundred dollars.

When it was understood that Mr. Stanly had failed to pay his expenses, some expressions of sympathy

were offered, but generally the matter was coolly dismissed by a single reference to his extra bills. No
one appeared to think that a preacher should have an
allowance sufficient to meet expenses of this kind, and
because his indebtedness arose from the sickness of
his wife, the official board felt under no obligation to
provide for it. They seemed to argue that such contingencies should not be allowed in a preacher's family, and if they were indulged in, the money to support them must come from private resources. Unlike all other men, ministers must calculate on uninterrupted health, in spite of long removals, and the
wear and tear of an Itinerant life. In such cases the
church will feel obligated to take care of them. Otherwise, like the worn-out beast of burden, they should
be turned on the commons and allowed to shift for
themselves. Happily for the clergy, this sentiment
of the Prattsville stewards, though quite general, is
far from being universal.

But the unkindest thing of all was yet to come.
The year closed, and Mr. Stanly had gone to the
conference with a heavy heart. He hoped to be
able to redeem himself before leaving his present locality, as he expected to return and resume his labors among those with whom he had so severely suffered. This prospect alone cheered and encouraged
him. To his surprise, he was now told by his presiding elder that the station had remonstrated against
his reäppointment. The brethren at Prattsville
wished a more " *efficient*" minister, thus throwing,
impliedly at least, the blame of their partial failure
entirely upon the preacher.

In view of this petition,.Mr. Stanly was more than
willing to be removed. It is true, he could not help
thinking of the expense that would arise, and more
especially of the health of his wife, who had not yet
recovered from the effects of their last change.

But nothing would induce him to stay where he
was not wanted. The brethren at Prattsville had
been the real cause of his want of success, and if
they were willing thus ungenerously to throw the reproach upon him and thereby add to his afflictions, he
felt that by the grace of God he could bear it. He
was accordingly removed.

CHAPTER XXVIII.

HERE AND THERE.

Mr. Stanly was at this time favored with an excellent appointment. Lisbon, to which he was sent, was but four miles from his recent location, and was every way adapted to his circumstances. The parsonage was in good condition, and whether the people knew it or not, the reception which they gave him prepared the way for a prosperous year.

Few charges, perhaps, are aware of the influence which may be thus exerted. In most cases, stewards and others act as if they supposed the preacher to be above the common infirmities of human nature, and in no wise affected by the incidents which operate so powerfully on other minds. Hence, they have not thought that first impressions, as to the spirit and temper of a church, may be as powerful and lasting in their results, as those that are entertained in regard to an individual. But so it is. The pastor who goes on to his circuit or station, and is met with a cold and heartless spirit, cannot fail to be depressed himself, and partially discouraged at the very outset. In this state, his faith is weakened, his zeal becomes languid, and he looks forward only to an inauspicious conclusion. He can neither preach nor pray as he otherwise might, and even his pastoral visiting becomes a drudgery rather than a pleasure.

But let him be received in the opposite manner, and how widely different the effect produced. He sees those around him whose hearts beat in so intimate union with his own, that he can but be encouraged. There is at once a vivacity in his preaching, a pleasure in his pastoral intercourse, and a spiritual life in his social nature, that enlivens all the exercises in which he is engaged. He becomes an earnest and successful preacher, and the church is in the enjoyment of prosperity and peace.

Were this principle, so perfectly philosophical and consistent, better understood and practiced upon, there would be far less complaint of poor ministers than at present. Those charges that are never satisfied, would find their difficulties in a great measure removed, as their kind offices would inspire the laborer's heart, and call forth the latent energies of his being. That this is true, may be seen in the fact, that while some stations are always satisfied with their preachers, others never fail to complain, though both classes enjoy the services of the same men. Now, it is not to be supposed that pastors change in their habits and modes of working, as they remove from one place to another, without some controlling cause. Neither is it reasonable for us to conclude that they can avoid being influenced by the circumstances around them. A preacher received as was Mr. Stanly at Prattsville, must almost necessarily make a failure. He is unmanned, and unfitted for his work. The consequence is equally fatal, when his interests are neglected, and the impression is made that the people have no care for his comfort and convenience.

The Lisbon church seemed to understand these principles, and act accordingly. They unitedly strove to make their pastor feel at home, and such was their bearing toward him, that they seldom failed of success. Mr. Stanly's term was exceedingly pleasant. Emily rapidly recovered her health, and was soon restored to her wonted bodily and mental vigor. Their financial difficulties were also in a great measure removed, and hope became once more in the ascendant.

We next find them located at Asbury. Here a most powerful revival crowned the efforts of God's people, and the faithful pastor saw a multitude giving evidence of having passed from death unto life. The work continued during the greater part of his term. Taken altogether, it was the most triumphant scene that had occurred in connection with his ministry. More than a hundred permanent additions were made to the church, and a hallowed influence widely exerted.

Asbury was in the vicinity of Prattsville, and the brethren from the latter place frequently attended the services held in connection with this revival. They were greatly surprised at the manner in which Mr. Stanly labored. It was so unlike what they had witnessed when he was among them, that they could not fail to see and wonder at the change. Had they properly understood the cause of the difference between the past and the present, they would have had occasion for deep humiliation and shame. As it was, they never once suspected that the difficulty was primarily with themselves, and that during the first week of his incumbency at Prattsville, they had raised an almost impassable barrier to his success.

A little incident may here be named to illustrate the bearing and influence of persons who become so completely absorbed with some single idea, as to be oblivious to everything else. . Mrs. Norton was a Methodist of several years standing, and was remarkable for her zeal in behalf of the regulations concerning dress which have been entered into by the church of her choice. Indeed, her hatred of finery was so intense, that it sometimes got the better of her discretion, and she had on several occasions rudely approached the converts on this subject, and done them serious harm. Two or three seekers had been driven from the altar altogether by her ill-timed efforts, and few opportunities were allowed to pass, when she did not bear testimony against the evil, which in her estimation was the crying sin of the age. Mr. Stanly once or twice sought to restrain her efforts, so as to keep them in proper bounds, but this only led her to suppose that he apologized for the delinquents, and indirectly approved their course.

As the revival continued, it was found necessary to invite several of the neighboring clergymen to assist the pastor in his arduous labors. Among them, was the Rev. Mr. Bush, a young man of fine personal appearance and pleasing address,. who preached with a good degree of success. As it happened, his wife was considered rather dressy, and Sister Norton, always on the alert, watched closely for some pin, or

key, or button, that offended against the rule, that
the preacher also might be put under the ban. She
was sure so good looking and talented a man as he,
must have pride in his heart. Still, some little time
passed, and nothing tangible was found, on which her
wished for criticisms could be based.

At length the long sought discovery was made.
Brother Bush was in the pulpit with a gold pin on
his shirt bosom. Sister Norton was horrified. She
could not remain in church and hear him even pray,
and while the first hymn was being sung, she departed
in great haste for her home. Such was her grief, that
she spoke to no one on the subject, but her resolution
was fixed to go early on the following morning, and
have a plain talk with Mr. Stanly, and if he did not
dismiss the offender, ask a withdrawal from the
church. So scandalous an affair was the consummation of the worst fears she had ever entertained.

Breakfast was scarcely dispatched at the parsonage,
when Mrs. Norton appeared and asked to have a talk
with the minister. The privilege was readily granted,
and she at once began her complaints against the
times in which she lived.

"What has happened now, Sister Norton?" said
Mr. Stanly, in his mild, pleasant manner.

"Don't you know?" asked the excited lady in
return.

"I have discovered nothing particularly out of
place," he replied.

"What! such a thing occur right before your face
and eyes, and you not discover it?"

"What thing! what do you mean, Sister Norton!" he again asked.

"O dear!" said the good woman, as she turned her face aside to hide her tears.

Mr. Stanly's sympathies began to be aroused, and he feared some terrible calamity had befallen his parishioner. He again pressed her to give an explanation of what she meant.

"Can it be possible," said she, "that you did not see what Brother Bush had on last night."

"I saw nothing unusual," was the reply.

"It must be because you didn't want to, then," said she.

"You know, sister," added the pastor, "that I have told you before, I never keep a suspicious eye on my brethren. I confess I saw nothing wrong in Brother Bush. Come, now, tell me what *you* saw that so afflicts you."

"It's no use; I see you justify him."

"He preached a good sermon, and a large number came forward for prayers, at least," said Mr. Stanly.

"I wouldn't give much for conversions that occur under his preaching, I assure you," said the sister. "I always had my fears that he was not right. I felt it last night as soon as I went into the church."

"I thought," said the pastor, "we had a most excellent spirit in the meeting."

"I didn't stay after I saw *that*, but went home and wept and prayed all night," said the sister in a melancholy tone.

"Saw what?" once more inquired Mr. Stanly.

"Why, that bosom pin which Brother Bush wore," said she emphatically.

"Bosom pin!" repeated the pastor, "I saw nothing of the kind."

"There's none so blind as those that won't see," said the sister earnestly, being now fully resolved to deal plainly with her minister.

"I don't think he wore anything of the kind," said Mr. Stanly.

"I know he did," added Mrs. Norton.

"You are certainly mistaken," said her pastor.

"Not in the least," insisted the sister.

"Well, we can settle the question very easily by calling on Brother Bush himself," said Mr. Stanly, stepping toward the door.

"I wish you *would* call him in," said she, "and I'll tell him all that is in my mind."

Mr. Bush came into the room, altogether unconscious of the storm he had awakened, and when interrogated on the subject, replied that he had never worn such an article in his life. Mrs. Norton looked surprised and almost incredulous, while Mr. Stanly burst forth into a more hearty laugh than he had enjoyed for many years. He began to suspect the true cause of the excitement, and the scene was too ludicrous for him to be able to restrain his merriment.

"Look here, Sister Norton," said he, pulling his ministerial brother round by the shoulder; "hasn't he got it on now?"

"That's it, truly," said she, in a stammering tone.

"What! that spot?" said Mr. Bush, beginning likewise to laugh. "Why, sister, that is a spot that was

K 16

made by some mud which my horse spattered on me when riding yesterday. My wife tried to persuade me to change my linen, but I did not think it of sufficient consequence. I beg a thousand pardons if I did wrong."

Mrs. Norton apologized as best she could, and was glad to get away. Her eyesight was poor and she did not see distinctly, and her overmuch righteous soul had been deeply afflicted by the mistake into which she had fallen. The ministers wisely concluded to have the merriment all to themselves, and consequently made no revelations of what had taken place. Mrs. Norton was a good woman, and they wished her no harm. She was evidently sufficiently humbled without having the affair given to the public. The lesson learned was not altogether in vain, and from that day many people wondered why Sister Norton was not as particular about dress as formerly, without in the least suspecting the cause.

Mr. Stanly was next appointed to Hillsdale. Here he found an active and wide awake, though not very intelligent membership, embracing in all about two hundred persons. These received him with warm hearts, and many expressions of welcome, and from the first the pastor and his wife were full of hope.

When the quarterly conference came to make out the preacher's salary, it was seen that the committee reported an exceedingly small and insufficient sum. They did so, as they stated, because of the large donation usually made, which with the quarterage would be sufficient to give him a living. In this manner, the stewards sought to appropriate the benefits

of this annual visit to their own advantage. Though
the proceeds were not to be reckoned on the salary,
they were practically made to come out of it by this
arrangement. It was only a plan by which the community might be made to believe they were giving
something to the preacher, when in fact they were
aiding the church in paying her legitimate bills. Mr.
Stanly plainly saw what was intended to be effected,
but for fear of giving offense, said nothing, and allowed
the scheme to be consummated.

The winter months passed away, and nothing was
heard at the parsonage of the contemplated visit. The
season for such occasions had already gone by, when,
at the third quarterly conference, the presiding elder
called for the financial report, and on learning the
state of the case, inquired if the promised donation
was not to be made. No one answered until he called
on a leading brother by name, who replied that he
knew nothing about it, as he was personally opposed
to such parties. Two or three others then expressed
themselves in the same manner, though these were
the very men who, at the beginning of the year, had
fixed the salary where it was, in view of such a
contingency.

"But you don't mean to repudiate your pledges?"
said the chairman.

"I have made no pledges," said one.

"Neither have I;" responded several others.

"Practically you did, in reporting the salary and
fixing it at three hundred and fifty dollars," replied
the elder. "You knew and admitted that sum to be

insufficient, and referred to the donation visit to make up the lack."

" We didn't regard ourselves pledged to make one," said a steward. "I am conscientiously opposed to them, and do all I can to prevent their being made."

" You did much at the beginning of the year to create a necessity for one," said the chairman.

After much discussion it was agreed that a donation visit should be made, or a hundred dollars added to the salary. As soon as this resolution passed, conscientious scuples rapidly disappeared, and several of the objectors voted to appoint a committee to take the matter in hand. Though refusing to serve themselves, or even attend the party, all now seemed anxious to have it held, and arrangements were accordingly made.

At the appointed time, the minister's house is full of company. But few of the leading church members are present, and there is far more rudeness than our friends have ever before witnessed at such times. The company take the most perfect liberty with everything around them. They ransack the old parsonage from cellar to garret, not allowing a cupboard, clothespress, or even a bookcase to escape their investigations.

The ladies find a scarcity for their table, and not willing that their reputation shall suffer, they search out Mrs. Stanly's preserve and pickle jars, empty them of their contents, and thus add to their stock. A jar of butter is also taken and made use of, with such other articles as can be found. Her new set of stone china is imperiled in the hands of the crowd, and she is pained to see several pieces more or less

broken. She would speak if she dared, but it is plain
the preacher and his wife are not expected to be particular, when receiving such favors as this. Thus
matters continue below, while occasional peals of
laughter from the chambers tell the character of the
scene above.

Soon after twelve o'clock, the company dispersed.
Glad to have a season of silence and rest, George and
Emily sat down and talked over the occurrences of the
evening. The secretary had left his papers and the
money received, in a drawer to which he had conde-
scendingly pointed the pastor as he withdrew, and
these were now examined. The other articles were
also brought together, and their value computed.

There was found in cash just twenty dollars, gathered in sums of from ten to fifty cents, from the various donors whose names were recorded. The estimated value of the other items, according to the papers left, was forty dollars, making sixty in all. But
on examination, they saw that most of these articles
were of no practical consequence. Among them was
a beautiful doll for the little girl, to which a large
number had contributed, put down at three dollars,
a pair of flower vases procured in the same way and
reckoned at ten; two or three worked collars from
the ladies, at a high figure; besides little fancy articles almost without number. Thus the sum total was
easily made up.

In looking on the other side, they found one valuable set of dishes nearly ruined, and one jar of butter
gone, in addition to the preserved fruit, dried beef,
and other eatables which had been laid in for future

use. The conclusion was soon reached that the loss was greater than the gain, and that they had been made the dupes of those who ought to have been, and actually professed to be, their brethren and friends. In business matters of a private character, such a course would have been downright dishonesty, but the official board, many of whom professed to enjoy too much religion to do otherwise, seemed gratified with the advantage they had gained. A hundred dollars had been saved on the allowance, and their burdens correspondingly lightened, and what matter was it to them how the preacher fared in the final result? Though they could so plan as to make the donation visit a necessity, they were altogether too religious to attend it. Hence the character of the occasion, considered in both its social and financial aspects.

The next day found the pastor's family busily engaged in cleaning house, and seeking to recover from the effects of the visit. No one proposed to assist them, though Mr. Stanly justly felt that the parties who had actually made money by the operation, and had not contributed a farthing, some of whom were his near neighbors, might have helped at least to bear this burden. They seemed to think otherwise, and the injustice of the affair was borne without eliciting remark from the deeply injured pastor.

Notwithstanding the results of this donation were plainly to be seen, it was evident that many of the people supposed they had done a fine thing for their preacher. Sixty dollars was an offering not to be despised, when it came as a present free and clear of salary. The payment of quarterage might now be dispensed with for several months, as there could certainly be no want at the parsonage.

And it was dispensed with almost to the end of the year, when Mr. Stanly found against him a ballance of one hundred dollars, after his salary should have been fully paid. The stewards had some difficulty in raising the arrearages, and not being willing to devote any time to such a cause, they proposed to reckon, in the end, a part of the donation in this way. The preacher was accordingly asked to report himself paid in full, when he should go up to the conference, and not allow the reputation of his charge to suffer. This he positively refused to do. He had already paid dearly for the privilege enjoyed, without meeting a second installment.

Mr. Stanly was pleased to be removed from Hillsdale at the end of the first year. He felt that he had been grossly wronged, and had no desire to repeat the experiment. The people complained that he was not allowed to stay, and with the exception of the official members, could divine no reason for the change. These were in fact nearly all the poor members which the church contained. Had there been a respectable board of officers, the station would have been widely different. As it was, their want of enterprise and liberal feeling gave tone to the whole, and allowed the society but a stinted growth.

CHAPTER XXIX.

NEW DIFFICULTIES.

WE next see our minister surrounded by circumstances of a peculiar character. He has generally regarded himself as highly favored in his appointments, and with the exceptions already noted, has been happily situated in all his charges. In this respect few Itinerant preachers have been more blessed than he.

Mr. Stanly is now located at a place known as Easton, and is spending his second year in charge of a large and interesting station. He has had time to become acquainted with his people, and is well pleased with the position assigned him. It has long been considered one of the best appointments in the conference.

For some time past, the American people have been quite generally excited on the subject of slavery. The iniquity of that diabolic system, as it exists in some sections of the country, had awakened numerous inquiries as to the best method of seeking its extirpation, and called forth the fierce invectives of many in the north, who had become more particularly acquainted with its real or supposed abominations. As a true follower of the immortal Wesley, Mr. Stanly had ever felt a strong repugnance to the "peculiar institution," and borne an unswerving testimony against it. At every place where he had labored, he found the majority of his membership agreeing with him in sentiment, and had encouraged them in their opposition to the great evil now generally under consideration.

It so happened at the time of which we speak, that a Mr. Green, somewhat celebrated as an antislavery lecturer, visited Easton and applied for the Methodist chapel in which to promulgate his views. The lecturer was known as a decided skeptic, bitterly opposed to the various religious denominations, which he everywhere unscrupuously denounced, and it was often suspected that his desire to overthrow the church, was greater than that which he felt for the abolition of slavery. As it was on Sabbath evening that Mr. Green solicited the privilege of the pulpit, the trustees referred him to the pastor, who at that hour usually held a social service.

Under circumstances of this character, Mr. Stanly did not think it proper to displace one of the established means of grace. He knew the applicant to be a vilifier of the church, and especially of the ministry, and had reason to suppose that he would pursue the same course here as in other towns. He could not, therefore, consent to the proposed arrangement, and gave a decided but respectful refusal. This awakened the wrath of the lecturer, who at once proceeded to argue the general question, by roundly abusing every one who seemed to stand in the way of his personal aggrandizement. At first, Mr. Stanly endeavored to conciliate him, but the effort was altogether fruitless. He was determined to be displeased, and seemed glad of an opportunity to denounce the
K*

churches as the bulwark of slavery, and at the same
time charge ministers with being the defenders and
apologists of the system.

Mr. Green was a fair representative of the class of
reformers to which he belonged. The reasoning element had no place in his constitution. All that he
could do was to indulge in vituperation and abuse.
His remarks on this occasion were sufficient to show
the wisdom of Mr. Stanly's course, and justify the
propriety of his decision.

At length, the disappointed lecturer withdrew from
the parsonage, and sought an interview with several
of the trustees and leading members of the society,
who were known to have strong antislavery feelings,
and who were supposed to be willing to hear his complaint. These were greatly surprised at his representation of Mr. Stanly's position. They had looked
upon their pastor as true to the spirit of reform, and
were accordingly disappointed at the apparent want
of sympathy which he now manifested. To most
of them, his course was altogether inexplicable.

Not so with Mr. Green. He claimed to understand the secret of the whole matter. All the pastor's antislavery professions were for mere effect. He
was at heart decidedly pro-slavery as his present position clearly indicated. With an expression of these
views, the lecturer went from one to another of Mr.
Stanly's friends, professing great concern for the welfare of the church, and slily hinting the impropriety
of allowing such a man to be a teacher of religion.

It was soon evident that several of the brethren
were seriously affected by this manner of procedure.

Until now, they had never doubted Mr. Stanly's sincerity, and were really at a loss what to do. A few called on him to learn his reasons, and were satisfied; but others insisted as the only way of making reparation, that he should give up his appointment and admit Mr. Green. This he could not consistently do, as he saw the bearing of that gentleman's effort, and the prayer meeting was accordingly held at the usual time.

Mr. Green also held a meeting at the same hour, in another place procured for the occasion. The disaffected party went to hear him, and returned boiling with indignation against " pro-slavery churches," and such ministers and members as gave them their support. As the result proved, Mr. Stanly was right in his opinion, as to the character of the contemplated lecture. Scarcely a word had been said against slavery, while the whole evening was occupied in a tirade against the churches of Christ. A portion of those who heard it were satisfied that the livery of heaven was being used for unholy purposes, and these gave the affair no further countenance. Another portion had their feelings embittered toward those institutions which they had heretofore loved, and through whose instrumentality they had been converted, and kept in the path of life.

Week after week the agitation and excitement thus begun continued to increase. The infidel philanthropist was in his element. With the help of such books and pamphlets as "The Brotherhood of Thieves," which he kept on sale, he proceded from house to house, making a hundred per cent. on his wares, and living without expense on the hospitality of his friends and sympathizers. This, added to occasional collections for the benefit of " the cause," gave him a fair salary while he remained at Easton.

With this emissary of Satan, Mr. Stanly thought to have as little to do as possible. He therefore pursued his usual course in the pulpit, at the same time doing all he could in his personal intercourse with the brethren, to counteract the unfavorable influence around him. With the larger and better portion of society, he had but little difficulty. They readily saw the true state of the case, and acted accordingly. But there were quite a number of inflammable spirits beyond the reach of reason. Their conclusions were drawn without forethought, and maintained without judgment. They were naturally well disposed men, of a warm and hasty temperament, and honest in their convictions, but had not sufficient balance of mind to be interested in more than one subject at a time. That idea had now eaten them up. They saw the abominations of slavery, believed the church to be in the way of emancipation, and were accordingly aroused.

After some time, Mr. Stanly consented, at the request of his friends, to preach on the subject of slavery. He did so by maintaining the positions he had been known to occupy from the first, and which had heretofore been satisfactory to all his hearers. It was a clear, able, and consistent antislavery discourse. But the followers of Mr. Green were no better satisfied than before, because it did not recommend secession from the church, which had now begun to be their watchword. No man, said they, can be antislavery, and belong to the corrupt churches which everywhere exist.

This sermon awakened also a feeling of an opposite character. A few, who gloried in their conservatism, were highly displeased that he should touch such a subject at all. Slavery, they argued, was a political question, and not appropriate for the pulpit. They did not believe in having a minister preach politics, especially on Sunday. Thus he was doomed to suffer, as most true men are, from both extremes.

Mr. Green and his co-laborers were, during several months, frequently at Easton. Among the number was one or two disaffected preachers, who had all at once learned that the government of the church was tyrannical and despotic, and this was now added to the causes of complaint. Men who had lived in this communion almost from childhood, and had never dreamed but what they enjoyed the largest liberty, now suddenly awoke to find themselves the victims of a spiritual aristocracy, too intolerable to be endured. They talked incessantly of the duty of secession, but made no move toward its accomplishment, until several were arrested and held to trial, when a general stampede took place. About thirty were dismissed, who soon after formed themselves into a new society.

During the months that this agitation prevailed, hard times were seen at the parsonage. The minister was not alone in being assailed by the disaffected parties. His family circle was also rudely assaulted. Private matters were dragged out to the public gaze, and every means taken to destroy the standing and influence of one who stood firmly in the way of faction, and maintained with a strong hand the character and reputation of an outraged church. This course was doubtless essential to the accomplishment of the end proposed ; for so long as there was confidence in the ministry, infidelity had not completely triumphed.

Mr. Stanly was painfully conscious that much of this whole difficulty might have been avoided, had the trustees originally exercised a proper control over the house of worship. The habit had long been indulged in Easton, of admitting all sorts of so-called benevolent and scientific lecturers into the meeting-house, and the refusal to make way for Mr. Green, had given the present movement its first and principal impetus. Had a standing rule been adopted, by which a temple dedicated to the service of Almighty God, should be used for that purpose alone, the result might have been widely different. As it was, every applicant was referred to the pastor, and he was thus made to bear the responsibilities in no wise connected with his office, and which he could not discharge without giving offense.

Too many of these traveling lecturers are like Mr. Green, full of hatred to the institutions of religion, and seeking their overthrow as the primary object of their labors. The garb of philanthropy is assumed for no other purpose than to give them currency among the people, and prepare the way for bringing religion into disrepute. Said one of this class of men in an "infidel convention," after a series of railings against God and the bible, " I never deliver lectures on infidelity ; but I am constantly lecturing on the various reforms of the age. I lecture on temperance, on antislavery, on peace, on moral reform, on socialism &c. &c., but wherever I go, I lecture on *infidel principles.* Thus our cause is promoted continually."

The new organization at Easton was a short-lived affair. Its leaders did not even design it to be permanent. It was only formed as a means of luring men from the fold of Christ, and when this work could be no longer successfully done, the society was allowed to go down. A few of the dupes of infidelity saw their error, and returned to the church of their early love, wiser if not better men, while others launched boldly off on the boundless sea of skepticism, and still pursue their cheerless voyage, without God and without hope in the world.

CHAPTER XXX.

THE PASTOR'S FAMILY.

IF at this period we take a look at the pastor's family, we shall see that the changes wrought by the hand of time are neither few nor small. Mr. and Mrs. Stanly are looking older and graver than when we last saw them in the family circle, and may now be regarded as having reached that age when the intellectual faculties are in the fullest exercise, and can be brought most successfully to bear upon the accomplishment of a desired end. Those who knew them twenty years since, when they entered the ranks of the Itinerancy, and devoted their lives to this sacred calling, would scarcely recognize the youthful couple in the persons before us. Their countenances are somewhat care-worn, and it is clearly evident that they have borne heavy responsibilities; yet the liveliness of their temperament is scarcely diminished, and the ardor of their zeal is in no wise quenched. Amid all their trials and sufferings, they have never regretted their devotion to this cause.

They are now the parents of five children. The eldest, a daughter bearing the mother's name, is almost eighteen years old, and is a fine representative of what her mother was at the same age. She is a member of the church, as is her sister Mary, just

blushing into sweet sixteen, both of whom are orna-
ments in our minister's household. The two next
are boys; the first named George, from his father,
the second called Wesley, after the honored instru-
ment of the second great reformation. George is wild,
and, as his parents have sometimes thought, almost
reckless; and yet their faith has ever claimed him as
a subject of redeeming grace. Thus far, he has steadily rejected the proffers of religion, grasping rather
for the pleasures and joys of earth, than the sublimer
and more enduring bliss of heaven. The inclination
of Wesley's mind is scarcely yet unfolded, though,
like his brother, he is somewhat impetuous and dar-
ing in his preferences and dislikes. The baby, as it
is called, though three years old, is the family pet; as
all babies are, and rejoices in the name of Ellen.

Mr. Stanly has sought, from the first, to give his
children the advantages of a good education. Three
of them have been connected with the conference
seminary, at which they propose to remain for some
time, with the exception of Emily, who intends to go
south and engage in teaching. She will graduate at
the close of the next term, and is already acquainted
with a favorable opening in Tennessee, to which she
is invited. Mary has taught one summer in a small
district school, and George is fitting himself for the
same work. They enter upon this business thus early
in life, because they have no other method of paying
their current expenses. Their father's salary is not
sufficient to enable him to keep them steadily at
school, though he manages to aid them to a considerable extent. For several years every dollar that

17

could be spared has been scrupulously devoted to this cherished object. He is well aware that they will be thrown on their own resources in the future, and that he can do no more for them than to aid in furnishing means for their mental improvement. Silver and gold are not within his reach. This must, therefore, be their only legacy.

Fortunately, the children of Mr. Stanly saw and appreciated their circumstances. They have consented, therefore, to submit to many inconveniences which the more wealthy can easily avoid. The prices of the boarding hall are beyond their reach, and they have accordingly hired a room where they may do their own work, and provide for their own wants at far less expense. Mrs. Stanly has some time since given up her hired girl at home, as an item of economy, and deprived herself of many little luxuries, that she might add to the comfort of the daughters abroad. Thus they have combined in carrying out the plan adopted, with high hopes of a successful result.

Though there were some unpleasant features connected with this method of securing an education, which girls of their age would have gladly avoided, yet both Emily and Mary have made rapid progress in their studies. It is true, but very few young ladies board themselves, and fewer still dress as cheaply as they, and though this is sometimes a source of mortification, they are willing to endure it, rather than be deprived of the blessings they seek.

George is not equally submissive. He understands the true cause of his father's poverty, and does not hesitate to complain. With him, the Itinerancy is no favorite, either in theory or practice. In his boyishness, he is unable to see the justice of the church in her inadequate support of the ministry.

"If my father had not been a preacher," said he on one occasion, "he might have sent me to school like other boys, without compelling me to work for my board. I don't think much of a minister's life, anyhow."

"I expect to see you on a circuit, some day," said Mary playfully.

"Never," was the response. "I'd be a wood-chopper first. Then I could be my own man; but a preacher must run at every man's call, and work at half price in the bargain."

"Don't be so fast, my dear brother," said Mary. "If you were to become a christian, your opinions would undergo a change in this respect, as well as in others."

"If I thought it would make me believe this way of doing business was right, I'd never be one, I assure you. I don't believe in a religion that makes wrong into right, no matter what you call it."

"It may be that you are wrong, instead of what you condemn," said his sister. "I hope you will yet live to see your error."

"Well, you may be a minister's wife, if you want to and can get a chance, which is doubtful, but I shall never be a minister;" and away he went, leaving the girls to their own reflections.

George Stanly jun. was not the only preacher's son that has seen injustice in the treatment of his father and those who have been dependent on him. It has been felt by thousands beside; and the number of such sons to be found in other christian communions shows the feeling to have been neither superficial nor transient. It is quite possible that many ministers themselves, in changing their church relations, have been driven to such a course by similar convictions.

It may also be well to inquire whether this has anything to do with the opinion so frequently expressed, that minister's children are more inclined to be irreligious than are those of others. The youthful mind is quick to learn, and if there be any correctness in the sentiment referred to, possibly the unwelcome fact may thus be explained.

CHAPTER XXXI.

THE CITY STATIONS.

AGAIN we see our preacher at the session of his conference. He has long since reached an honorable position among his brethren as an able and efficient minister, and as it is his moving year, several congregations are making efforts to secure his services. Among others, there is a petition from Jay street, one of the oldest and most important stations in the city from which the conference is named, and a committee is also present to secure, if possible a favorable response. Mr. Stanly's personal preferences are in favor of another charge, to which he is also invited; but as he ever holds himself in readiness to go where he is most wanted, the matter on his part is very properly left in the hands of those to whom it legitimately belongs.

The Jay street church had of late enjoyed a reputation of no enviable character. Evidently feeling its importance as the leading city appointment, it had taken the selection of pastors into its own hands, and like such societies in general, had become very difficult to to be suited. For a number of years the supposed interests of the station had been so peculiar that they could not be committed to the constituted authorities of the church, and at almost every session of the conference, the official board was accordingly

represented in the lobby. Though seldom satisfied
with their present incumbent, these committees had
always some one in view precisely adapted to their
wants. At this particular time, Mr. Stanly was their
man, and they were quite sure no one else would
meet their necessities. The result shows that they
were once more gratified, and our friend is accordingly thus appointed.

The first business on reaching his new field of labor, was to look up a house. There was no parsonage,
and strange as it may appear, the people made no arrangements to give the preacher and his family a home,
as he came among them. The late pastor had moved
twice during his connection with the station, and being
unwilling to take a house for a year, when he knew he
could occupy it but for a few months, had hired his
board since the first of May at a hotel. There was,
consequently, no vacancy from his removal, and as
the renting season was gone by, it was with considerable difficulty that an opening could be found.

Under the circumstances, the only resort was to
the newspapers. For two days every tenement that
was advertised to let was faithfully visited. Some
were held at too high a price, others were in the wrong
location, and still others were so out of repair as to
be unfit for use. At length, when weary of going for
and returning keys, climbing stairways and examin-
ing apartments, a fair house was engaged, though at
an exorbitant price. The lease extended only to the
first of May, when a cheaper one must be secured,
so that another removal was early in prospect.

It was soon found that the life of a Methodist

preacher in the city, was greatly unlike that in country towns. In the first place, the brethren and sisters seemed more shy and unsociable. A number of days passed, and no one came to extend a welcome, or aid in effecting a settlement. To the preacher and his wife, this was entirely unusual, though the lack was more easily supplied by the abundance of proffered help, at moderate charges, on the part of carmen and day-laborers, than they could have at first supposed.

Another wide difference was found in the expenses of living. The market was now their daily resort, where everything was held at prices unheard of in the places where they had heretofore resided. For the first time they had no garden, and no farmers to supply such articles as theirs should lack. They were also obliged to make a purchase of stoves, a species of heavy furniture which they had found supplied by their poorest charges, and which they had hoped never to be obliged to own. In short, not the slightest arrangement was found for the convenience, or comfort, or economy of the minister's family. Still it was Jay street, and the new pastor saw, by the bearing of his people, that those whom he served regarded it in the light of a favor, to be allowed to fill so distinguished and honorable an appointment.

The visiting was also conducted on a different principle from that to which he had been accustomed. A certain time must elapse before it would be in order to make calls at the minister's residence, and then they must be made according to the strictest rules of etiquette. Fashion and ceremony took the place of the warm, perhaps blunt, but hearty greeting usually extended, and it need not be wondered that Mrs. Stanly felt homesick in her new location. Her husband understood her, when in answer to inquiries extended, she expressed the opinion that the country air was more agreeable than that of the city, and better adapted to the peculiarities of her constitution. It had, however, a hidden meaning, not so easily comprehended by others.

The first quarterly meeting did not occur until nearly three months after conference. Various circumstances combined, during this time, to convince Mr. and Mrs. Stanly that the largest and richest station in the conference was not necessarily the most pleasant and agreeable. The official board had in several instances assumed prerogatives not properly belonging to them, which Mr. Stanly looked upon as disrespectful to himself and the ministry in general; and he now appealed to the presiding elder, and in each case obtained decisions in his favor. This act awakened more feeling than he had ever before witnessed in a quarterly conference, and he saw plainly that he was rendering himself obnoxious to such as were unwilling to conform to the disciplinary regulations of the church, which he thus sought to maintain. Still he was resolute in his purpose, and firm in maintaining the positions taken.

At the close of the quarterly conference, a steward came to him in an excited manner, and stated that great dissatisfaction was being awakened by the course pursued.

"I am very sorry to hear it," said Mr. Stanly.

"You must manage a litle different," added the brother, " if you think of sustaining yourself *here*."

"I will try and do right," was the response.

"You must do as *we* want you to, while you remain in our employ," said a class-leader by his side. "If you can't do that, we cannot give you our support."

"You can do as you please as to that matter," said Mr. Stanly. "It will make no difference with my convictions of duty."

" A preacher needn't think of coming to Jay street and setting himself up against the official board," said the steward, "without anticipating trouble. Brother Smith began in that way, and we gave him a walking paper at the end of the first year."

"And so you may do by me if you please," answered Mr. Stanly, quite aroused, "but you cannot bring me to any such terms as you have dictated. While I stay, I shall try to be a Methodist preacher, and hope to maintain the integrity of my calling. I did not ask to come to Jay street, and am not particularly desirous of remaining a second year. My respect for no appointment will lead me to sacrifice the principles which I am pledged to support. You understand me, gentlemen, and can take such action as you think proper."

As Mr. Stanly withdrew, an earnest conversation was begun as to the merits of the question at issue. Opinions were freely expressed, and it was soon ascertained, that while a few were for carrying things forward with a high hand, the majority were disposed to yield to the demands of the discipline by

L

which they professed to be governed. The counsels
of the latter class finally prevailed, and nothing more
was heard in the way of complaint, concerning the
straight-forward course which the preacher pursued.
Mr. Stanly saw, and was highly gratified at the result. Though a few were temporarily disaffected, he
was conscious of having won the respect and esteem of
the many, by his adherence to the right.

The year, as it would seem thus inauspiciously begun, was more prosperous than could at first have
been anticipated. The congregation was well pleased
with their minister, and in most cases not the less so
for the firmness which he manifested. Mr. Stanly
soon became quite reconciled to the circumstances
around him, and proceeded with his usual energy and
success, in carrying forward the work of the gospel.
In matters of finance he was subjected to more than
his usual embarrassment, for though his salary was
larger than in the country, it was far from being increased in proportion to his expenses. The times
were also getting hard. Prices were higher than
ever, and the innumerable little presents of fruit,
fresh meat, vegetables, and the like, ordinarily sent
in from farming communities, were now wholly with-
held. This made an essential difference in the support of the family, and though a fine donation was
given, Mr. Stanly found himself largely behind.

At the close of the year, the official board requested
their pastor's return, and though aware of his financial deficiencies, insisted on a compliance with their
wishes. Numerous apologies were made, and ex-
planations offered in view of the past, and it was

generally agreed that they would be able to do much better for the year to come, so that he need have no fears in continuing in their midst. Under the impression that these hopeful indications would be fulfilled, Mr. Stanly raised no objection to his reäppointment, and was accordingly returned.

At the appropriate time, the committee appointed to estimate the preacher's table expenses, and thereby make out his allowance, reported to the quarterly conference the same aggregate as had been given the previous year. Mr. Clark, the chairman, a man worth fifty thousand dollars, confessed it was not what it should be, but thought it was all that could be raised without embarrassing the society. This seemed to be the general feeling among the brethren present, nearly all of whom regretted that they could not afford to pay a larger sum. The presiding elder, who understood the preacher's circumstances, remonstrated in his behalf; but Jay street thought it a virtue to hold this officer in contempt, and accordingly disregarded his advice. The vote was taken, and the report adopted by a unanimous voice.

"I guess," said Mr. Clark, turning to his preacher with a look of satisfaction, "that you can live on what we have allowed."

"No sir," answered Mr. Stanly; "the brethren all know I cannot."

"I wish we could do better," added Mr. Clark. "I am sure we are willing a preacher shall get all he can. It is only a necessity that causes us to fix the salary at what we have."

"Yes," said another steward, "we should all be glad to do more if we could."

" I wish you to understand, gentlemen, that I cannot live on what you have voted," said Mr. Stanly. " I have nothing to fall back on to make up deficiencies, and I would now inquire what you would have me do ? "

" I wish we *could* raise more," said a rich class-leader.

" There is no use of *talking* about this matter any longer," said Mr. Clark. "The report has been adopted, and it is getting late. I move we adjourn."

" Wait a moment," said Mr. Stanly. " I don't want to be a burden to you, and if my presence as your pastor at a salary sufficient to support my family is regarded in that light, I will endeavor to relieve you. Perhaps the presiding elder, using the power vested in him, could make an arrangement satisfactory to both parties."

"What do you mean by that ?" asked a member.

" I mean that if you cannot support me, we had better request the presiding elder to move me to some charge that can, and for one, I shall insist on such a change."

Had a bomb shell been suddenly thrown in among them, the members of the quarterly conference would not have been more surprised. They had never dreamed that Jay street was not the most desirable place for a Methodist preacher which the conference afforded. They really supposed they were conferring a favor on Brother Stanly, in allowing him to stay a second year. To hear him now talk of asking a better appointment, was to be treated with vile ingratitude.

"I think we shall not be moved by any threats," said a brother.

" I think not, either," put in another.

" Just as you please," answered Mr. Stanly. "I don't ask you to allow me *anything ;* but if you wish me to stay, you must support me."

The subject was discussed for a full hour, but with no change in the result. So important a station as this was not to be dictated to by a preacher. Mr. Stanly said nothing further, but his resolution was fixed.

The presiding elder conducted the services on the Sabbath following, as is customary on quarterly meeting occasions. He knew, as did all others, that the plea of inability on the part of the Jay street members was a sheer invention. They were abundantly able, but had fallen into the habit of paying just so much each, and their unwillingness to do more was construed as we have seen above. True, they could not make out a larger salary without increasing their subscriptions, and despite all that could be said, this was the only difficulty. They were no doubt willing the preacher should have a comfortable support *if he could get it,* but not as willing to put their hands in their pockets, like real christians, and contribute according to their abundance.

"Early on Monday morning, the little words "To Let," so frequently seen in cities, were found suspended over Mr. Stanly's door. In the course of the day several of the members called, and inquired the meaning of this, and were surprised to learn that he intended to give up his house, though, with the ex-

ception of the official members, none could divine
the reason of this strange proceeding. These began
to suspect that matters were coming to an unexpected crisis, and upon consultation, concluded to
hold an extra meeting and try to effect a compromise.
They accordingly came together, and deputed one of
their number to go for Mr. Stanly, who at first declined, but afterward consented to meet them, according to their wishes.

It was evident, at once, that the brethren were not
in the happiest mood, and one or two exhibited a de-
fiant air as he made his appearance. "I thought,"
said Mr. Clark, "that you were a great admirer of
discipline. Is not this a little contrary to usage in
our church?"

"It certainly is," replied Mr. Stanly. "The economy of our church provides that the preachers give
up their right of choosing places and bargaining for
salaries, and that the members give up theirs of se-
lecting preachers; so that, for the good of the whole,
the appointing power is lodged with a third party.
As you see, it is a species of compromise, in which
there is a mutual surrender of privileges. But Jay
street has practically repudiated this arrangement.
You choose your preachers in advance, insist on having them, without reference to the feelings of others,
and have generally carried your point. You need
not be surprised, then, if the other party to the contract begins to act on the same principle. You nul-
lify your obligations, and you leave me free with regard to mine.

"I should not have been here, had you left the

appointments where the discipline directs. In that
case my embarrassment might have been avoided,
and the burdens of which you complain lightened.
As it is, the infraction of the spirit of the discipline
has brought us into difficulty, and I am obliged to
seek another appointment."

"You don't really intend to leave us, though?"
said a steward.

"That is with my presiding elder. He knows the
facts of the case, and has signified a willingness to
accommodate both you and myself."

"I supposed," said Mr. Clark, "that Methodist
preachers were not very particular about their salary. I have known Presbyterians and Baptists to
stand out on that point, but never expected to see
such a thing in our church."

"I wish no further controversy. All I ask is
enough to feed and clothe my family, and I think I
should sin against God not to insist on such a provision for my household."

"I think so, too," said a brother who had thus far
kept silent.

"Understand me," added Mr. Stanly. "I do not
ask you to increase my allowance. I petition for no
mere *favor* at your hands. I am willing to labor
among you if you support me, and am willing to
labor somewhere else if you do not. You can make
your own election. I went in debt last year one
hundred and fifty dollars, and though not a Presbyterian or a Baptist, I seek to be sufficiently honest to
pay my bills."

Mr. Stanly declined arguing the points raised, and

left the board to take its own course. They wisely concluded to add two hundred dollars to the sum previously fixed upon, and thus the matter ended.

Immediately after the adjournment, Brother Clark approached the pastor, and remarked that he was satisfied, for one, that the salary ought to have been increased, but was sorry Mr. Stanly had taken such a course to secure it.

"You cannot regret its necessity more than I do," was the reply.

"I fear," said the former, "you will lose friends, and that the church will not coöperate with you as cordially as before."

"I am in no wise concerned about that," answered Mr. Stanly. "I am willing to forfeit any man's friendship who thinks it a sin to provide food for one's wife and children. Such a person's good will is not worth having. The church, of which you speak, will doubtless be all the more efficient for having done its duty."

"Well, we will hope for the best," said the old gentleman, at the same time bidding him good day.

The result of this affair was as Mr. Stanly anticipated. A very few niggardly souls blamed the preacher for not trusting in "Providence," but nearly all felt their respect for him greatly increased. Never before had he made so many friends by a single act. Even those who had withstood him, knew he was right, and in the end gave his course their approbation. So true is it, that a man never gains the esteem of those around him by sacrificing principle at their unrighteous demands.

The increased salary was raised without the slightest difficulty, and from that day everything passed off in harmony and peace. The year was prosperous almost without precedent in the history of Jay street. Mr. Stanly said no more on the subject of finance, and yet was enabled at the close of his incumbency to pay off the deficiencies of his first term. With this he expressed himself satisfied, though but few men in the prime of life, would be willing like him to live without making some provision for sickness and age.

His next appointment was also in the city. Elm street was less assuming and less wealthy than his last charge, and yet the church found no difficulty in supporting its pastor. A good parsonage, provided with heavy furniture, was furnished in addition to the salary given at Jay Street, and this enabled Mr. Stanly to lay up three hundred dollars from the two years of his incumbency, which was just about the sum received from his donation visits and wedding fees.

This second city station was blessed with an enterprising and efficient official board, through whose influence had been secured a corresponding membership. Though not as wealthy as many others, it had risen to a position of equality with the best stations in conference, and by most preachers was preferred to Jay street. From the period of its organization the members had sown with a liberal hand, and been favored with a perpetual harvest. Revival followed revival, and prosperity attended all their efforts.

Mr. Stanly now visited Colombia and made a payment toward relieving the debt on his little home. It was the first time in several years that he had come in possession of more than enough to meet his current expenses. Even now, it was almost snatched from his children, who were struggling for an education, and whose prosperity it might have greatly subserved.

CHAPTER XXXII.

CALLS FOR MONEY.

MANY persons wonder why it costs a minister so much to live; and after all that has been said on the subject, not a few are unable to see why his expenses should exceed their own. These are wholly unmindful of the peculiarities of his social position. They overlook the great number of visitors which frequent the parsonage; the consequent necessity of being always in readiness for company; the wear and tear of moving from place to place; the inability to take advantage of the markets; the cost of books and stationary; with numerous other incidentals from which ordinary householders are exempt. They forget, also, that above all others, he must be given to hospitality, and is expected to make a liberal as well as prompt response to all calls for charitable and benevolent objects, to which the religious public are constantly subject. It is well known that in most of these matters, christian ministers are expected to take the lead; and in no branch of the church so much so, as in the one which furnishes them the least competent support.

As proof of this, it is only necessary to turn our attention to the schools and colleges under the fostering care of this large and flourishing denomination.

It is well understood, that in almost every case these
have originated with the clergy, and to many of our
costliest institutions they have been not only the foremost but heaviest subscribers. Upon investigation,
the same will be found true in regard to nearly all the
benevolent and philanthropic organizations in our
midst.

In our cities and larger towns, the objects of charity
which press upon a minister's attention, are much
more numerous than in country appointments. Thus,
Mr. Stanly found many of the poor connected with
the societies he now served, and, as from time to
time he became acquainted with their wants, was
constrained to do something for their relief. More
than once has he found such extreme suffering while
visiting among this class, that his last dollar has been
freely tendered, though he knew it must be at the expense of his own family comforts. And then, too,
there were almost unnumbered applications at his
residence. Of the scores of traveling agents who
visit our important towns, none fail to make a call on
the ministers, with whose office there seems to be
connected a kind of professional hospitality. Of this
latter class, we will take the following literal case
as an illustration.

While Mr. Stanly was at the height of his money
pressure at Jay street, a gentleman called and introduced himself as the Rev. Mr. Evans, and stated that
he was pastor of an embarrassed seaman's church, for
which he was soliciting aid. He related the circumstances of the case, the difficulties they had surmount-
ed in building their house of worship, the good that

had been already accomplished, and the necessity of immediate help from the friends of the enterprise, in order to save their property from sheriff's sale. It was undoubtedly a clear case. The agent ought to be assisted; and Mr. Stanly did not hesitate to express his willingness to encourage the undertaking to the utmost of his ability. He invited Mr. Evans to a home in his family while he remained in the city, which was cheerfully accepted; and arrangements were immediately made for the successful prosecution of his mission. These included the proffer of the pastor's time, who consented to accompany the agent in calling on the leading families of his congregation.

Everything in readiness for the commencement of his work, as they were about to leave the parsonage, Mr. Evans unfolded his subscription paper, and turning to Mr. Stanly, remarked: "Well, brother, I suppose I must begin with you. How much are *you* willing to subscribe?"

Mr. Stanly explained his circumstances in brief, and stated his inability to contribute as he could wish; but pledged himself anew to use his influence with the people, many of whom were able to give without embarrassment.

"I need the influence of your name on the paper," said the agent. "Your example will tell more than your precepts in such a matter."

"I cannot do it," answered Mr. Stanly, "Some of my people are rich, many of them are in easy circumstances, while I am literally poor. I cannot set them an example as to what they should give."

"It will be of but little use for me to go among them, without your name as a contributor," was the reply.

"I *ought* not, but still I suppose I *can* give you a little. I want you to succeed in redeeming your church. You may put me down two dollars," said Mr. Stanly.

"O, but that will not answer," remarked the agent. "I presume it is all you are *able* to give, and am sorry to ask you for more. But I fear your members will not sign more than you do, and in that case I shall make a failure. Can't you say ten dollars?"

"I haven't ten dollars in the world."

"At least you must put down five for example's sake," persisted Mr. Evans. "You can trust in Providence for the result."

Mr. Stanly sincerely wished the agent success, and rather than be a party to his failure, headed the list with the last named sum. The paper was then circulated through the station and gained many signatures, but no one felt it his duty to give more than his pastor. In this, as in many other cases of like nature, men worth their ten thousands, measured themselves by one almost penniless, and considered it a virtue to equal his benevolence; so that Mr. Stanly gave on the whole as largely as the most wealthy of his hearers.

This case of Mr. Evans was by no means peculiar. Scarcely a week passed without applications for money, and a minister whose very life is devoted to the well-being ·of his fellows is not expected to refuse. In him the poor and needy look for a friend that shall

never turn them away. To many, it does not seem
to occur that his means are limited, and his expenses
unusually great. If he allows himself to turn a deaf
ear to their calls, the charge of penuriousness is at
once made, and his ministerial reputation badly
damaged. If he even attempts to provide for the vi-
cissitudes of human life, by saving from his dearly-
bought earnings a mere pittance for himself and his
children when sickness and infirmity shall come upon
them, he is at once liable to the suspicion of being
actuated by unworthy motives, in having entered the
ministry of the Lord Jesus Christ. He must therefore give, and keep himself poor, or lose that measure
of influence that crowns his labors with success.

CHAPTER XXXIII.

WE have now to trace the history of our minister in a comparatively new field. He has been appointed to the charge of Colombia district, and is about to enter upon the peculiar duties connected with the office of presiding elder. This is a position requiring great labor and care on the part of its occupant, and one which Mr. Stanly would have gladly avoided; but as he had been called to it by the constituted authorities of the church, he cheerfully sacrificed his private preferences, and prepared for the work assigned him.

Early in the history of the Methodist Episcopal church, the presiding eldership was held in high repute; and its occupant considered especially honored. Afterward, it came to be looked upon by large numbers of both clergy and laity as unnecessary and uncalled for; and the propriety of its abolition was long and earnestly discussed. The result of this agitation is well known. Some became embittered, and seceded; others changed their minds, and acquiesced in the existing arrangement, and in course of time peace and harmony were fully restored. Still, from that day, a distrustful eye has ever been kept on the office, and in many sections of the country it is yet quite generally regarded with indifference. This state of feeling, which pervades nearly all the eastern conferences in a greater or less degree, will account for many incidents connected with Mr. Stanly's administration.

The district was favorably located in a central portion of the conference, and contained several stations which Mr. Stanly had formerly served as pastor. It took its name from the village of Colombia, which was nearly its center, and in which the presiding elder had usually resided. This was a happy circumstance for the present incumbent, and especially so for his family, who were thus thrown into the society of friends and acquaintances to whom they were strongly attached.

Mr. Stanly had no sooner removed to his new home and become settled, than he entered upon his work. His district contained about twenty circuits and stations, and there was no time to be lost. His first quarterly meeting was held in the place where he lived; and he was happy to meet the friends of former years, and become once more associated with them. True, great changes had taken place in the lapse of time, and comparatively few remained at their post. Brother Tompkins had died in the triumphs of faith, and many others had followed him to the grave, so that the charm of going among old friends was in a measure broken. Enough remained, however, to remind him of the past, and revive the fond recollections of other days. Father Bennett was still alive, though obliged to retire from active life. Brothers Roberts, Dickson, and Jones, were left to extend a cordial welcome, and they were the same

good men as before, while Mr. Pindar had grown,
if possible, more fault-finding and garrulous than ever.
It seemed as if the good Lord had spared him to a
ripe old age, that the faith of the saints might be properly tried, and the blessings which accompany afflictions be conferred on his people.

Mrs. Stanly was also greatly pleased with a residence at Colombia. The fact of her being among acquaintances, with the prospect of remaining a term of
years in the same place, made up in part for the frequent necessity of her husband's absence. The children were now all at home. Emily had already engaged as a teacher in the village academy, and the
others were attendants upon its advantages.

The presiding elder's second quarterly meeting was
held at Jonesville. A very few only attended the
Saturday service, as it was said that most of the brethren could not find time to be present. Several of the
official members came in, however, at the close of the
sermon, so as to attend to the conference business
which was then to be transacted. Mr. Stanly had
reason to regard this course on the part of his brethren, as a poor compliment to himself, but indulged
in no disposition to complain.

The quarterly conference was called to order, and
proceeded to business in the usual manner. Nothing
worthy of note occurred, until the president named
the subject of appointing a delegate to the district
steward's convention. This is a meeting convened
on the appointment of each new presiding elder, and
as much oftener as the case shall require, to estimate
that officer's salary, and apportion it among the vari-

ous churches which he serves. It is composed of one representative from each charge, selected in the manner already indicated.

On this occasion the matter was no sooner broached, than several members seemed to manifest a little feeling. After a few moments' private consultation, one of the number suggested that a less amount for the support of the presiding elder than heretofore, should be set to Jonesville, and at the same time moved that the delegate be instructed to insist upon such an arrangement. To this resolution the preacher in charge raised an objection, expressing a preference to leave it to the brother chosen to do the best he could.

"It is possible," said he, "that the sum paid is no more than our proportion with the other charges."

"I don't know how that may be," said one, "but it is more than we can afford to pay."

"We can pay our part, can we not?" asked the pastor. "It's no more than right that each appointment should do its just proportion."

"I don't see as we get any benefit from presiding elders, anyway," said the brother. "What's the use of paying out money when no good comes from it."

"I think the office is unnecessary, and ought to be abolished," said another. "But while it is continued, I am in favor of sustaining it."

"Yes," put in a third, "our preachers could hold the quarterly meetings just as well as a presiding elder."

"But," said the pastor, "that is only a small part of his business. Have you considered his other duties, and found how they can be provided for, without impairing the Itinerant system?"

"I didn't know," said the first speaker, "that he
he had any other duties."

"Nor I, either," said another.

"Perhaps," added the minister, "if we were better
acquainted with the discipline, and the practical workings of our general economy, we should have less objections to its various parts than at present."

"I think so, too," said a venerable class-leader. "I
was among the number that sincerely believed presiding elders could be dispensed with, and, as you all
know to my shame, went off with the seceders, and
gave the opposite system a trial. But we soon found
that an Itinerancy without an efficient executive department, was a mere sham."

"I think we will not argue the point here," interrupted the elder, "as we have no authority to make
changes in the discipline. We must either be willing
to bear the burdens of the Itinerancy, or else give up
its advantages."

"That's it," said the class-leader who had just spoken. "The choice is between Congregationalism and
our own system. We cannot break in upon the Itinerancy here, without giving it up altogether. I have
witnessed a faithful trial of the experiment, and am
satisfied."

After a few moments' further conversation, the subject was dropped, and the delegate appointed without
any specific instructions. Sufficient had been said,
however, to awaken a new train of thought in the mind
of Mr. Stanly. Was he to be regarded as a burden on
his district, and go about his labors without the sympathy and affection of the people? Was it true, that

he was looked upon in his new position as an incumbrance rather than a blessing to the churches that he served! The remarks of the Jonesville brethren seemed, at least, to hint at this. And yet he saw clearly that he was as strictly in the line of duty as at any previous portion of his ministry.

When he went into the pulpit on the Sabbath, he could scarcely rid himself of these unpleasant reflections; and they were not without their influence on the sermon. At the close of his labors he was glad to leave those who seemed afflicted with his presence, and return to the quiet of his own family circle.

That the remarks referred to did not grow out of any personal ill-will to Mr. Stanly, is evident from the fact that he had never been at Jonesville before, and was therefore an entire stranger to all the parties concerned. They resulted from an altogether limited view of the nature and duties of his office. A better comprehension of the subject would have led to an entirely different opinion.

For several weeks following nothing of interest occurred. The quarterly meetings were held among those who gave a hearty support to the usages of the denomination, and Mr. Stanly began to be more highly pleased than at first with the work committed to his hands. Almost every charge that he visited was in the enjoyment of religious prosperity, and both pastors and people were successfully laboring in the vineyard of the Lord.

At one point he was greatly pleased with the occasion enjoyed, especially as it presented a strong contrast to similar services at other places. Since the di-

vision of the work into small and often feeble stations,
in the place of the old fashioned circuits, the quarterly
meetings have in a great measure lost their peculiar
interest. The love feast differs but little from the general class meeting, and the congregation on the Sabbath is necessarily the same as at other times. With
the exception therefore of the celebration of the Lord's
Supper, the whole passes off as an ordinary affair.

Weston circuit alone, in Colombia district, maintained almost its primitive dimensions; and Mr.
Stanly found, on visiting it, a different state of things
from what he had seen elsewhere. At the appointed
hour on Saturday, the house of worship was nearly
filled with pious and attentive worshipers, and in
preaching to them he enjoyed unusual liberty. In the
evening prayer meeting the Holy Spirit was gloriously
manifest in their midst. There was the shout of a
king in the camp, as sinners were converted and believers sanctified. Such a triumph had never before
been witnessed by our presiding elder on a quarterly
meeting occasion.

The love feast was of the same character. Brethren
were present from quite a distance, and as they now
came together, it was with holy greetings and triumphant songs. Altogether, it was a spiritual festival not
soon to be forgotten, and Mr. Stanly almost sighed
for those days of which the fathers spake, when similar scenes were everywhere enjoyed. He began to
doubt, before leaving Weston, the propriety of the
changes which Methodism has undergone in her effort to keep up with the spirit of the age, and conform to the maxims of the times.

Next in course came Freeville, a station of rather poor repute as to its financial character, and yet very difficult to be suited in the men appointed to its charge. For a number of years it had been supplied with young and inexperienced preachers, who had not given general satisfaction, until, at the last session of conference, a petition was forwarded for a minister of high standing, and in hopes of changing the character of the appointment, the wish of the applicants had been granted. The Rev. Mr. Smith was accordingly in charge of the station.

Unlike Weston, the preparatory sermon on quarterly meeting occasions was given up, and nothing farther was done on Saturday than to meet and transact the business of the quarterly conference. This was quickly dispatched with the exception of the single item of fixing the pastor's salary. The committee to whom this subject had been referred, made their report, awarding him the sum of three hundred dollars. The presiding elder took occasion to remind them, on its presentation, that it was not in due form.

"It is simply your duty," he remarked, "to estimate the amount of fuel and table expenses for the preacher's family, as the other items are otherwise fixed."

"We prefer to report simply the aggregate," said the chairman.

"The committee have to do only with those items," answered Mr. Stanly. "The aggregate will take care of itself."

"But this is the way we have always done at Freeville. I suppose it makes no difference," persisted the brother.

"Then let us do it according to discipline," remarked the president.

The report was recommitted by a vote of the conference, whereupon the committee proceeded to subtract the items required by the rule, to see what would be left for table expenses and fuel. The disciplinary claim was two hundred and fifty-six dollars; traveling expenses thus far, covering moving bills, thirty dollars; house rent fifty dollars; making thirty-six dollars more than the allowance proposed, and leaving the items which they were appointed to estimate still unprovided for. Some one now moved to allow, in all, three hundred and fifty dollars. This was objected to, for fear of inability to raise it, and the brethren seemed at a loss what do.

"Is it believed," inquired Mr. Stanly, "that Brother Smith can support his family on what you propose to give him."

"It is all we can afford to pay," responded one of the stewards.

"That is not the question," rejoined the presiding elder. "It is the business of this quarterly conference to estimate and allow what they think necessary. You certainly ought to be willing to do as much as that, and I think you should be satisfied, inasmuch as you have the matter entirely in your own hands."

"Then we'll fix it at three hundred, as we have always done before."

"That would be a fair estimate," said Mr. Stanly

with a roguish look, "and added to the items already fixed will make a good salary."

"I mean that for all," said the brother.

"Will you board Brother Smith and his family for three hundred dollars a year?" asked Mr. Stanly. "Will any of you do it?"

No one responded, and the chairman resumed his remarks. "Brethren, you seem to ask a preacher to board and clothe himself, pay his moving and traveling bills, and the incidentals growing out of his professional life, on a less sum than you would ask for his provisions alone. This station is well able to support its preacher, and I shall insist on your giving him an honorable allowance."

"I thought," said one, "the matter was in our own hands."

"And so it is. We send you a preacher, and you pay him what you please. He has no legal claim whatever. I trust you are not disposed to take advantage of such a circumstance to oppress him."

"We are willing to pay," said the leading steward, "all we are able. We generally have sufficient difficulty in securing the old salary."

"Few stations in the district have more financial ability," replied the presiding elder. "If you will not pay more than three hundred dollars, I shall be obliged to make an exchange, and give you a young man."

"We have had new beginners long enough," said a class-leader.

"But you cannot ask a man to bring his family here to suffer, as he must do on what you propose to

M   19

give. You may make your own election. Support
the man you have, or I shall take him away, and give
you one with a smaller claim."

" It would ruin us to have Brother Smith go away,"
said the steward, " and yet I don't see how we can
pay any more than we have done."

" Brother Smith is no longer your preacher, unless
you agree to give him a living," said Mr. Stanly,
decisively.

This was reaching a point which the conference
had not anticipated. Their pastor was beloved by
the whole church, and under his labors the congregation was rapidly increasing. The year upon which
they had entered had promised to be more than usually successful, and no one would listen for a moment
to a proposition for an exchange of pastors. The consultation was continued for some time, and it was
finally agreed to give Mr. Smith three hundred and
fifty dollars.

" Can you live on that ? " asked the elder turning
to the preacher.

" No sir," was the prompt reply. " It would be
impossible to pay the wages of a hired girl, and support five of us beside, on that sum."

" So I supposed. Come, brethren, redeem the
character of your station and pay your preacher as
you ought, and as you are abundantly able," said Mr.
Stanly.

" We can do no better than that," replied the leading member.

" I regret to hear it. You will certainly need a

change of a single man in place of Brother Smith. I suppose I can accommodate you."

After another conversation of an hour, the matter was adjusted, and an allowance agreed upon, that was pronounced satisfactory, though it was far from being, even then, what the circumstances demanded. As had been suspected, the difficulty in raising it was altogether imaginary. The official members took the lead in the increase of their subscriptions, and the congregation promptly followed. In a few months all were satisfied with the result, and Freeville assumed a position in the conference which it had never before occupied.

Mr. Stanly found it necessary, in the discharge of his duties, to spend a large portion of his time away from home. This was to him the most unpleasant feature of the presiding elder's work, yet it could in no wise be avoided. He was often gone from Friday to Tuesday, as there was much in the general oversight of the district, besides the quarterly meetings, to demand his attention. Occasionally, almost the whole week was in this manner employed, and he felt most keenly the loss of those kind and soothing influences which are alone found in the family circle.

This loss was in a measure made up by the proverbial hospitality of his brethren. The connectional features of the Methodist economy, and the frequent changes among its ministers, have given to this church a oneness which few others possess. The social element is also largely cultivated. Churches thus bound together, and dependent upon each other,

are not apt to become isolated in their position, or
sectional in their feelings.

Still there are instances which form partial exceptions to the general rule. These are quickly apparent
to one situated as is a presiding elder. Mr. Stanly
saw in the exercise of the rites of hospitality, among
those he visited, a wide and growing difference, as
he passed from place to place. He was generally
greeted with a cordial welcome in all his charges.
At one or two points, however, he met with such exhibitions of selfishness as would be a shame to any
people. For example: On visiting Salem, one of his
largest and most influential stations, he remained until ten o'clock in the evening, in attendance upon the
quarterly conference, and was then left, without an
invitation from a single brother, to seek his lodgings
for the night. The pastor was absent, and no provision being made, Mr. Stanly took his horse and
drove four miles to another charge, and put up with a
friend that he knew would be glad to entertain him.
The night was dark and stormy, and the circumstance
gave rise to anything but pleasant reflections. On
the following day, more than one of the Salem people
wondered why the presiding elder did not preach as
well as usual, without in the least suspecting the true
cause. To many persons it has never seemed to occur, that a preacher is affected, like other men, with
the circumstances around him. When this fact shall
be fully appreciated, it will account for many of the
comparative failures of the pulpit.

On another occasion, Mr. Stanly was on his way to
one of his distant quarterly meetings, and being over-

taken by a severe storm, thought it prudent, in view of the precarious state of his health, to put up for the night, before reaching the place of his destination. Just at hand was a wealthy farmer, known to belong to the church, whom he had occasionally met, and on him he now determined to call. Driving to the door, he went in, was very coolly made welcome, and asked to lay by his hat and coat, and seat himself by the fire. No allusion being made to his horse, he stated the object of his call, and inquired if it would be convenient to entertain him until the following morning.

" I suppose we shall have to keep you," said the farmer, indifferently.

" If it is not convenient, I will drive on," said Mr. Stanly.

" O, you can stay," was the reply. " It storms too bad to go farther to night."

Nothing was yet said of the horse which was standing exposed to the fierce winter blast, and Mr. Stanly, feeling a little uneasy for his beast, proposed to go out and see to it.

" We'll put him in the barn," said the brother, " though we are pretty short for fodder this winter. Hay and oats came in light last fall."

So saying, he went out and led the animal away, leaving Mr. Stanly to enjoy the luxury of the fire. Returning, after a few moments, he remarked that it was one of the most blustering nights he had ever known.

" You could have hardly got through if you had

tried," said the farmer. "The roads are drifting very full already."

"I experienced much difficulty in getting thus far," said Mr. Stanly. "I fear it will be no better in the morning."

"Chance if it is. You may have to stay in the neighborhood several days, at this rate;" and the old gentleman pointed to the driving snow. "There is Brother Campbell, living half a mile from here, would be glad to have you come and stay with him a day or. so, I presume. He has no place for a horse, though."

"I shall try to go on in the morning," remarked the presiding elder, feeling by this time a little uncomfortable.

"Well, maybe you can," answered the farmer.

The conversation here ended for the present. The different members of the family went about their appropriate business, leaving the preacher pretty much to himself. Thus matters continued until the early part of the evening, when Mr. Stanly had occasion to go to his sleigh for some article he had left in it, when he found, to his astonishment, his horse standing in an open shed, with the snow drifting upon and around him, and without a mouthful of hay or straw upon which to feed. His first impulse was to harness the animal and seek some other place. But on second thought, this was seen to be impracticable. The storm continued to increase, the darkness had come on, and the roads were litterally filled with the driven snow. The best he could do, was to call

attention to the fact, and ask that it might be
remedied.

"I have no room in the barn," said the farmer.
"My cattle must be housed such weather as this, and
every stall is full."

"Can you not feed him, at least?" asked Mr.
Stanly.

"O, certainly. I didn't know but the boys had
given him something to eat." So saying, one of the
young men was directed to go and give "the man's
horse" a lock of hay. This task was quickly performed. Mr. Stanly thought also of oats, but he remembered they had "come in light," and concluded
to say no more.

The morning revealed the unpleasant fact, that the
preacher's horse was without a mouthful of food. He
might have had some the night before, but no signs
of it remained. Certain it was, that no move was
made to supply the defect, until after breakfast and
prayers were over, when Mr. Stanly again requested
that he might be fed. This done, the presiding elder waited a little, resolved, as soon as possible, to
seek another place, though it was evident he could not
go far until the roads were opened.

After thinking the matter over, he concluded there
would be no love lost, if he should press his unwilling
host a little farther. He determined, at all events, to
make the experiment.

"Now that your cattle are turned out, can you not
put my horse in the barn?" inquired he.

"Y-e-s," answered the old man. "James, you go
and put it in the cow-stable."

" And can you not give him some oats?" said Mr.
Stanly.

"The boy will see that he has some.   Do you hear,
James?"

"Give him six quarts," added Mr. Stanly.   "I will
go out and assist you."

"That will not be necessary," said the farmer.
"He can do it just as well."

With the experience of the past night fresh in
mind, the presiding elder chose to go in person, and
did so.   In this manner, he managed to get enough
for his faithful beast, in spite of the penuriousness of
the rich old farmer with whom he stopped.   As soon
as it was possible, he started for some more congenial
place.   He bid adieu to his host, and set out in his
journey, without receiving the least intimation that
he was at liberty to remain until the roads should be
opened.   It may as well be confessed, that he was as
glad to get away, as was his host to have him
gone.

By dint of perseverance and much hard labor, Mr.
Stanly reached another stopping place, where he met
with a widely different reception.   It was also with
a farmer belonging to the same society as the last.
Here everything was pleasant and agreeable.   Neither oats, hay, nor a christian good will were wanting.
It was such a reception as he usually enjoyed when
thrown among his brethren, in the discharge of the
duties assigned him.

From these friends he learned that the brother with
whom he first stopped was the wealthiest man in the
neighborhood.   He was a steward in the church ; and

when it was stated that he was a leading man in the society, Mr. Stanly did not wonder that the station to which he belonged was the poorest in the district. One single rich, penurious steward will not unfrequently, as in this case, be the ruin of the charge which he represents.

For reasons which can be easily imagined, the presiding elder made no mention of the circumstances here narrated. He kept his own secret, but was careful not to be caught again where he had been once exposed to such unmitigated meanness.

M*

CHAPTER XXXIV.

THE DISTRICT APPOINTMENTS.

By the discipline of the Methodist Episcopal church, the power to make the appointments is very properly vested in the general superintendents, or bishops. These are to travel at large through the connection, visit all the conferences and preside at their sessions, and exercise, as far as possible, a general oversight of the spiritual and temporal affairs of the whole church. It belongs to their office to make distribution of the ministers to their several fields of labor; though in this respect they are subject to various rules and regulations that have been agreed upon, by which their authority is limited, and their course directed. It will be seen, however, as they never exceed six or eight in number, that their personal observation cannot possibly extend to all the circuits and stations under their supervision; and that even to many of the preachers themselves, they must necessarily remain entire strangers. Under these circumstances, the employment of some subsidiary agency is demanded, by which this difficulty may be remedied, and intelligent decisions reached, in the general arrangement of the work.

This want is intended to be supplied by the office of presiding elder. The conferences are divided into districts, to whose charge efficient men are appointed,

whose duty it is to visit all the churches, mingle freely with the preachers and members, and thus become
thoroughly acquainted with the qualifications of both
parties, and their adaptation to each other. By calling these men together in any given conference, the
bishop forms his cabinet, and becomes associated with
capable advisers. Thus, in the public mind, the presiding elders are made to bear, in a great measure,
the burden and responsibility of the appointments.
Their representation is supposed to govern the action
of the superintendent, and in most cases the supposi-
tion is doubtless correct.

While discharging the duties of his present position, Mr. Stanly found this to be the most important
and difficult part of his work. Governed by a sincere wish to promote the prosperity of every appointment within his district, he was often at a loss what
course to pursue. Interests were found to conflict
with each other, as he took into consideration the necessities of the preacher as well as the wants of the
people, and almost from the beginning of his incumbency he was oppressed with anxiety and care. The
efforts of a single year fully convinced him that the
office of presiding elder was no sinecure, however it
may be regarded by others, less experienced in its
intricate perplexities and trials.

It so happened at the close of the first year of Mr.
Stanly's superintendency, that most of the preachers
on Colombia district were to be removed. As a
change of pastors is an affair of no small importance,
when viewed in the light of its possible results, it is
not strange that many of the charges manifested a

deep interest in the occasion at hand. Several of them forwarded petitions for such men as they desired, and others sent delegations to the seat of the conference to watch the progress of events, and shape their plans to the best possible advantage. To many it might seem, at first view, that this would relieve the appointing power, in part, at least, of its delicate responsibility; but the result will show, that the embarrassment of the work was thereby greatly increased.

It is scarcely necessary to say in this connection, that in every conference there is a great variety of ministerial talent. Some who are called of God are far more gifted and useful than others; and it is perfectly natural and right that every station should wish the presence and labors of the most successful preachers. This innocent and praiseworthy desire on the part of the people, often leads them in different localites to ask for the same men; and Mr. Stanly now found himself beset with numerous petitions of this character.

The Rev. Mr. Cone, for example, was an able and eloquent divine, whose services for the coming year were asked for in five different charges. The official members from each of these appointments presented what they supposed to be peculiar claims, and earnestly insisted upon their gratification. In such a case, it required great wisdom to exercise a proper discrimination, and make an arrangement that should be most conducive to the good of the church.

Two or three delegations were present, asking the appointment of Rev. Mr. Wallace, a brother distinguished for his devotion to pastoral visiting, and whose labors were consequently in great demand. Each of these claimed that the church represented was peculiarly situated, and hinted that it would be little short of injustice not to furnish relief, when it could be so easily done. Thus, conflicting claims were constantly pressed, and the difficulty of making the appointments greatly increased.

In this manner, all the leading men of the district were spoken for, each in several different quarters; and as a consequence, for nearly half the preachers, no petition was preferred. This was not because the latter class were not able and useful ministers, for some of them were among the best in the conference; but that they were comparatively unknown, and accordingly unappreciated. Now, let it be remembered, the bishop and his cabinet must give all these a place, and that, too, without showing any partiality, or exhibiting any signs of favoritism.

And then there were other difficulties. Some charges did not petition at all. They considered themselves bound by the compromises which resulted in the establishment of the Itinerancy, to leave the whole matter to the judgment of the party agreed upon as arbiters between the preachers and the people. This was undoubtedly the original design of the compact, and the opposite course was an innovation on Methodist economy. It is plain that these appointments should not be allowed to suffer by the encroachments made by others, on the primitive usages of the church. Their wants were to be met with the same faithfulness as were those of the stations that petitioned. Indeed, Mr. Stanly felt inclined to care for them all the more, since they had left the subject entirely in his hands. As may be readily seen, it was sometimes found necessary, in order to do them justice, to appoint to such places men petitioned for by other but less deserving localities.

Even this was not all. The preachers had preferences as well as the people, and these were also to be consulted. The presiding elder found himself between two fires. Several of his men wanted the same charge, when perhaps the station asked for still another, and insisted upon his appointment. It sometimes happened that neither the preachers nor the station could be gratified, without doing injustice to some other part of the work, and as the reasons for the decision could not with propriety be made public, a considerable number would be disappointed and grieved. The peculiar circumstances connected with these cases, were often known only to the appointing power. They were frequently of such a nature, that they could not be disclosed without seriously prejudicing the character and reputation of the aggrieved parties. In all such cases the presiding elder must consent to bear undeserved censure, as an offset to the honors of his office.

Such were some of the difficulties which Mr. Stanly encountered, in his first attempt to give the necessary direction to the appointments in his district. Long before the conference closed its session, he became painfully conscious that some of his friends would be disappointed, if not afflicted by the decisions reached. After doing all within his power, he could not hope to avoid blame.

The result was as he anticipated. Though most of the ministers, having an apprehension of the difficulties of the case, submitted without a murmur, the appointments were scarcely announced, when several laymen began to utter their complaints. These brethren could not see why their wishes had not been gratified. Being local in their feelings, and having no knowledge of the wants of other charges, they could not understand the reasons that had governed in the case, and were very naturally aggrieved. Still, as a general thing, they possessed enough of religion and good sense to quietly fall in with the existing arrangement, and move forward in harmony with the general plan. The only disaffection that was allowed to remain, was an alienation of good feeling from the presiding elder, and on several charges, Mr. Stanly was ever after regarded as unfriendly to their best interests.

Two or three of the preachers also entertained suspicions of unfair dealing. The Rev. Mr. Henry, upon whom Mr. Stanly had looked with the highest respect, was of this number. He was an aged man, and had asked to go to Lyndon, where he had a son residing; and finding himself appointed elsewhere, now demanded the reason that his request had not been granted. For his own part, he could imagine no cause for the treatment he had received. He claimed to have faithfully served the church during many years, and several times hinted at the ingratitude with which he was thus turned aside.

It would have been very easy for Mr. Stanly to have explained matters so as to relieve himself from censure; but not without inflicting on the old gentleman's feelings a deeper wound than the one already received. The Lyndon brethren had petitioned for another man, and when Mr. Henry had been proposed to them, had forwarded a stern remonstrance against his coming. To have sent him under these circumstances would have been to involve both him and the station in most disastrous difficulties. In mercy to the preacher, therefore, his request had been refused; but it was not thought proper to make a statement of the reasons governing the case. The interests of all the parties would doubtless be better subserved by maintaining an unbroken silence. And yet from that hour, Mr. Stanly lost the friendship of the brother he had so faithfully attempted to serve.

The Rev. Mr. Benson was so fortunate as to be the owner of a farm. For a number of years he had not been obliged to move his family, as appointments had been secured in the immediate vicinity of his home; and he now asked to be stationed for the second time in the place where he resided. The members of the church in that locality, suspecting his wish, had taken the precaution to remonstrate, on the plea that he was too secular. The adjoining stations entertained similar feelings, and Mr. Stanly found it impossible to comply with the brother's request. He frankly stated the difficulties of the case to Mr. Benson, and at the same time urged him to devote his time fully to the work of the ministry, but without obtaining any favorable response.

Now that Mr. Benson found himself assigned to a distant field, he claimed to be greatly injured by the course of his presiding elder. No criticism was too severe, as the motives of that official were freely and openly discussed. He forgot that circuits and stations have rights as well as preachers, and that one appointed to watch over the interests of both, must guard with a jealous eye aga nst the encroachments of either.

Amid all these reproaches, our presiding elder moved steadily forward, fully conscious of the purity of his motives and the integrity of his heart. In most cases, he could have easily removed the suspicions that rested upon himself, but not without doing a greater injury to the happiness and prosperity of those whom he had been appointed to serve. He greatly preferred himself to suffer, than have that suffering fall upon the church of God.

There were circumstances, however, in which he felt at liberty to depart from this general rule. Soon after conference, he fell in company with the Rev. Mr. Bunday, who was in charge of one of the smaller stations, and who took the liberty to indulge in bitter complaints against his appointment. With a sort of fault-finding and censorious tone, this gentleman abruptly turned upon Mr. Stanly and asked,

. "Why is it that I can never be sent to the place I want? Others select their stations, and have their wishes gratified; but I am forever turned off with some poor appointment."

"We try to do the very best we can," said the presiding elder.

"Why, then, do such men as Brother Cone and Brother Wallace go just where they please, and why

20

are others left to suffer merely to accommodate them ?" asked Mr. Bunday.

"Nothing of the kind has ever been done, I assure you," answered Mr. Stanly.

"At least, some of our men always figure for prominent places, and are never disappointed," continued Mr. Bunday.

"You are entirely mistaken, brother. Neither of the preachers you name have ever indicated to me, nor, so far as I know, to the bishop, the slightest preference for any appointment. You do them injustice by such remarks."

"How do they always come to take the best charges, then ?"

"There are at least two reasons why they are sent to good stations. In the first place they merit them; and in the second, the people quite generally ask for their services," replied Mr. Stanly.

"You know I wanted to go to Salem this year; but instead of sending me, you have put Brother Cone there. Now I should like to know the reason for your preference."

"The bishop, doubtless, had satisfactory reasons for his course," answered the presiding elder, evasively.

"But I want to know what they were. I claim that I have a right to know," continued the preacher, evidently a little excited.

"I prefer to make no disclosures concerning these affairs," said Mr. Stanly. "Still, if you insist upon it, I will give you the reasons you ask."

"I do," said Mr. Bunday.

"Well, then,—the official board at Salem earnestly

petitioned for Brother Cone, and as earnestly remonstrated against you. The brethren distinctly stated, in their letter to the bishop, that they would prefer to be left without a preacher, than to have him send them Mr. Bunday. They also stated, that they had understood you asked for the appointment, and had consequently taken considerable pains to learn your qualifications as a pastor, and had unanimously come to the conclusion that you could not sustain their interests."

" What reasons did they give ? " asked Mr. Bunday, after a few moments' silence.

" They did not give the reason in their letter," was the reply.

" I confess I am astonished they should have taken such a course," said the preacher, somewhat agitated.

" I also greatly regretted it," added Mr. Stanly.

" I certainly might have gone to Frankfort," said Mr. Bunday, not yet fully satisfied.   " I should have been as well pleased with that place as with Salem."

" There was the same difficulty in this case as in the other," remarked the presiding elder.

" What ! they did not remonstrate ?"

" They did, most assuredly."

" For what reason ? "

" They simply stated that you were not the man they needed."

" What do they know about me ?   I never preached there in my life."

" They understood you wanted to come, and for that reason proceeded to your last station and made inquiries."

"I have no doubt but what I could have sustained myself at Frankfort."

"Nor I either. But you see the difficulty in the way of your appointment."

"Did any other place remonstrate?"

"Yes."

"Against me?"

"Two or three others."

"How does it happen that they came to think of me at all?"

"Because you kept talking about your appointment during almost the whole year. The brethren on these charges heard of your uneasiness, and came to the conclusion that a man who had to worry himself out of breath to get a suitable place, was no man for them. Besides you had been known to express a wish to go to these appointments, and hence their action."

"I don't believe I do half as much to control my appointments as do some others," said Mr. Bunday, almost out of patience.

"You have emphatically controlled them, however. Had you kept quiet, you would have doubtless gone to Frankfort, and all parties would have been satisfied. You are also mistaken, Brother Bunday, in suppposing the preachers to whom you have just referred, to be engaged in seeking places. Neither Brother Cone nor Brother Wallace have ever expressed a preference in regard to their places of labor. If they had done as you suppose, in years gone by, I am sure they would not have been so great favorites with the people."

"Perhaps I am mistaken."

"You are, indeed."

"I trust, Brother Stanly, you will say nothing about these remonstrances," said Mr. Bunday, after a thoughtful pause.

"Certainly not. I should have never named them to you, had you not so severely blamed me, and at the same time insisted on knowing the reasons for my action."

"I am glad you gave me the facts of the case, and will try to merit better appointments hereafter, rather than petition for them," said Mr. Bunday.

"That is undoubtedly the true course," replied Mr. Stanly. "This undue anxiety always awakens suspicion in the minds of the people, and will generally hinder, rather than add to a preacher's success."

"I have no doubt erred in that direction," said the brother in a serious tone. "By the grace of God I will try to leave this matter where it belongs, for time to come."

The conversation continued yet some time, with increased exhibitions of friendly feelings on both sides. Mr. Bunday felt deeply humbled by the facts which he elicited, and which were to him entirely unexpected. He had learned a lesson of no small value, which was not soon forgotten.

It was seldom that Mr. Stanly made these developments, even when his own justification seemed to demand them. It was a painful task thus to add affliction to the feelings of his brethren, and he consented, rather than do it, to bear even undeserved censure.

CHAPTER XXXV.

THE SACRIFICE.

Dûring the years of Mr. Stanly's presiding eldership, his temporal affairs remained much the same as
before. Nominally, his salary was greater than when
in charge of a station, but really, his income was con-
siderably less. Then, his perquisites amounted to no
inconsiderable sum; but as he was now cut off from
the pastorate, sustaining a general relation to so many
churches, and a particular connection with none, these
had almost entirely ceased. Weddings had become
quite a rarity, except as he was called to an occasional
one among his preachers, which was usually attended
without the acceptance of a fee, and the flow of little
presents and donations, so grateful to the settled
minister, was no longer enjoyed. Every appointment had its own preacher to look after, and the presiding elder was very naturally left to himself.

In addition to this, he found his expenses considera-
bly increased. About three hundred dollars had
to be invested in traveling equipage, the interest of
which, with the cost of keeping it in repair and furnishing feed for his horse, demanded no small part of
his entire receipts. It was only by the closest frugality that he could manage to keep out of debt.

Mrs. Stanly had become, by this time, so accustomed to the study of household economy, that she

almost regarded it a great part of her business to watch the various family outgoes, and keep them, if possible, within her husband's means. To accomplish this, she had been compelled to plan and labor from the day of her marriage. It sometimes seemed to her, as if it had been made the great end of her earthly existence.

The time had now come, when George, the oldest son, had reached the proper age, and made sufficient advancement, to be prepared to enter college. Mr. Stanly had wished to have Wesley accompany him, that the two might pursue their studies together ; but after all his efforts, he found it impossible to provide the means for carrying out his desire. Indeed, it was often considered doubtful whether the privilege could be granted to either.

George might have completed his college course before this, had it not been for the difficulty named. He had struggled through obstacles incident to a life of poverty, until he had reached his present position, and was now waiting an opportunity to complete his cherished design. The delays that had been forced upon him, were awakening in his mind an unusual degree of dissatisfaction. His feelings were constantly chafed, and so sensitive was he to the wrongs of his position, that Mr. Stanly, who was a close observer, began to fear the result. The father could but look with deep concern upon every influence brought to bear upon the young mind committed to his care, and was sometimes almost alarmed at the lessons inculcated and seized upon with such avidity, by one so susceptible to their control.

In this state of things, one only remedy presented itself. That was to sell the house and lot for which they had so long toiled, and apply its proceeds to this object. To this place their attention had been turned for a number of years, as their future home, and though it was not yet fully paid for, enough had been advanced to make its final clearance probable; and in that case secure a spot where they might dwell in their declining years. They were already on the down hill slope, and Mr. Stanly was anticipating at no distant day, the necessity of retiring from the effective ranks. To obtain a home of their own against such a time of need, both himself and companion had long and earnestly labored, often depriving themselves and their children of the common necessaries of life.

They now saw it necessary to abandon the plan which they had thus sought to execute, or withhold the advantages of an education from the children that God had given them. Mrs. Stanly had always hoped and prayed that George might be a minister, and though he was still unconverted, she had not abandoned the thought. Perhaps this might be the means, in the hand of God, of bringing about the wished for result. And then, how gladly would she look upon the offering of the required sacrifice. Thus she reasoned ; and, as in most cases, the love of her offspring triumphed over her fears for the future.

Mr. Stanly saw in the plan proposed, the only way in which he could make provision for his children; and let what would happen to himself, this was a duty he did not feel at liberty to shun. The house was accordingly sold, and George furnished the means to continue his studies. The young man fully appreciated the circumstances of his situation, and went forward with the resolution to make the best possible improvement of the opportunities enjoyed.

The parents were highly pleased to witness his progress in his studies, and soon felt richly repaid for their sacrifice, by his constant and steady advancement. The sisters were also gratified. They seemed to vie with each other in promoting the end in which they all felt so intense an interest. Many a busy hour was employed at home, in providing articles for the comfort of the absent one, and the loss which all had suffered was forgotten in the benefits which all seemed to share.

A year or two passed, and George continued his course in college, full of ambition and intellectual energy, but still a stranger to the joys of religion. The excitement of his present mode of life impelled him onward, without allowing him to pause and seriously attend to the higher interests of his being. This circumstance caused great anxiety at the parsonage home in the country, from which went up many prayers and earnest pleadings in his behalf.

As the result proved, these were not in vain. During his senior year, the gratifying intelligence was received, that the absent son was numbered among the fruits of a revival, with which the college was being favored. Mr. and Mrs. Stanly obtained the first intimation of this, in a letter from George, wherein he made a clear and open profession of faith in our Lord Jesus Christ. It may well be imagined that the

N

joy of the christian parents scarcely knew any bounds
at this auspicious event. The hope at once sprung
up anew, that the one in whom so much of their affection centered, might now be led into the moral
vineyard, as a devoted and successful minister of the
cross. Nothing was known, however, of his feelings
on this subject, and vacation was anxiously waited
for, when he might return and be once more in their
midst. Though a free correspondence was kept up, in
which George uniformly referred to his religious experience, it was thought best by the parents to leave
him to his own convictions, and the tuition of that
Eternal Spirit, who calls and sends forth whomsoever
He will.

The vacation came, and its happy weeks were swift-
ly flying away, as all the members of our pastor's
family were again together, in the enjoyment of each
other's love. Emily had been recently married, and
was about to become settled in the immediate neighborhood of their present residence, and George was
soon to go out from under the parental oversight, and
engage in the busy scenes of life; so that they were
never likely to meet again as they now met, and
mingle as heretofore in the loved associations of home.
Taken all in all, it was one of the most interesting
scenes ever enjoyed at the parsonage.

Soon it was time for George to return, and yet his
intentions as to the future were as much unknown as
before. The subject in which his friends had been so
deeply interested was a delicate one, and none of
their number had yet ventured to introduce it. He
had seemed to cautiously avoid all allusions that might

even hint his preferences, and no ·means were left but to interrogate him accordingly.

The evening before his departure, as his mother and himself were alone, when the conversation had touched upon various subjects, Mrs. Stanly plainly asked him what course he purposed to pursue after leaving college.

"I am all unsettled as to that," answered George.

"And have you no thoughts as to the future, should God spare your life?" she inquired again.

"No *settled* convictions," said he, evasively.

"I trust you have no disposition to shun the path of duty, whenever it is made known," continued his mother.

"I am often at a loss to know what is my duty. I hope to be willing to do it whenever it is understood," was the reply.

"It has long been my desire that God will make you a minister," said Mrs. Stanly.

"And mine, too," said Em ly, stepping into the room just in time to hear the last remark.

"Tell me frankly, George," said his mother, "have you not had serious thoughts of entering this work? You will soon graduate, and it is none too early to consider these things."

A tear stood in the young man's eye, as he hesitated what to answer. At length he replied, assuming an air of indifference.

"I have thought of it, of course, among many other things."

"Have you never felt that God called you to the work?" asked Emily, unwilling to let him go.

"I might have thought so, were it not for certain circumstances in my case," said he.

"What are they? Come, now, tell me the whole matter," added Emily.

"I cannot name them, now," was the reply; "but if you wish, I will write and explain the whole."

"Do so, then, by all means," said his sister, highly pleased with the promise. The subject was here dropped. Other topics were introduced, and the mother and sister were content to wait until they could hear from him at college.

Not many weeks had gone by, after the above conversation, when a letter was received from George, containing a full account of his feelings on the subject just named. The communication was long, and evidently written after much earnest thought, from which his conclusions had been reached. It was directed to Emily, and from its pages, we will make the following extracts:

"In regard to the inquiries which you made when I was at home, I have hesitated what to say. Ever since my conversion, I have felt a sincere desire to labor for the salvation of sinners, and my humble efforts in that direction, have brought rich blessings to my soul. I have been subject to a great variety of mental exercises, and confess that I am often at a loss what to do. I should love to preach the gospel, if it were clearly my duty, but on this point I cannot be fully satisfied.

"I confess, my dear sister, I see but one insurmountable difficulty. I am sure you will sympathize with my feelings in regard to that. It is upon a point concerning which I would say nothing, had you not sought my views. As it is, I will permit you to understand the whole.

"You and I are not strangers to the trials and perplexities of the Itinerant ministry. From our childhood we have watched the course of our parents, as they have struggled on, often in penury and want, while faithfully serving the church of God. Though we have never heard them complain, we could not fail to see the wrong, and as you know, I have felt it keenly. You have many times heard me say, I would never be a minister, but on this subject my mind has undergone a great change. I do not now hesitate in the least, in view of the personal sacrifices that would be demanded.

"To my mind, there is a difficulty in my way, of a much more serious character. My parents are in the decline of life. They have no means of support when failing health shall compel them to go into retirement, and if I enter the ministry, I must give up all hope of rendering them assistance. I do not feel that the other children ought to take care of them alone, even if they had the means, for I have shared more largely than you all in the distribution of their dear-bought earnings.

"It seems a duty, then, devolving on me, to seek, in time to come, a supply for their wants. The funds of the conference for its superannuated preachers are altogether inadequate, and I do not, *cannot*, think God requires me to leave them in destitution. More than that,—I cannot think the religion of the bible *permits* me to pursue such a course. It would be far from honoring my father and my mother as the scriptures enjoin. They have sacrificed and suffered for me, and I feel now called upon to care for them. When the little home, for the possession of which they had toiled so many years, was freely given up, I vowed in my heart that while I had a hand to work or a tongue to plead, they should not be left to suffer.

"Here then, dear Emily, is the real difficulty in the case. If it were not for this, I might feel it my duty to preach, and if the church had provided for them as I think it should, I could consistently go forward and identify myself with the Itinerant ministry. As it is, I cannot think it my duty. I cannot even think I could stand approved in the sight of God, were I to pursue such a course.

"A day or two since, one of our college professors interrogated me on this subject, and I gave him the same reasons I have named to you. He frankly admitted that it was a hard case, but quoted the following passage from our Savior, as if to give direction to my course: 'He that loveth father and mother more than me, is not worthy of me.' I confess I felt not a little grieved at such an application of the text. He certainly could not have supposed that our Divine Teacher intended to authorize children to forsake their parents in age, and leave them in their feebleness to the cold charities of the world, and yet his language implied it. Neither could he think it an evidence of disrespect to the Son of God, or of want of affection to the blessed Redeemer, to pursue the opposite course, though he could not have more plainly made the assertion. I shall hereafter consider the professor a very good teacher of mathematics, but not equally happy as an expositor of the scriptures.

"Thus, my sister, you have in brief the answer to your question. I cannot adopt the sentiment which prevails among certain savage and idolatrous tribes, that I am at liberty to leave my parents to themselves, and pursue the course best adapted to my own feelings. I am quite confident you will not blame me for engaging at present in other pursuits. The ministry would be my choice, were it not that both the laws of nature and revelation establish a claim which necessarily precedes all others."

This letter from George produced deep feeling at the parsonage. Each member of the preacher's family rejoiced in the evidences which it gave of pure and holy affection, but at the same time equally regretted the decision to which he felt driven by the circumstances around him. Numerous efforts were made to move him from his purpose, but he steadily replied that it could not be his duty to preach, while paramount obligations were yet unfulfilled.

CHAPTER XXXVI.

THE CHILDREN.

THE reader will not be surprised to learn that Mr. Stanly was highly pleased in being again appointed to the charge of a station. Though in the opinion of his brethren, well fitted for the post he had recently occupied, and which he had filled with credit to himself and success to his district, he had ever felt himself inadequate to the responsibilities of his position. He preferred the less conspicuous and equally useful life of a pastor, where he might go in and out before a people that he could call his own, and in whose sympathies and prayers he might be assured of a prominent place. He was therefore glad of an opportunity to withdraw into comparative retirement and rest.

To the different members of our minister's household, it was equally pleasant to be once more united in the unbroken associations of the family circle. For a term of years, Mr. Stanly had spent nearly all his Sabbaths from home. Indeed, the cares of his district had demanded and received a large portion of his time in the transaction of business abroad, aside from the proper work of preaching the gospel. The reunion in the services of the sanctuary, was therefore of the most delightful character, and could not fail to be highly appreciated.

Mr. Stanly and his companion were now in the autumn of life, but they were permitted by a gracious Providence to continue several years in their chosen work. These were mostly spent in connection with the better class of appointments, and among a people who cared for their temporal wants and looked well to their supply. The children were of that age that they could mostly provide for themselves, and they had severally engaged in employments where they could secure an honest livelihood.

In due time, George had graduated with the highest honors of his class, and at once engaged in teaching. Nothing had yet transpired to change the purpose which he had previously expressed, and he accordingly continued in his secular business. He accepted the office of local preacher, and availed himself of numerous opportunities to minister in word and doctrine, and everywhere with the happiest results. Among his acquaintances, it was almost a universal opinion that he ought to give himself wholly to the duties of the ministry, but he still regarded the obstacle before him as insurmountable.

His brother Wesley chose to engage in trade, and was already hired as clerk in a city store, where he resolved to deserve, and then wait for, a favorable promotion. He was a member of the church, though his religious character was not as decided as his parents could wish. Mr. Stanly had found it impossible to carry both his sons through college, and Wesley did not feel exactly satisfied that his privileges had been less than those of his brother.

Of the daughters, Emily was married to a farmer,

well to do in life, and settled near the village of Colombia. Ellen alone had become identified with the
Itinerancy. She was the wife of the Rev. Mr. Barnes,
a member of the same conference with her father,
and at present residing in his immediate vicinity.

Mary continued yet at home. In many respects
she was the special joy and hope of her parents, for
whom she manifested, in return, the most tender affection. In childhood she had given her heart to
God, and from the hour of her conversion, had steadily pursued the christian pathway. Her sweet and
joyous disposition was well calculated to enliven the
hearts of those around her, and soothe the wounded
feelings of such as were in affliction and sorrow. She
was indeed the light of the parsonage, now that, of
the children, she alone remained.

Fears had sometimes been entertained of the stability of Mary's health. It had been thought that
consumption had marked her for its early victim, but
the impression was not yet confirmed. Of late, the
indications had appeared more favorable, and these
thoughts were quite generally dismissed. There was
now a freshness in her countenance, and an elas-
ticity in her step, that gave promise of yet many
years.

On one occasion, Mr. and Mrs. Stanly were sitting
quietly in their little parlor, when Mary chanced to
come into the room. She was no sooner gone, than
the mother called attention to the improvement in
her daughter's appearance, and congratulated herself that their former fears had proved so groundless.
Mr. Stanly had also marked the recent changes that

had been taking place, but his practiced eye was
fast leading him to a different conclusion. He
almost involuntarily started from his seat as his
attention was now called to the color in her cheeks,
which was supposed to be an evidence of health
and vigor. The mother saw the mental agitation
which her words had awakened, and was not slow to
inquire after its cause.

"I fear," said he, "that she is unusually fragile."

"But, my dear, she is constantly improving. Just
think how much better she looks to-day than she did
a year since."

"Those favorable tokens, as you call them, are
to me the most alarming symptoms. I am afraid
it is the terrible hectic flush upon which you base
your hopes."

"O, do not say so. It cannot be. God will surely
spare her to us in our declining years."

"The impression is as sad to me as to you, but
I fear that before the flowers come again she will be
gone."

Mr. Stanly was so affected in thus giving utterance to his feelings, that he bowed his head and
wept like a child. The emotions of his companion
were also at their height, and neither of them dared
speak further. It was some time before they fell
into a calmer mood, and even then, they did not
venture another allusion to the painful subject.

It required but a very few weeks to prove that
the father was not mistaken. Mary was laboring
under the influence of a severe cold, when she was
suddenly taken with bleeding at the lungs. At once

all hope of her recovery was gone. Her attack was
followed by an unremitting and rapid decline.

During Mary's sickness, the beauty and glory of
religion were strikingly exhibited. From the first,
her confidence in the Redeemer's love was unshaken,
and as she approached the grave, she rose to be a
triumphant conqueror. One by one she bade her
father, mother, brothers and sisters a long and final
farewell. Death had lost its sting, and the grave
had been robbed of its victory, and the dying girl
triumphed over both. Almost in her last moments she spoke of "the blessed Jesus," and beck-
oned her friends to follow her to his loved embrace.
Gently she sunk away from earth, and was numbered
among the angel spirits in heaven.

Thus Mr. and Mrs. Stanly were once more alone.
Their children had all gone out from under the
parental roof,—one of their number to the home of
the saints above, the others to contend with the ills
and storms of life, and win a passport to the same
blest abode.

In their loneliness, the minister and his wife continued their usual labors in the Master's vineyard;
but how unlike the years of their earlier history,
when they were equally by themselves. Then, they
were launching out upon what was to them an un-
tried sea; now, they were slowly but surely approaching the haven. Then, hope sat as queen of
the passions, pointing to a joyous and sunny future; now, resignation is enthroned, and faith bears
up the drooping spirits. Then, the whole earth was
bright with promise; now, heaven alone can re-

compense their sorrows. Mournfully, and yet joyfully, they travel on, having a regard to that better inheritance which has been provided for them above. Heaven has now an additional attraction, and to it they look as their long-sought home.

CHAPTER XXXVII.

THE LAST APPOINTMENT.

ONCE more we see Mr. Stanly at the session of his conference. He is now becoming enfeebled by age and constitutional debility, and for the first time in his ministry, asks a favor as to his appointment. The state of his health is such that he can no longer endure the labor and fatigue of a large charge, and he requests a small station, where he has formed an agreeable acquaintance, and which he hopes to be able to serve. His wish is granted, and he accordingly becomes settled in the village of Lansing.

This station has a small but convenient parsonage, well suited to the wants of its present occupants, and Mrs. Stanly seeks again to dispense with hired help, and do her work alone. By the occasional assistance of her husband, her effort proves successful, and the hope is entertained that by such frugality, a few dollars may be saved from their income, for the supply of their wants in a future day. The people prove to be kind and considerate, and though not rich, they find no difficulty in supplying the pastor's wants, which in his present circumstances are comparatively few.

Farther than this, no one seemed to entertain a thought. The official members appeared to think their duty fully attended to, when the preacher was not allowed to suffer; not once suspecting that he had a care for the morrow like other men, and was under the same obligation to provide for its contingencies.

Mr. Stanly had previously come to the conclusion that it was of but little use for a Methodist preacher to go without the necessaries of life, from a desire to lay up something against sickness and age. His experience had shown him that the people aimed simply at the supply of present wants. If those wants were curtailed, his income was limited accordingly. The church sought to appropriate all the benefits of such economy to itself; or rather the individual members of the church availed themselves of its advantages.

He now saw this principle in the financial arrangements of the official board more clearly developed than ever before. It was known that the expenses of Father Stanly, as he began to be familiarly called, were light, and the salary was estimated accordingly. The sum which was originally in contemplation, was reduced fifty dollars, when it was understood that the labor of a hired girl was to be dispensed with, so that the object had in view by the sacrifice was completely defeated. It was soon evident that nothing could be saved from the two hundred and fifty dollars in addition to the parsonage, which was now granted.

The donation visit also revealed the existence of the same feeling. It was the smallest ever made by the station, not because of any want of respect or affection for the preacher, but because his family was so limited that he did not need it. The fact that he was liable at any time to be thrown out of employment

by his failing health, was in no wise considered. To-
day his wants were met, and he was expected to be
satisfied.

This was not the development of a new state of
feeling to Mr. Stanly, for he had seen it, and suffered
from it, during the whole course of his ministry. Too
many times it had seemed as if the stewards only
sought to keep the pastor along on the shortest allowance possible, until the time should come when
they could shove him on, penniless as he was, to the
next station, and begin the same process with his
successor. These men, with all the circumstances
before them, generally opposed an increase of salary,
and then not unfrequently stood in the way of donation visits, for fear they might conflict with the work
of raising the regular allowance. To this rule, however, honorable exceptions had been found on almost
every charge, and they were remembered with
gratitude.

Several months passed away, and the preacher and
his people were in the enjoyment of a quiet and uni-
form prosperity. Mr. Stanly's increasing infirmities
frequently admonished him that what he had to do
must be done quickly, as his ability to continue his
labors another year was already beginning to be
doubted. Though the health of Mrs. Stanly was better than that of her husband, she, too, was prema-
turely broken and worn down, by the excitement
and anxieties of her past life.

During the latter part of the year, Father Stanly
was attacked with a severe fit of sickness. He continued along for some time unable to leave his house,

and of course another was engaged to supply the pulpit. All hope of remaining in the regular work was
now abandoned, and the long dreaded hour in the
life of a Methodist preacher had fully come. He
must hereafter be laid aside, and suffer, rather than
do, the will of God.

During the preacher's sickness, a large bill of expense was quickly run up at the parsonage. To meet
this, an effort was made among the people to raise
the arrearages of his salary, which was promptly met,
with the addition of nearly a hundred dollars as a
gratuitous contribution. This afforded present relief, for which the pastor and his wife were truly grateful. Before the year closed, several small sums were
received from George—who, true to his purpose,
stood ready to minister to his father's wants. All
the children visited him at Lansing, with whose presence he was also greatly comforted.

Mr. Stanly sufficiently recovered to be able to attend conference at its following session. He received
many marks of kindness and respect from the brethren among whom he had labored, and with a sad
heart took his final leave of the active duties of the
Itinerancy. Henceforth he was known only as a superannuated or worn-out preacher, belonging to the
past rather than the present, in the affairs of the
church to which he belonged.

CHAPTER XXXVIII.

SUPERANNUATION.

Now that Mr. Stanly has withdrawn from the regular work of the ministry, and is left without an appointment, we have but to trace him to his place of rest. Though having faithfully labored in the service of the church for a long and eventful series of years, he found himself, at the close of his term of active life, with no spot that he could call his own, and no means of procuring the blessings of a permanent home. Thus situated, he truly felt that his only treasure was in heaven; and while the prospects connected with the world to come were bright and glorious, he could see but little in his earthly circumstances in which to hope. It was the day above all others for the trial of his faith; and he slowly, sadly, turned away from the battle field in which he had gained so many moral victories, and sought his home in the retirement of private life.

There were many reasons that led him to decide, without difficulty, on the place of his future residence. The village of Colombia, in which he had lived at several periods of his Itinerant labors, contained numerous inducements that justified his choice of that locality, as the place where the remainder of his days should be spent. For a long time both himself and compan: 1 had instinctively turned to it as their home, when no longer able to do effective work. Latterly it had come to possess additional interest, in view of the fact that two of their children were there located. George was still in charge of the Academy in that town, and Emily with her family resided but a little distance from the village, while the grave of the lovely Mary did not fail to present a strong though mournful attraction.

By the aid of his children and several friends who interested themselves in his behalf, a house was soon hired at a cheap rent, into which he moved and became settled. George so arranged his business that he could board with his parents, and in a good degree make their interests identical with his own. In this manner a ready provision was made for their necessities, and Mr. and Mrs. Stanly found their circumstances more favorable than their highest anticipations had allowed them to hope.

Our minister was no sooner left to himself in his superannuated relation, than he became painfully oppressed with a sense of loneliness. Though surrounded with numerous tried and familiar friends, he was illy at ease so long as he could not engage in his appropriate work. It was altogether the most difficult task he had ever undertaken, to sit down and become a mere looker on, while stirring scenes, in which he had long been a participant, were transpiring around him. Accustomed to a life of activity, and to an intimate association with his brethren, he could scarcely content himself in his present position. His only relief was obtained in keeping up an interest in the general affairs of the church, and laboring,

as strength and opportunity would allow, in the vineyard of the Lord.   In so doing, he had the satisfaction of believing that his efforts were still blessed in
advancing the cause he so ardently loved.

Thus matters continued, until Mrs. Stanly found it
impossible to do the work of the family, and the necessity arose for the employment of help.   This so
greatly increased their expenses, that it was decided
to break up housekeeping.   By the advice of the
children, the parents took up their abode with the
eldest daughter, where it was hoped they might pass
the remnant of their days.   George was soon after
married, and began housekeeping for himself.

The only income which Mr. Stanly now enjoyed,
consisted of the dividend made by the annual conference to its superannuated ministers.   It is well
known that the discipline of the M. E. church contemplates the payment of a sufficient sum to her
worn-out clergymen, to keep them from coming to
want.   This provision is based upon a previous one,
by which the amount paid to effective men is limited
to their current expenses.   From the salary given, it
is not expected they can properly provide for sickness
and age, and hence the arrangement to which we refer.

The contract virtually entered into by the church
on the one hand, and the clergy on the other, is simply
this : The church is to have the entire time and talents
of the ministry devoted to her interests, and is to give
in return the means of subsistence, and no more.
With this the clergy are to be satisfied, in view of the
further provision, by which themselves, their widows
and orphans are to be provided for, when they shall be

compelled to leave the regular work. This plan was
expected to remove from the minds of the preachers
all anxiety in regard to worldly things, and make
them men strictly devoted to the interest of their
calling. They could well consent to give their lives
to this work without accumulating for the future, with
this assurance that their actual wants should be properly met.

The arrangement was certainly well calculated to
promote the desired end. No other could so completely shut out worldly care from those whose sacred
office demands all their energies, and calls for the
uninterrupted exercise of the noblest and purest principles of the christian religion. But unfortunately,
it has been observed only in part. The stinted salary
has been given from year to year according to discipline, but when the self-sacrificing minister has been
so unfortunate as to become disabled, he has found to
his sorrow the provisions for his further support entirely inadequate. From ten to fifty per cent. only
of the sum allowed has been received. The collections for this purpose invariably come short of meeting the demand. Thus, the compromise comes doubly
severe on such as are compelled to share all its losses,
while reaping but few if any of its benefits.

Mr. Stanly now had a claim of two hundred dollars
per year. It was met by the payment of about sixty,
which was all the conference funds would allow. With
this sum he must get along as best he could. Had it
not been for his children, he must have been left to
suffer. Their assistance alone kept him from actual
want, and though neither of them was blessed with

an abundance of means, they cheerfully shared their substance with the parents they so tenderly loved. Those parents felt richly rewarded for the sacrifices of other years, in the evidences of sympathy and affection which they now received.

About five years after Mr. Stanly took a superannuated relation, he was called with his companion to endure an affliction more severe, if possible, than any through which they had yet passed. Their daughter Emily suddenly sickened and died, leaving them once more to suffer a loss which none but those who are parents can fully appreciate. Thus, two of their children had gone before them to the spirit land, and though they expected soon to follow after, their sufferings were most intense. With Emily they had hoped to live and die, and they now saw their fondest expectations cut off by this mysterious stroke. Once more they were deprived of a home, as they could not consistently remain where they were.

Bowed down and stricken, they undertook again to live by themselves. Their receipts from conference were sufficient to pay their rent and furnish fuel, and the proffered assistance of George and Wesley made up the balance. Here they continued for several years, dependent on their sons and the charities of the people with whom they were surrounded, who on several occasions contributed liberally for their relief.

During all this period, their religious experience was deep and satisfactory. No complaints were uttered, and no regrets indulged. Their lives had been given to a blessed cause, and they felt richly rewarded in being permitted to look out on the fields they had cultivated, and witness the triumphs of the cross. On every hand the church was making rapid progress, and these aged pilgrims could exclaim with the dying Wesley, "The best of all is, God is with us." While assured of his presence, nothing could make them unhappy; and notwithstanding all their trials, if they were to commence life again, it would be devoted to this same blessed work. Such was their confidence in God, such was their faith in his word, and such was the character of their personal experience, that they were constantly joyous and happy. They gladly looked forward to that blessed day when God should take them to himself, and crown them heirs of eternal life.

Mr. Stanly was first called to his eternal reward. In holy triumph he passed over the swelling Jordan, exemplifying in his death the power and glory of the religion he had so faithfully preached in his life. His companion spent a little time longer on earth, mostly in company with her only remaining daughter, and then passed gently away, conscious that through the riches of grace she had not lived in vain.

THE END.

THE METHODIST PREACHER,

CONTAINING

TWENTY-EIGHT SERMONS UPON DOCTRINAL SUBJECTS.

BY

BISHOP HEDDING, DR. FISK, DR. BANGS, DR. DURBIN,

AND OTHER EMINENT PREACHERS OF THE M. E. CHURCH.

One Volume, 400 pp., 8vo., Muslin. Price $1 00.

This volume contains twenty-eight different sermons by twenty-three different ministers. The subjects discussed in these sermons, are the most important within the
whole range of Bible Theology; and they are discussed with an ability, clearness and
force rarely equaled. Their authors are among the most eminent ministers of the
church, living or dead. These sermons embody the most careful deductions of their
mature minds, and are at once the enunciation and the evidence of their pure and benevolent hearts.

EPISCOPAL METHODISM,

AS IT WAS AND IS;

BEING

A History of the M. E. Church in the United States.

INCLUDING THE

Origin, Progress, Doctrines, Church Polity,

USAGES, INSTITUTIONS AND STATISTICS,

OF THE

METHODIST EPISCOPAL CHURCH IN THE UNITED STATES.

EMBRACING, ALSO, AN ACCOUNT OF THE RISE OF METHODISM IN EUROPE, AND OF
ITS ORIGIN AND PROGRESS IN CANADA.

BY REV. P. DOUGLASS GORRIE.

One Volume, 354 Pages, 12mo., Muslin. Price $1 00.

The following are its leading divisions:

Book I.—HISTORY OF METHODISM.
Book II.—DOCTRINES OF METHODISM.
Book III.—POLITY OF EPISCOPAL METHODISM.
Book IV.—BENEVOLENT AND LITERARY INSTITUTIONS.

MILLER, ORTON & CO., Publishers,
25 Park Row, New York, and 107 Genesee-st., Auburn.

LaVergne, TN USA
01 December 2010
206981LV00005B/73/P